JUDAISM, PHYSICS AND GOD

JUDAISM, PHYSICS AND GOD

Searching for Sacred Metaphors in a Post-Einstein World

RABBI DAVID W. NELSON

For People of All Faiths, All Backgrounds

JEWISH LIGHTS Publishing

Woodstock, Vermont

Judaism, Physics and God:
Searching for Sacred Metaphors in a Post-Einstein World

2006 First Quality Paperback Printing
2005 First Hardcover Printing
© 2005 by Rabbi David W. Nelson

For information regarding permission to reprint material from this book, please write or fax your request to Jewish Lights Publishing, Permissions Department, at the address / fax number listed below, or e-mail your request to permissions@jewishlights.com.

Library of Congress Cataloging-in-Publication Data
Nelson, David W. (David William)
Judaism, physics and God : searching for sacred metaphors in a post-Einstein world / David W. Nelson.
p. cm.
Includes bibliographical references and index.
ISBN-13: 978-1-58023-252-4
ISBN-10: 1-58023-252-3 (HC)
ISBN-13: 978-1-58023-306-4
ISBN-10: 1-58023-306-6 (PB)

1. Judaism and science. 2. Physics—Religious aspects—Judaism.
3. Metaphor—Religious aspects—Judaism. I. Title.
BM538.S3N45 2005
296.3'75—dc22
2004026716
10 9 8 7 6 5 4 3 2 1
Manufactured in the United States of America
Cover Design: Tim Holtz
Cover Art: Fractal image © Paul Bourke, visualization researcher, Swinburne University

Published by Jewish Lights Publishing
A Division of LongHill Partners, Inc.
Sunset Farm Offices, Route 4, P.O. Box 237
Woodstock, VT 05091
Tel: (802) 457-4000   Fax: (802) 457-4004
www.jewishlights.com

Dedicated to my father, Sol Nelson *z"l*, who died weeks before this book first appeared. He would have been so proud! And to all those with the courage to confront new and strange ideas. Such ideas stretch the mind and the soul and challenge what we thought we knew. Looking them in the eye can be exhilarating—and scary.

CONTENTS

PREFACE

It has been said that all writing is, in some way, autobiographical. And although I never thought of this book as being connected with my life's story, it now seems that the links are deeper than I realized. My father was born in New York City to recent immigrants from Eastern Europe. He grew up in a highly traditional, immigrant Jewish community. Yiddish was his first language, and Shabbat afternoons were often spent with his grandfather, a very pious Jew for whom I was named. As a teenager, my father became disenchanted with much of traditional Jewish culture and left it all behind. He went to New York's City College, became a chemist, and embarked on a professional career in science that lasted until his retirement. Shortly before I was born, when my father was in his early thirties, he resumed active participation in Jewish life, joining and eventually becoming quite involved with Reform congregations. Nevertheless, the intellectual tone of the household in which I grew up was clearly scientific, rational, and liberal.

As a child, I was certain that I would become a scientist, like my father. Throughout elementary school, I read voraciously about the space program, physics, and chemistry. I remember with particular fondness a book called *The Story of the Atom* and another called *The How and Why Wonder Book of Chemistry*. The latter title was one of a series, each of which was devoted to a different branch of science. I had them all and had read them all so many times that I had essentially committed them to memory. My course in life was clearly laid out before me. During these same years, I attended Sunday school, prepared for and celebrated my Bar Mitzvah, and led an active, if not terribly traditional or well-informed, Jewish life. My family had wonderful Passover seders and lit Hanukkah candles. Jewish identity was unquestionably a part of my life. Even so, it was the ethos of scientific rationality that shaped my sense of self.

When I was fourteen years old, my father changed jobs and relocated, and for several months we saw him only on weekends. That put a tremendous amount of stress on the family, and that stress exacerbated the early adolescent rebellion that was already brewing in me. By the beginning of high school, I was much less committed to a future in science.

Then, during high school, I became involved with a synagogue youth group and the movement (NFTY, the umbrella of youth programs run by the Reform synagogues of North America) of which it was a part. I got to know several young rabbinical students who worked as youth group advisers and came to admire them tremendously. I spent summers at Jewish summer camps where worship services, Israeli songs and dances, and Jewish study were a core part of the daily schedule. These experiences had a profound impact on my sense of who I was and what I cared about in life. For my sixteenth birthday, I asked my parents for a copy of the Soncino edition of the Pentateuch, with commentary by Rabbi J. H. Hertz. I had come quite a long way from *The Story of the Atom* and *The How and Why Wonder Books*. Thus, just as I was turning away from my interest in science, I began turning more and more toward Judaism. I decided to become a rabbi and spent a great deal of time and energy, as an undergraduate at Wesleyan University, with the campus rabbi. After college, I enrolled at Hebrew Union College–Jewish Institute of Religion and received rabbinical ordination five years later.

The conflicts and tensions in our lives often drive us to do what we do. This book arose from my own need to reconcile science and Judaism, for they represented some of the fundamental personal tensions in my own family life. My father left the Judaism of the Eastern European immigrant world and embraced a life of science. I left childhood dreams of following in his scientific footsteps and developed a love of Judaism that links me more closely to the legacy of the great-grandfather for whom I am named than to anyone else. Now, in the pages that follow, I have searched for a way to integrate and harmonize these two worlds.

ACKNOWLEDGMENTS

Because the writing of this book required me to learn and ponder deeply so many things about which I am not an expert, I am especially grateful to those who encouraged me and who provided technical assistance. Professors Bob Dorfman, Jerry Gollub, and Saul Perlmutter were especially generous with their time and expertise.

I am thankful for the time and efforts of the members of the roundtable, whose insights and analysis made the final chapter possible: Professor Bob Dorfman, Dr. Ilan Chabay, Rev. Jim Miller, Rabbi Michael Paley, and Professor Neil Gillman.

Professor Bruce Lewenstein, of Cornell University, has always been willing to listen to ideas, make suggestions, and provide thoughtful guidance throughout this project. I appreciate his friendship and his willingness to help.

My family shared my enthusiasm for the project from the first, and lovingly tolerated my obsession with the mysteries of physics for years. Without their understanding and support I would never have tried anything so ambitious.

Because I am a first-time author, the tender loving care given me throughout the final year of the book's gestation by the professionals at Jewish Lights Publishing was most welcome.

I am grateful also to all my friends and former colleagues on the staff of CLAL—the National Jewish Center for Learning and Leadership, who, for more than fifteen years, provided me with an environment that nurtured my mind and encouraged me to think in new and creative ways.

And finally, I must make special mention of National Public Radio. I have lost track of the number of news stories, interviews, and features over the years that made me drop what I was doing and scribble a few notes about some part of what was to become this book.

Introduction

JEWISH TRADITION AND FROGS' LEGS

"*Metaphor is the currency of knowledge. I have spent my life learning incredible amounts of disparate, disconnected, obscure, useless pieces of knowledge, and they have turned out to be, almost all of them, extremely useful. Why? Because there is no such thing as disconnected facts. There is only complex structure. And both to explain complex structure to others and, perhaps more important—this is forgotten, usually—to understand them oneself, one needs better metaphors....*

"*My father always said if you translate a proverb from one language into another, you pass for a poet. The same for science. Work strictly within one area, and it's diminishing returns, hard to make progress. But translate a concept from its field for use where it is unknown, and it is always fresh and powerful.*"

—Luca Turin, quoted in Chandler Burr's
The Emperor of Scent[1]

NORMAL JEWS AND
NONEXPERT SCIENCE

This book is about science and Judaism and how they relate. But most of all, it is about ordinary people. Not scientists or theologians but average, normal, ordinary people. You might ask: What do normal people have to do with either Judaism or science? Isn't Judaism run by pious old men with long beards who spend all their time studying Talmud? And isn't science the exclusive domain of brilliant thinkers who can't seem to explain anything without using a computer and lots of very sophisticated math that *I* never learned in high school? My answer to both is: no.

As far as Judaism goes, it is normal people who run the show. Or to be a bit more precise, such Jewish folks *are* Judaism. To a significant extent, Judaism ends up being what the Jews say (or think, or believe) it is. Occasionally, Jewish leaders have admitted that this is true, as in the talmudic prohibition, "A court may not issue a decree that is not likely to be upheld by the majority of the community" (*Horayot* 3b).[2] This means that, while a rabbinic court may prohibit one practice or require some other practice, it *may not* do so unless the court senses that the majority of the community will be willing to accept and abide by the ruling. Thus the legislative process, which generates the rules that define Jewish life, is itself limited and constrained by the will of the people.

A second example of the power of ordinary Jewish people to shape Judaism comes from what my Bible professor, Dr. Harry Orlinsky (of blessed memory), used to teach about the holiday of Purim. The Rabbis certainly wouldn't have invented Purim! The holiday is based on the biblical Book of Esther, a bawdy and funny and deeply secular story (God's name appears not a single time in the entire book). Dr. Orlinsky used to say that, in his opinion, this hilarious story of palace intrigue and sex contests was a folktale deeply beloved by the people. The leaders had two choices: They could approve the book and the festival it created, then shape and interpret them to teach "correct" lessons, or they could try to get rid of the book and the holiday as well. Although they would have loved to have taken the latter course, they knew that such an attempt to censor a story or suppress a holiday that the people loved so much could never succeed. Any attempt would only undermine the power and credibility of the leaders. So the story stayed, as did the festival, and both were imbued with positive, valuable messages.

We find a third example from our own time in the issue of intermarriage. In the 1970s and the 1980s, when the problem began to be serious, rabbis would give rip-roaring sermons about how terrible intermarriage was. It didn't help. Intermarriage rates climbed steadily, and the rabbis lost credibility. In the past few years, rabbis have begun to realize that the phenomenon is here to stay, a consequence of the Jews' great success at becoming integrated into every aspect of American life and society. So more and more, rabbis have begun to change their tune. Now they support programs of "outreach to the intermarried" and try to figure out how to come to grips with the phenomenon (which they still oppose) in the best possible way. All these examples teach us that it is the Jews—the grassroots, average, not-so-scholarly Jews—who ultimately decide where Judaism goes, what it does, and how it believes.

With regard to science, the issue is a bit more complicated. It is true that science, with its fascinating ideas and its intriguing theories, is initially developed by scientists. They are the ones who do the research, write the papers, and win the Nobel Prizes. But my interest here is in a different level of science. For although scientists come up with the ideas, the ideas take on a life of their own and have an impact on society independent of the scientists. It is the impact of scientific ideas on average people that interests me precisely because it shapes the way average people think about the world. When your mother told you, "Put your coat and hat on! Do you know how cold it is out there? Do you want to catch pneumonia?" she was expressing a scientific view. It may not have been correct, but it was scientific, for it was based on a popular understanding (or misunderstanding) of a scientific model of how disease works. Or how about the disparaging observation, "What do you expect from him? Of course he's a bum! His father was a bum. The apple doesn't fall far from the tree, you know!" Again, we see the expression of a scientific view of how personality or character traits are passed on from parent to child. It may not be a sophisticated or correct understanding of the process, but it reflects the impact of a scientific understanding, as it has filtered down to the level of common knowledge. Thus, it is not the cutting-edge discoveries and breakthroughs made by the ivory tower elite that interest me, but rather the basic truths that slowly filter down from those developments and breakthroughs to affect the way ordinary people perceive and understand the world.

My purpose in this book can now be stated clearly: I am interested in exploring how the "truths" of science, filtered down to the level where normal, intelligent adults can understand them, affect our understanding of God and some of the basic tenets and beliefs of Judaism. To put it another way, I focus on how our modern understanding of the natural world came to be and how that understanding shapes the metaphors that comprise Judaism.

WHAT MAKES METAPHORS MEANINGFUL?

This is a book about Judaism. The processes and phenomena that fuel the need for this book, however, are true for all religions. At its core, religion—any religion—is a human search for meaning. We live in a very large, highly complex, often terrifying world. Its size and complexity would surely overwhelm us if we could not maintain some semblance of control over it. But how do we control a world that is so much larger than we are? Throughout the ages, humans have achieved that control through understanding. One of the most effective methods for understanding that which mystifies us is metaphor. Many of us recall from our school days learning about the difference between similes (comparisons using *like* or *as*), metaphors (directly equating one thing with another), and analogies (*father* is to *boy* as *mother* is to *girl*). But since all these devices ultimately stem from the same reasoning process, I do not distinguish among them here. For our purposes, then, a metaphor is a comparison of one object, A, to another object, B, where B is more familiar to us than A. Metaphors help us understand a less familiar thing by likening it to a more familiar thing. "Her dress was the color of the sky just after sunset." "I've never tasted it before, but it reminds me of a cross between cinnamon and chocolate." "He shows up here every morning, regular as clockwork." For a metaphor to be effective, object B *must* really be familiar. This may seem obvious, but its importance will become crucial later on. So, the foregoing examples only make sense if you have seen the sky just after sunset, know the flavors of cinnamon and chocolate, and are familiar with clocks and their workings. Or, in a classic example, you may describe the taste of frogs' legs by saying, "No kidding, they taste just like chicken," but one would probably not say, "You know, they taste just like rattlesnake." While the latter may be true (never having tasted either frogs' legs or rattlesnake, I couldn't say), it is less helpful because the average listener *has* tasted chicken, but has *not* tasted rattlesnake. So metaphors, to be useful, *must* be drawn from the set of familiar things.

It will be important later on to bear in mind another feature of metaphor: A metaphor is an approximate, suggestive device, *not* a precise or exact one. The thought process behind metaphorical language (or thinking) is a sort of shorthand. When I say, "He shows up here every morning, regular as clockwork," what I *really* mean is that his arrival every morning has a regularity and dependability that remind me of the regularity and dependability of a clock. I do *not* mean that he has numbers set in a circle on his face, or that he needs to be reset after every power failure! The metaphor is useful as a suggestive device to give a sense of the qualities being described. The value of metaphor in human life in general, and in religion in particular, can hardly be overestimated. In our search for meaning in an overwhelming world, we use this sort of thought process to bring within our grasp that which would otherwise remain unbearably large and incomprehensible.

Let us take a simple example. The ancient Greeks and Romans looked at a sky full of stars and sought to organize them. They did so by seeing constellations as pictures of animals, people, and inanimate objects. They even told stories about how the pictures got into the sky. This was a highly sophisticated form of metaphorical analysis. I do not think that the ancients really believed, literally, that there were bears or hunters or twins in the sky. The stories helped the ancients orient themselves in the universe and understand their place in a cosmos so large that it made them feel very small. The stories had great practical value. Almost every child's first astronomy lesson takes place on a warm summer night when a parent or older sibling points out the Big Dipper. Often the next part of the lesson involves using the end of the Dipper's handle to find the North Star. In a society where navigation is important, this orientation to the stars and their positions is a crucial bit of technological knowledge. So aside from calming the existential discomfort of gazing at a bewildering and disorganized skyful of stars, the metaphorical analysis that leads to constellations contributed in a substantial way to the culture of the peoples who first used it.

Essentially, this sort of metaphorical thinking involves recognizing or identifying patterns in things that we observe and labeling those patterns with *familiar* (remember the chicken and the clockwork) meaningful images that immediately convey the patterns. Thus, a scientist, on an elementary teaching level, will refer to the stars "in the Big Dipper," though no one infers from this that the teacher really thinks there is a huge kitchen utensil up there in the sky, outlined by stars. It is merely convenient pattern recognition. Patterns, and their recognition, are very important in human thinking. In fact, astronomer John Barrow has written that "the heart of the scientific process" is "the transformation of lists of observational data into abbreviated form by the recognition of patterns."[3] The technical term for this process of pattern recognition in lists of observational data is *algorithmic compression*. In mathematics, the core of the idea is that a string of numbers of a particular length can be expressed in a briefer, more efficient form if patterns can be identified and labeled. If no pattern can be identified, that is, if there is no way to describe the string of numbers short of writing it out in full, the string is said to be "random" in the technical sense. Randomness implies meaninglessness, and for human beings, meaninglessness is a source of great anxiety and discomfort. Religion is a search for meaning. And though metaphorical thinking is not mathematical in its form, it is no different in spirit from the scientific process of finding algorithmic compressibility. To describe the seven stars of the Big Dipper as a dipper is far shorter (algorithmically more compressed) than to have to describe the relative position of each star: "Imagine four stars in a roughly square configuration, actually more of a trapezoid with the bottom shorter than the top, then three other stars arranged in a crooked line near the top." Not only is the description long, it's also hard to follow and clumsy. "A dipper, with four stars in the bowl and three more making a crooked handle" is far more efficient.

Given the importance of pattern recognition for both science and ordinary human thought, including religious thought, it is interesting that scientists often reject its value when it is dressed in nontechnical garb. Such a rejection can be seen in what physicist Paul Davies writes of the eighteenth-century image of the universe as a watch, which must therefore imply the existence, intelligence, and skill of some cosmic watchmaker. Davies critiques both the image and the thought process that produces it:

> The weakness of this argument ... is that it proceeds by analogy. The mechanistic universe is analogous to the watch; the watch had a designer, so therefore the universe must have had a designer. One might as well say that the universe is like an organism, so therefore it must have grown from a fetus in a cosmic womb! Clearly no analogical argument can amount to a proof. The best it can do is offer support for a hypothesis.[4]

Davies makes two mistakes here. First, he comes perilously close to forgetting the rule, described above, about the imprecise nature of metaphors. Describing the world as a watch, or, for that matter, as an organism, is not meant to imply that the two are identical, but to suggest certain characteristics with respect to which the two are similar. Thus, likening the world to an organism does not necessarily mean it grew like a fetus in a cosmic womb,[5] but it may imply that the world or the universe, like an organism, grows, matures, develops, ages, evolves, or perhaps even has awareness or consciousness. Second, Davies is mistaken when he claims that, at best, such analogies can only offer support for a hypothesis. In fact, metaphorical thinking can do far more than that! It can offer, in "algorithmically compressed" (though nontechnical) form, a description of a vast system (the universe) by which many features of that system can be quickly and easily grasped. This makes analogy a tremendously powerful tool for communicating and for thinking. Thus, to return yet again to frogs' legs, suppose you ask a friend who has tasted these amphibious delicacies, "So what do they taste like?" If your friend says, "They're not like anything else I've ever tasted. You just have to try them," he has said, in essence, that the "data set" that comprises the taste of frogs' legs is not algorithmically compressible. The answer "sort of like chicken," on the other hand, provides you with a great deal of information in highly compressed form. Similarly, typical religious statements rooted in metaphor, for example, "The Lord is my shepherd" (Ps. 23:1), are highly effective tools for communicating complex ideas in compressed form. We are not sheep, nor does God carry a crooked staff. But the image of "shepherd" represents, for the psalmist, caring, protection, guidance, and perhaps much more.

If religious metaphors have such great communicative value, why would such a sophisticated thinker as Davies discount their usefulness so completely? Should we not expect that a scientist, trained and conditioned to evaluate phenomena objectively, would grasp the importance of religious thought in human life? Before proceeding with our analysis, it may be worthwhile to spend a moment on this important issue.

SCIENCE AND RELIGION: NATURAL ENEMIES?

Davies's disparagement of the value of analogy seems to imply that religion is incompatible with science. His attitude, I think, is evident when he comments that "Einstein was not religious in the conventional sense, but he liked to use God as a metaphor for expressing deep questions of existence."[6] In so saying, Davies seems to be expressing a discomfort with conventional religion. I think he's suggesting that no one as brilliant and as deeply committed to scientific truth as Einstein could ever be *really* religious (even though Davies often quotes statements made by Einstein that suggest that the latter was, indeed, deeply religious). I suspect that Davies imagines religion "in the conventional sense" to be an arcane set of outmoded traditions, rituals, and dogmatic beliefs that no really intelligent person (a category of which Einstein, in our day, still stands as an outstanding exemplar) would value. This view is not uncommon. Michael Shermer, in his book *How We Believe: The Search for God in an Age of Science*, comments that "higher education is associated with lower religiosity" and that "interest in science corresponds to lower religious intensity."[7] In another passage, Davies imagines a theist and an atheist debating the usefulness of describing God as the cause of the Big Bang.[8] The atheist (who, I suspect, speaks for Davies himself) claims that the idea is useless because it does not meet the criteria for a good scientific theory. The problem with this claim is not its accuracy but its relevance. In fact, the goal of religion is not (or ought not to be) the construction of good scientific theories. The goal of religion is to seek good and useful—that is, meaningful— metaphors that will, as Davies put it, express "deep questions of existence." The highly respected physicist Murray Gell-Mann comes close to allowing this view (though he stops short of endorsing it) when he concludes a lengthy discussion of belief systems, myth, superstition, and magic:

> We can look upon myth and magic, then, in at least three different and complementary ways:
>
> 1. as attractive but unscientific theories, comforting but false regularities imposed on nature;
>
> 2. as cultural schemata that help to give identity to societies, for better or for worse; and

3. as part of the grand search for pattern, for creative association, that includes artistic work and that enriches human life.[9]

I am willing to go even further than Gell-Mann and say that, although we *could* view religion in any of these three ways, I *choose* to take the most optimistic (and, I admit, an ideally prescriptive rather than realistically descriptive) view, that is to say, his third option. If it is to be taken seriously in our time, religion, and specifically Judaism, *must* be seen as "part of the grand search for patterns, for creative association" and, most important, for meaning.

RELIGION AT ITS BEST OR NOT

Of course, the reality of religious life and thought, of Jewish life and thought, has not always matched this aspiration. Religion has often turned into a closed, narrow system of dogmatic beliefs and prescribed, rote practices that lend little meaning to followers' lives beyond the social cohesion and societal control that such a tightly run system affords. A classic example comes from a legal issue concerning the eating of *matzah* (unleavened bread) and *maror* (bitter herbs) at the Passover seder. These two ritual eating events resonate deeply with the story of the Israelite enslavement in and liberation from Egypt. The *matzah* reminds the participants both of the meager food on which their enslaved ancestors had to subsist and of the hardships they endured as refugees in the desert after the Exodus. The bitter herbs are symbolic of the bitterness of slavery for any society. Eating both is a potentially powerful piece of religious "theater" whereby the seder participants actually taste the memories of which the Haggadah speaks. Against the background of this tremendously compelling ritual, the following texts, which are typical of an entire genre of religious writing, are startling:

How big a piece of *Matzah* corresponds to an olive? The exact answer will, of course, depend on the thickness of the *Matzahs*; however, the Chazon Ish considered a piece the size of half a machine baked *Matzah* generally sufficient, while according to Rabbi Moshe Feinstein a piece of about 4" by 7" (roughly two-thirds of a machine *Matzah*) is needed. (When a double portion is called for, he considers a piece of about 6 1/4" by 7" sufficient.)

The quantity of *Maror* to be eaten on each occasion also has to be equal to an olive. In the case of Romaine Lettuce, this requires (according to Rabbi Moshe Feinstein) enough center ribs to cover an area 3-by-5 inches. If whole leaves are used, they should cover an area 8-by-10 inches). In the case of pure, grated horseradish, it should be the amount that can be packed into a vessel measuring 1.1 fluid ounces.

It is suggested that, for measuring purposes, one prepare before the seder a piece of cardboard on which is marked off the area to be covered with Romaine Lettuce and *Matzah*.[10]

[T]he *k'zias* [volume equivalent to an olive's bulk] of *matzahh* and *maror* must be eaten in a span of four minutes. Since eating definitely involves ingesting, and does not necessarily involve chewing, we suggest that people continue to chew the *matzahh* without swallowing, until their mouths are full to capacity. Thus, the time from which one is considered to have begun eating is deferred.[11]

These texts, and the religious culture that they represent, seem to drain all the meaning, drama, and power out of the seder, leaving behind only a strict set of narrow behavioral prescriptions. Focusing on the number of square inches of *matzah* or *maror* poses a threat to the search for meaning in life. If these texts were the sole paradigm for "religion in the conventional sense," I would agree wholeheartedly with Paul Davies. I could not imagine why anyone who is really intelligent, and certainly anyone who is seriously committed to science, would ever be attracted to such a system that limits inquiry and is threatened by whole categories of questions.

I believe deeply, however, that religion, like any other human system of belief, understanding, or behavior, is not an all-or-nothing sort of thing. Rather, it is a complex structure, with many components. In any given religious system, we may find some components compelling, others repelling or horrifying, and still others that leave us indifferent. I believe that we need *not* buy the whole package; we can ignore or reject elements of the system that we find objectionable. For example, the minute laws about how much *matzah* and *maror* one must eat, and how many minutes one may have to do so are a part of Jewish tradition that I do not incorporate into my personal Jewish life. For me, they do not reflect religion at its best.

For me, religion at its best is a concerted attempt to understand God, the world, and our own lives and how these three elements interact. It is a search for meaning and for guidance that is never afraid of posing ultimate questions. Its goal is to achieve a tiny bit of control over an overwhelmingly vast and complex universe by finding patterns and meanings in it. In the interest of fairness I must admit that this view is *not* shared by all who care about religion. Many would disagree, arguing that religion is about finding the Truth as revealed by God, or by ancestors, to their particular faith community. Once the adherents to the religion are firmly in possession of the Truth, they are willing to defend it (tragically, often to the death) against all other candidates for truth or meaning. Many even insist that the veracity of their Truth is "proved" by science, as when they search the fields of cosmology or evolutionary biology for indications that the creation story of Genesis is, in fact the Truth. I disagree strongly with such approaches. They miss the most important point of religion. Religion is an ongoing attempt—one of many devised by humans—to find patterns, and therefore meaning, in life.

RESISTANCE TO CHANGE
IN SCIENCE AND RELIGION

In science, one must always stand ready to abandon completely positions or theories formulated in the past when they are over-turned by new data, new theories, or new understandings. Ultimately, the goal of scientists is to express the most precise, insightful, and complete explanation possible *now* for the ele-ments of the natural world that those scientists are investigat-ing. Thus, no matter how firmly earlier scientists held a view of a given facet of nature, contemporary scientists *must* abandon that view if it is disproved or simply becomes a less convincing explanation of the phenomenon than a new, alternative expla-nation. (Of course, abandoning the old in the face of a new, bet-ter explanation is the ideal, science at its best. In reality, we know that scientists, like other human beings, cling tenaciously to familiar views, despite the pressure of new information or new theories. A classic example is Einstein's own inability to fully accept quantum theory!)

Religion is somewhat different. The main goal of religion is to provide explanations, structures, and metaphors that enhance the meaning of human life. Because meaning for human beings always has a great deal to do with relationships to and identity with a larger social unit than the self, religion tends to value ancient truths simply because they are ancient. In other words, if my ancestors (in a religious tradition structured around familial transmission) or my master's master's master (in a religion transmitted primarily through the master-disciple relationship) held a particular view, I cherish that view in part because doing so connects me with the ancients. That connection gives me a clearer picture of who I am, what group I belong to, and why I am here—all these are important parts of the elusive "meaning" that we humans crave. This being so, religious thinkers, unlike scientists, tend to be extremely cautious about discarding ancient views in favor of new ones. Because a decision to abandon a traditional belief tends to dissociate the contemporary religious person from his or her ancestors, such a decision would likely *reduce* the amount of meaning in life. Thus, such a drastic step should generally be reserved for cases in which adopting a new position benefits the community so much that the benefit outweighs the cost of breaking links with the past. Such might be the case, for example, if the traditional view has become so highly implausible that it has lost its power to convince the community of its truth, or if it has come to be seen as anathema to generally accepted contemporary norms and values.

Although adhering strictly to traditional belief is a natural part of religion, it is also important for religion (again, religion at its best, not at its worst) to recast traditional views in the conceptual and metaphorical language of the day. Doing so allows each new generation to feel personally connected with ancient traditions. After all, ancient traditions, whose only claim to authenticity is that they are old, run the risk of becoming old-fashioned. But if an ancient tradition can claim to be not only ancient but also timeless and contemporary as well, it has a far greater chance of convincing each new, young generation of its value. Such a claim requires that each generation's retelling use the new metaphors of the new generation. Unfortunately, it seems that this often does not happen, as can be seen in the story of a young boy who came home from Sunday school and reported to his father that they had learned the story of the Exodus from Egypt. "So the Israelites left

Egypt, then they got to the Red Sea. They turned around and saw that the Egyptians had changed their minds about letting them leave and were in hot pursuit. Moses quickly organized several teams of skilled combat engineers who constructed pontoon bridges. All the Israelites crossed the sea on the bridges, then, just as the Egyptians were starting across, the engineers blew up the bridges."

"Are you *sure* that's the way you learned the story?" asked his incredulous father.

"No," the boy answered, "but the way they told us the story you wouldn't believe it in a million years!"

What makes the joke funny is that we postmodern folks are all familiar with a certain level of disbelief that engages when we read biblical stories of miracles. They *don't* make sense to us, and even our children are aware of that. Often we react to these unbelievable tales by continuing to tell them, while taking them *and the entire system they represent* less and less seriously. The result is a world in which many people, even if they still participate nominally in some aspects of religious life, do not see religion as a source of truth. That has become the domain of science. Research, experiments, laboratories—these are the realm of truth.

A primary goal of this book is to restore some of the credibility that religion has lost in our era by exploring how the ideas, beliefs, and norms that we inherit from our ancestors might be understood in the context of a world in which space flight, atom smashing, and black holes are common features of our metaphorical landscape.

THE GOD QUESTION

What is God? To the ears of traditional Jews, this question is audacious, foolish, and perhaps even blasphemous. The Jewish people, in their roughly three millennia of literary productivity, have rarely asked it. The Torah itself opens with the words, "When God began to create,"[12] or, in the older, more familiar translation, "In the beginning, God created." Either way, God is the first assumption, the starting point. The text never questions who or what God is (not to mention whether God is), but rather immediately takes up the question of what God *does*. The situation is similar in rabbinic literature—Talmud, *midrash,* and so on. In the medieval period, the great Jewish Aristotelian philosopher Moses Maimonides (1135–1204), along with most of the other philosophers of the period, did ask a closely related question, namely, "How can we prove whether God exists?" The answer, rooted in the first principles of Aristotelian thought, was based on the fact that the world exists, that every effect has a cause, and that the philosophers rejected the possibility of an infinite regress of any chain of causality. Thus the chain of cause and effect had to start somewhere, so God's existence as the uncaused cause is proved.[13] But this is not quite the same question as the one I have posed. Maimonides avoids answering the "what is God?" question as much as possible. The closest he comes to answering it is the development of a system of "negative attributes," that is, things we can say that God is *not*. Ultimately, however, we can say very little of what God *is*. In the early decades of the twentieth century, the great American Jewish thinker Mordecai M. Kaplan did ask the question and answered that God is the power of goodness and salvation in the world.[14]

Can I presume to stand with the likes of Maimonides, Kaplan, and the other luminaries of Jewish philosophical history? The answer is simple: no. My purpose, my interest, and my questions are not philosophical in any technical sense. I am not trying to plumb the inner essence of the Divine, or figure out what God "really" is. I do not think that we can know with any certainty. Such limitation of knowledge is part of what being human is all about. But another part of being human, a primary and critical part, is our propensity to think and to speak. So what I am asking is: How do we *think* about and *speak* about God? In other words, given the vast mystery of God, what *metaphors* shall we use to describe God?

The question is important, in part, because in the last century or so we Jews, together with many others, have found the ancient traditional metaphors less and less convincing and tenable. We inherited metaphors for God from our ancestors— God as king, shepherd, protector of the weak, healer of the sick, and so on—that have sounded increasingly hollow as the modern age has progressed. As our scientific understanding of the world grew, we increasingly identified forces in nature, politics, or other areas of life as being responsible for control, protection, disaster, and healing. Two brief examples of this will suffice.

When our enemies attacked and persecuted us in ancient times, we attributed their success, or failure, to God's grand plan. When we were attacked and decimated, our enemies were the rod with which God delivered chastisements or punishments because of our sins. On the other hand, if we were attacked but we successfully repelled the enemy and inflicted great losses on them, we understood this as a sign of God's grace and protection. In modern times, however, we have developed all manner of sophisticated theories citing psychological, political, economic, and even religious reasons for these outcomes. And we have responded, in part, by asking ourselves, "What can *we* do to prevent further persecution?" As we piled answer upon answer, we developed quite a large repertoire of responses. Some Jews thought it best to assimilate. Others felt the pressing need to fight back, with physical force or political or economic power. Still others chose to respond by establishing a Jewish state where we could be safe (and where, by the logic of some early Zionists, we would not be bothered by the nations of the world, since the gentiles' hatred of us came from our constant presence as an unwelcome "guest" in their world). But among all the creative, bold responses, rarely did modern Jews ever say, "Let's pray to God to protect us." Some of the soldiers in the Israeli army certainly pray, as do some of the Jewish activists who lobby Congress, march on the United Nations, or encourage others to bring economic pressure to bear on countries that oppress Jews. But their prayers are never more than an adjunct to their primary activity. The model of prayer as the sole strategy for coping with crisis, which had been a mainstay of Jewish response for centuries, had lost credibility. This loss, though reflected in many large and small ways, is nowhere more painfully heard than in the question "Where was God during the Holocaust?" It is not my intention here to address the question. I raise it simply because the frequency with which it is asked is an indication that one of the old metaphors for God seems to have stopped working. "The Guardian of Israel neither slumbers nor sleeps," proclaims the psalmist (Ps. 121:4), but the modern Jew, who learned as a child to recite the litany of persecutions, pogroms, and murderous attacks which we have suffered throughout the ages, is unconvinced.

A second example: Throughout many centuries of Jewish life, the physical fragility of the human body was often interpreted as being in the hands of God. Deuteronomy promised that if we violated the terms of the Covenant, we would be stricken with plagues of all sorts.

> But if you do not heed the word of the Eternal your God, to observe faithfully all His commandments and laws which I enjoin upon you this day, all these curses shall come upon you and take effect: ... The Eternal will strike you with consumption, fever, and inflammation, with scorching heat and drought, with blight and mildew.... The Eternal will strike you with the Egyptian

inflammation, with hemorrhoids, boil-scars, and itch
from which you shall never recover. (Deut. 8:15, 22, 27)

The Rabbis composed numerous prayers and blessings
asking God for healing and identifying God as "the healer of
the sick." Yet as the modern age moved along and medical science flourished, we came increasingly to believe that diseases
are caused by germs, or genetic mutations, or environmental
toxins and that healing can come through drugs, surgery, or
other high-tech human interventions. True, even now we are
able to control only a small fraction of the ills that plague us,
but our *belief* has shifted so that we rarely assume that the diseases still left uncured or the ailments still unalleviated are
God's domain. Instead we raise money for research and read
the newspapers daily, always expecting the next medical miracle or technological breakthrough. And despite the recent trend
toward focusing on nontechnological spiritual sources of "healing,"[15] most Jews, I think, still see medicine, human technology,
and the body's own power to heal itself (that is, nature) as the
source of healing, not God.

These intellectual and cultural developments of modernity
that have convinced most people of the truth of science and the
untruth of ancient beliefs leave us with a limited number of
choices. The first, and by far the most common, response is to
conclude that religion in general and Judaism in particular are
deeply mired in a set of obsolete, archaic, and completely meaningless ideas that therefore have no claim on our lives and
deserve neither our time nor our attention, not to mention our
respect. It is an interesting historical curiosity that people once
believed that the sun was a fiery chariot driven through the sky
by Apollo, or that disease and health were once thought to be
meted out and controlled by gods or demons, but these ideas
are so completely outmoded that the average person is not
likely to spend much time or energy on them. The same

response or, more precisely, lack of response applies to Judaism. It is filled with interesting historical curiosities—that the rainbow was God's bow, placed in the cloud as a reminder for God never again to destroy the earth by flood—but can have little real meaning for us or our lives. The second response is to conclude that the old religions—including Judaism—are, not surprisingly, cast in old and obsolete molds and that we should look for new religions. Either of these first two responses leads, obviously, away from any interest in or commitment to Judaism.

I want to propose a third response. I propose that what has collapsed in the last few centuries of astounding growth in human technology and scientific understanding is not the *essence* of ancient religion, but rather the ancient metaphors in which ancient religions were framed, studied, and expressed. This is a critical distinction that is often missed by those who disparage religious belief. For example, Michael Shermer, the founder of the Skeptics Society, writes about his conversion as a young man to "born again" Christian belief. After describing the process of his conversion and the passion that accompanied it, he describes the problems that he encountered. Not surprisingly, one major issue was "the 'Problem of Evil': If God is omnibenevolent (all good) and omnipotent, then why is there evil in the world?"[16] After a very brief review of the problem, Shermer laments that "God is not the plenipotent Yahweh of Abraham, the King of Kings and Lord of Lords Sovereign of the Universe."[17] His conclusion is that belief in God is somehow outmoded and silly, or at the very least obsolete in an age of science. Never does he consider the possibility that an age of science may simply call for new metaphors, new ways of thinking about God. The collapse of ancient, inherited metaphors for God—healer, protector, shepherd, and so on— does not *necessarily* imply the collapse of God or of our belief in God. Rather, I take it as a challenge to develop a new set of metaphors for thinking and talking about God. If they are to prove useful, these new metaphors will have to be based on plausible, current ideas about the world and how it works. This is the task ahead.

I must add a note of warning here: While the language of physics suggests new metaphors that—at least to me—seem to do a better job of communicating ancient beliefs or ideas than some of the old metaphors, these new metaphors occasionally lead to brand-new ideas or beliefs that are sometimes incompatible with ancient components of Jewish tradition. When this happens, you may find yourself rejecting the new idea simply because it is new and uncomfortable. I make this observation from personal experience. But I urge you: Try as hard as you can to listen to the new possibilities with an open mind. You may ultimately reject them, but try not to do so without first giving them a fair hearing. Jewish tradition has *not* survived and flourished for these many centuries by being static. It has evolved and developed new ideas, sometimes requiring old ideas to be consigned to the dustbin of Jewish history. However, I believe that Judaism will ultimately be strengthened, and not weakened, by creativity and change.

THE METHOD

It may be helpful to describe briefly the journey that took me from my first ideas for this book to its completion. First of all, I am not a scientist. I have not taken a course in hard science or math since high school. But I *do* know quite a lot about Judaism, having studied for five very full-time years at rabbinical school followed by eleven part-time years in graduate school and having continued my studies constantly since then on a less formal level. The result of all that study is that, while I don't know everything, I do know where to look everything up.

After initially conceiving of the idea for this project, I obviously had to read a lot of science. But because of my limited academic background in science and math, I was limited in my reading to nontechnical, nonmathematical, purely descriptive books. These are tough, but not impossible, to find. I soon learned that there are some brilliant physicists in the world who seem to take great pride in being able to explain their fields of expertise without resorting to formulas or technical jargon. As I read book after book of physics, I allowed myself to free-associate the material I was reading with the Jewish ideas, texts, religious practices, and beliefs that I carry around in my head. I looked for anything in the world of physics that seemed in any way relevant to the world of Jewish life and thought. Each time I found a connection, I followed it to see where it would lead—often ending up in some surprising places. I then organized those connections so that each chapter of the book focuses on one particular area of physics.

This is not a finished product, for two reasons. First of all, my intention is that the ideas I am presenting here regarding new ways of thinking about and expressing Jewish ideas and beliefs will begin a discussion. I am quite certain that I have not exhausted the ways in which the metaphoric language of physics can shed light on being Jewish. It is more likely that I have only scratched the surface. I hope that others will rise to the challenge and continue to explore these linkages, for I believe that the more connections we find between ancient Jewish life and contemporary experience, the healthier Jewish life will be. The second reason for the unfinished nature of this work is the eternally unfinished nature of science. Especially when dealing with the newest developments, it is not unusual for new fields to be developed or, occasionally, for old ones to be discarded. If the *method* that I have used here is a productive one, however, then it will allow the discussion and the exploration to proceed.

A NOTE ON THE TRANSLATION

The Bible translation I have used in this book is almost entirely from the Jewish Publication Society's translation of *The Tanakh* (1985). This translation uses what we today recognize as "masculine God language." This is in contrast to the language that I have used in my text throughout the book, but I leave the masculine God language intact to preserve the authenticity of the citations.

1
COSMOLOGY AND CREATION
In Search of Beginnings

ANCIENT COSMOLOGY

One of the most important roles of God in the history of religion is that of creator of the world. According to the beliefs of many religious systems, God's status as creator precedes (both logically and chronologically) any revelation of self, issuance of moral law, or initiation of special relationship with any group, family, or nation. The biblical view of how this happened is typical—and typically unclear. According to the first chapter of Genesis, the creation took six days; it started with the creation of light and culminated in the creation of human beings. Chapter 2 of Genesis suggests a different process; it begins with the creation of humans (or perhaps a single human male), then moves on to the creation of a garden, animals, and, finally, a woman. In various psalms and the closing chapters of Job, the story includes images of God subduing various primordial monsters.[1] Though the details vary throughout the Bible, some elements of the story remain fairly constant: An intelligent

1

being, that is, God, created the world in a deliberate manner. That being existed before the creation and *chose* to create the world. Finally, all this happened within the last few thousand years (the reckoning of the traditional Jewish calendar sets the creation in about the year 3761 B.C.E.).

This biblical portrayal of creation seems incredible to many contemporary readers for several reasons. First, numerous forms of scientific evidence, including data from biology, geology, anthropology, paleontology, and other disciplines, suggest that our planet is far older than the nearly six thousand years allowed for by the traditional Jewish calendar—probably four to five *billion* years older!—and that the universe is at least ten billion years older than that. Second, the biblical accounts all place the earth and its human inhabitants at the center of the creative process, while modern science tells us that our planet is, on a cosmic scale, a rather insignificant bit of stuff orbiting a medium-sized star in a galaxy of billions of stars, which is only one among billions of galaxies. Thus, the privileged position of our planet or our species in the Bible seems unlikely and myopic at best. Finally, the idea of a thinking, deliberate, pre-existing God sitting "out there" (out where?—modern scientific notions of the universe do not permit us to imagine any "place" outside it) somewhere before the creation and deciding how many species of hawk to create or whether to give humans opposable thumbs flies in the face of everything that we have believed about the evolution of life since Darwin's time. In addition, such a portrayal raises nasty, unanswerable (and, therefore, in some quarters, religiously unaskable) questions such as: Where did God come from? When and by what creative agency was God created? Where did God reside before creating the universe? and so on and on.

These and many other questions lead many contemporary readers of the Bible to one of two conclusions. One is that the biblical account reflects the best, most scientific guesses available to the ancient Israelites in the second and first millennia

B.C.E. but has little explanatory value for us today. God had nothing to do with creation. The biblical account makes a great, simple story for children (or primitive adults) but is not much use to sophisticated modern adults like us. Therefore, religion in general and Judaism in particular have nothing substantial to say about the aching human quest to understand the universe in which we live, its origins, or our place in it. This view is typical of religious and intellectual liberals. Such people view creationists (who espouse a belief that the biblical creation narrative is literally true) as either foolish or crazy, no more deserving of serious intellectual attention than the members of the Flat Earth Society. The second possible conclusion (one which I generally have espoused myself) is that the biblical creation stories have nothing to do with the science of cosmology. Rather, they are poetic pieces of literature meant to convey values, moral beliefs, and social philosophy. This view makes it easier to read the Bible sympathetically and to gain wisdom and understanding from it, but leads nevertheless to the conclusion, once again, that religion has nothing to tell us of cosmology.

Either of these approaches leads the best intentioned of modern people to a sort of split-personality approach to religion. They may value religious teachings for moral lessons but switch out of religious thought mode and into scientific thought mode when they turn to questions of the origins of life and the universe. Religion is seen as an aid to a limited part of our lives, but not as having relevance to every aspect of the human condition. This view and the narrow strictures it places on the role and relevance of religion disturb me. The Judaism that I value and teach urges me to find a way to apply it to every area of life. It resists being restricted to the limited (though important) realm of social behavior. Intuitively, it seems to me that if the truths of Judaism—or of any other religious tradition—are ultimate truths, then they ought to have something to say about the most basic ultimate human questions, including those about the historical origins of the universe. This chapter explores the possible relevance of Jewish religious ideas to creation. It sketches out very briefly some of the teachings of modern scientific cosmology, and then discuss how those teachings might relate to the Jewish religious metaphors by which Jewish tradition has described the world.

SCIENTIFIC COSMOLOGY

The general consensus among cosmologists today[2] places the beginning of creation in an event known as the Big Bang, a term first used in 1950 by British physicist Fred Hoyle. The Big Bang was a violent explosion, about fifteen billion years ago, that began as an infinitesimal area of energy, infinitely compressed by the pressure of gravity—that is, its size was zero—and therefore infinitely dense. Physicists call this situation a *singularity*.[3]

Four questions occur to me right at the start, because of their specific relevance to a whole set of theological issues with which traditional Jewish texts have a great deal of difficulty. If the scientific account of creation cannot address them any more comfortably than Jewish tradition, then we will have gained little by abandoning Genesis in favor of theoretical physics. The questions are: (1) Where did the Big Bang occur? (2) What was the situation *before* the Big Bang? (3) What, exactly, exploded during the Big Bang? (That is, if the Big Bang resulted in the creation of all "stuff," then what stuff was there to explode?) (4) What caused the Big Bang to occur?

WHERE DID IT ALL BEGIN?

Paradoxically, the answer to the first question seems to be that the Big Bang occurred *everywhere*. How can this be so if the size of the Big Bang (the singularity) was zero? In our day-to-day lives, we think of "space" as an endlessly huge, empty expanse filled with an infinite number of locations at which things can occur. Every location is "somewhere" in the emptiness. Imagine an immense room in which any spot can be defined precisely as being a certain distance from one wall, a certain distance from a second wall, at right angles to the first wall, and a certain distance up from the floor (or down from the ceiling—it doesn't matter). With this system, I can locate any spot, whether in my bedroom, in a gigantic sports stadium, or in the state of Texas—or anywhere else. It is important to realize that we generally assume space to be a static, fixed background through which things move. We distinguish between the "stuff" in the world and the "space" it occupies. I can move things around, shift them from one location to another, but the space through which they move does not change.

Modern cosmology does not share these everyday assumptions about space. For decades, physicists have been quite certain that the space of the universe is expanding. The possibility of this expansion first occurred to astronomers in the 1920s when they realized that the color of the light from all distant stars is red-shifted (that is, it looks a bit redder than expected), or moved a bit toward the red end of the visible spectrum.

What does this mean? First of all, it's important to realize that modern science understands light to be energy that travels in waves (see figure 1.1A). We all learned in grade school that the spectrum of visible light, as seen in a rainbow or cast on a wall when sunlight passes through a prism, is designated as ROY-G-BIV, that is, *Red Orange Yellow Green Blue Indigo Violet*. These colors represent a range of wavelengths from the longest (red) to the shortest (violet). *Wavelength* is the distance between the crest of one energy wave and the crest of the next. It is this property of light that determines what color our eyes perceive any given light source to be. When heated to very high temperatures, different materials emit different wavelengths, or colors, of light in a precisely predictable way.

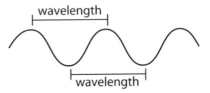

Figure 1.1A: The wavelength is the distance between the crest of one wave and the crest of the next, or the trough of one wave and the trough of the next.

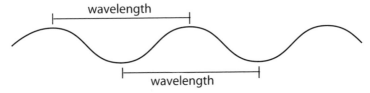

Figure 1.1B: The longer the wavelength, the redder the light.

Astronomers who had studied many stars had good reason to expect certain wavelengths to be emitted under certain conditions. They expected to see certain specific colors, but their expectations were not met. The light from distant stars had a longer wavelength than it should have (compare figure 1.1A to figure 1.1B); the stars appeared too red. Eventually, scientists determined that this shift toward red is caused by the Doppler effect. The stars are moving away from us, and so the light waves, as they reach us, are more stretched out and appear redder. This is the optical equivalent of the apparent drop in pitch of an ambulance siren as the ambulance speeds away from us. As the distance between the vehicle and our ear increases, the sound waves "stretch out" and the pitch of the sound (pitch in sound, like color in light, is determined by wavelength) seems lower than it would if the vehicle were not moving away. Although there is some controversy among cosmologists as to exactly how fast the universe is expanding, the fact of its expansion is virtually undisputed.

Perhaps the strangest part of the idea of the expanding universe is the assertion that the stars and galaxies themselves are *not* moving away from each other through empty space, the way an ambulance speeds off through the space of the city. Rather, the *space* in which the stars and galaxies are located is *itself* expanding, stretching, becoming larger. An analogy commonly used by physicists to explain this idea to nonphysicists is that of a balloon with polka dots drawn all over it. As the balloon is inflated, the "space" of the balloon expands, causing each dot to move away from every other dot. This analogy is somewhat unsatisfying, however, since we know that the balloon is expanding *into* the space of the room in which it is being inflated. If we imagine blowing up a very large balloon in a very small room, we can visualize how, as the balloon inflates, it occupies more and more of the space in the room. Eventually it will fill the whole room and (assuming the inflation pressure is insufficient to break apart the walls of the room) stop growing. Unlike the balloon, however, the expanding universe is *not* expanding "into" any pre-existing space. Rather, space itself is expanding.

Based on the study of this expansion, scientists are able to plot the history of the size of the universe in reverse. They know roughly the size of the universe now (though there is some controversy over that as well), and they know roughly the speed at which it is expanding. Knowing these two things, cosmologists imagine the expansion in reverse and calculate what would happen if the universe *contracted* at the same rate starting from its present state. These calculations are like running a videotape backward to see how the movie began. After about fifteen billion years of "rewinding the tape" of history, they arrive at the Big Bang. At that instant, the universe, which today measures at least fifteen billion light-years across,[4] was crowded into an unimaginably tiny spot whose size at the very instant of the Big Bang was zero. At that instant, there was no space, no expanse, no emptiness outside that point of zero size. All space that we experience, every bit of every expanse that ever has been or ever will be, was condensed into that spot. That *was* the universe, and there was nothing outside it. The problem in imagining this, of course, is that if the entire universe was far, far smaller than the period at the end of a sentence on this page, I'm forced by my everyday experiences to ask what was next to it, above it, or below it. The idea that the entire universe could have been microscopically small, that there might have been nothing else, is one of the leaps of "faith"—an interesting term in the realm of science!—that modern physics asks us to make. Thus, the answer to the first question is that the Big Bang happened everywhere. All places that can be identified as being "somewhere" in the universe were, at the moment of the Big Bang, all squashed into the same place.

WHAT CAME BEFORE THE BEGINNING?

The second question leads, unfortunately, to no less paradoxical an answer. What was the situation *before* the Big Bang? The answer is that there was no "before." Words such as *before* and *after* only have meaning and can only be used in an environment that has *time* as one of its essential attributes. One of the revolutionary realizations that came out of Einstein's general theory of relativity (which is discussed at length in chapter 5), however, was that time is inextricably bound up with space. In fact, just as space is often defined with reference to three (spatial) dimensions, namely height, width, and depth, so time is often referred to as the fourth dimension. Since Einstein's day, the two have been so closely linked that it has become common to refer not to "space" and "time" separately, but to a single entity known as *space-time*. This being so, there could have been no time before the Big Bang because time came into existence together with space as a *result* of the Big Bang.

We now find ourselves face-to-face with another concept that defies visualization, namely, the creation of time. At a certain point in the finite past, time came into existence, thereby allowing the use, from that point onward, of ideas such as "before," "after," "duration," and so on. We are accustomed, in everyday life, to think about existence occurring on a stage of space and time. Just as we know that the stage in the theater was there before the actors in a given performance stood on it, we "know" intuitively that this stage of time and space was here before we were. The problem is that modern cosmology asks us to imagine that the stage of time and space was created at a particular instant. With a theater, such imagining is easy. We know that the theater was built in, say, 1958. But we also know that *before* the theater was built, the location that it now occupies was a parking lot, or a tenement, or a wheat field. In the case of space-time, we are being asked to imagine that there was a time when the stage—space and time—did not exist; in fact, nothing existed. This violates our common sense and is hard to do. But it is no harder than other leaps of imagination that human beings have made in the past and that we now take for granted. Any schoolchild "knows" that the sun is stationary relative to the earth and the earth rotates. Yet our practical experience tells us just the opposite, that the earth is stationary and the sun moves, "rising" in the east every morning and "setting" in the west each evening. Many people in the past (Galileo being the best known of the lot) suffered quite a lot for professing their belief in the counterintuitive picture of reality, but in the end we have gotten used to it. We take it for granted. The same process will eventually occur with regard to the counterintuitive reality that modern cosmology describes regarding the interconnectedness of space and time and the fact that both came into existence as a result of the Big Bang. It still feels rather strange, however, because we aren't used to it yet.

There is a rabbinic *midrash*, an interpretive comment on the Torah from the period of the Talmud, in which the homilist raises the question of why the first letter of the Torah was a *bet* ‎ב‎ (that is, the second letter of the Hebrew alphabet) instead of an *aleph* ‎א‎ (the first letter of the alphabet, which would have made more sense). The question is an important one from the point of view of the Rabbis, for if the Torah is the document at the foundation of the world, it is important to know something about the cornerstone of that foundation. Essentially, the question is an ancient Jewish equivalent to asking, "Why did the world begin the way it did?" Among the several answers offered in the *midrash*, we find the following:

> Rabbi Jonah said in the name of Rabbi Levi: Why was the world created with a *"bet"*? The *"bet"* is closed on three sides and open only on the fourth. This teaches that one should not question what is above or what is below, or what came before, but only what transpired from the day of the world's creation forward. (*Bereshit Rabbah* 1:10)

This *midrash*, in its original context, is a rather disturbing limitation on "permitted questions." But in the context of the present discussion, about the absurdity of certain kinds of questions about the Big Bang, the *midrash* takes on new meaning. Perhaps the shape of the letter *bet* does not prohibit the asking of questions. Rather, it shows us which questions have meaning and which do not! In the case of questions regarding space and time, it is only meaningful to ask them about events that occurred "from this point—that is, the point of the Big Bang—forth."[5]

THE RAW MATERIALS OF CREATION

Having dealt with the issues of where and when the Big Bang happened, the third question becomes, at least superficially, far easier to answer. What *stuff* exploded in the Big Bang? The answer is that there was no "stuff" since all "stuff," all matter, came into existence as a result of the Big Bang. The explosion was not one of "stuff" at all, but only an explosive and sudden release of a massive amount of pure energy, which later cooled and "congealed" into matter.

What is fascinating to me about these last two questions— the question of what preceded the beginning and that of what raw materials were present at the beginning—is their close parallels in ancient religious debates. Since the dawn of systematic philosophical thinking (which we may conveniently, if not precisely, date to the fifth century B.C.E. in Athens, the era of Plato and Aristotle), philosophers have argued often about whether time was created or whether it always existed and about whether the universe was created ex nihilo—Latin for "out of nothing"—or from some preexisting but chaotic and unrecognizable matter. Both questions were debated over and over again, especially among the Jewish medieval philosophers who were influenced by the Muslim revival of Aristotle's thinking (Maimonides being the best known of these). The parallels are instructive to me because they demonstrate the extent to which the questions being addressed by modern science are the exact same questions that have made us wonder for many centuries. The language, the tools, and the metaphors we use to ask and to answer them have changed, but the questions, at their core, are comforting in their familiarity.

THE CAUSE OF CREATION

However, Aristotle and all those who followed in his footsteps were unable or unwilling to ask our fourth, prickliest question:

What caused the Big Bang? For the philosophers, the question was absurd, because they started with the assumption that the Creator (God) was the uncaused cause, the only element in the otherwise endless regression of cause-effect-cause-effect that was itself a cause but not an effect. Unlike our other questions, this question may not be any easier to address in the system of scientific cosmology than it was for Aristotle or Maimonides. Physicist Paul Davies puts it in rather clear terms:

> If one accepts the idea that space, time, and matter had their origin in a singularity that represents an absolute boundary to the physical universe in the past, a number of puzzles follow. There is still the problem of what caused the big bang. However, this question must now be seen in a new light, for it is not possible to attribute the big bang to anything that happened *before* it, as is usually the case in discussions of causation. Does this mean the big bang was an event without a cause? If the laws of physics break down at the singularity, there can be no explanation in terms of those laws. Therefore, if one insists on a reason for the big bang, then this reason must lie beyond physics.[6]

In other words, if we think of physics as the human effort to understand the workings of matter in space and time in a systematic fashion, and we conclude that the Big Bang singularity was the point at which the entire structure of matter, space, and time had its origin, then science does not appear to be much use in finding the reason for that singularity.

THE BIG BANG FROM A RELIGIOUS PERSPECTIVE

What if we were to accept the idea that the Big Bang was *the* beginning of the universe, that it stands at the head of the chain of causation leading to any conceivable structure or event that exists in the fabric of matter, space, and time, but that the Big Bang itself cannot in any meaningful way be discussed as having had some other "cause"? In other words, what happens if we posit that the Big Bang is the first (or uncaused) cause? This would lead us, by traditional theological paths, to the conclusion that somehow God the creator *is* (or perhaps is *in*) the Big Bang. The impact of this statement cannot be overestimated. We began our inquiry by rejecting the idea that God was some sentient being, existing outside the structure of what we commonly know as "reality," who decided at a particular moment to create the universe. We have seen, however, that, in scientific terms, it makes no sense to speak of causation before the singularity that marks the beginning of the structures of matter, space, and time that determine causality. But does it help our religious thinking at all to think of God as somehow *synonymous* with the Big Bang? In other words, does using a system of metaphors that is rooted in the scientific theory of the Big Bang[7] singularity provide us with any useful religious insight into God, the creation, or our relationship to it all?

Paul Davies is skeptical. Shortly after concluding that it is meaningless to discuss causation before the Big Bang, he spins out an imagined debate between a theist and an atheist about whether it makes sense to say that God caused the Big Bang. The coup de grâce of the atheist's argument is delivered as follows:

> ATHEIST: But unless you have other reasons to believe in God's existence, then merely proclaiming "God created the universe" is totally *ad hoc.* It is no explanation at all. Indeed, the statement is essentially devoid of meaning, for you are merely defining God to be that agency which creates the universe. My understanding is no further advanced by this device. One mystery (the origin of the universe) is explained only in terms of another

(God). As a scientist I appeal to Occam's razor,[8] which then dictates that the God hypothesis be rejected as an unnecessary complication. After all, I am bound to ask, what created God?

THEIST: God needs no creator. He is a necessary being— he must exist. There is no choice in the matter.

ATHEIST: But one might as well assert that the universe needs no creator. Whatever logic is used to justify God's necessary existence could equally well, and with an advantageous gain in simplicity, be applied to the universe.[9]

In this hypothetical exchange, Davies's atheist claims (and rightly so) that our understanding of how the universe came into being is not advanced, once we agree on the Big Bang as creation's source, by further saying that God is the cause of the Big Bang. But my agenda is different from that of Davies and his atheist. I am not seeking deeper or more complete understanding of what caused the universe to come into being, but rather a deeper and more compelling understanding of God and how religious thought and life can relate to God. I want to know: If God is (or is in) the Big Bang, what does that mean for me as a modern heir to an ancient set of Jewish religious, spiritual, and theological traditions? As I peruse the repertoire of traditional God metaphors, I am unmoved, for reasons already discussed, by "king" or "shepherd." But does the metaphor of "creator," as used by the Rabbis in the talmudic age, make more sense? Specifically, is its meaning enhanced by dressing up the generic idea of "creator" in the modern cosmological garb of the Big Bang?

I am proposing a metaphorical identity between the Big Bang and God, whereby we speak and think of God as the Big

Bang, just as, in earlier eras, we spoke and thought a
as father or shepherd. Does this proposition make it easier for
me to be a modern Jew? I am *not* asking whether the proposed
identity between God and the Big Bang is true or factual, as in,
"It is true that the sun is about ninety-three million miles from
the earth." Rather, I am asking if it is *useful*. We are dealing
here with metaphors used to aid our understanding of ourselves
and our relationship to Jewish tradition. If my proposition
helps deepen or enhance our understanding, it will be a useful
source of religious metaphors. If not, we may discard it.

In our initial explorations of the question, let us put aside
the nagging issue of what caused the Big Bang and simply
regard it as "the beginning." According to the standard description furnished by modern cosmology, "the beginning" was
characterized by a very high level of energy (it was *infinitely*
hot) in a very tiny spot (its size was zero) that contained all
space that would ever exist. In that first instant, there was no
matter; no physical stuff had yet been formed. But that distinction is no longer the serious concern it would have been a century or more ago, for Einstein taught us that matter and energy
are simply[10] different forms of the same thing and can be trans-
formed from one into the other and back again. We are normally familiar only with the transformation of matter into
energy—this is essentially what happens when we "create" heat
by exploding a nuclear bomb. But the process (theoretically)
works the other way as well. Timothy Ferris puts it succinctly:
"What we call *matter* is frozen energy. It froze because the universe, owing to its expansion, cooled."[11] Thus, all the (yet-to-
be-unfolded) time of the universe and all the (not-yet-expanded)
space of the universe and all the (not-yet-frozen-solid) matter of
the universe were there in the Big Bang. These three ingredients—time, space, and matter—make up reality as we know it.
So *everything* that is—and that ever was or ever will be—was
there at the Big Bang. The atoms that make up my body and the

neuroelectrical impulses that I experience as my thoughts were there at the Big Bang. The electrical charges that are, as I write, making my computer screen glow in a pattern of light and dark that I interpret as letters and words were there. The space in which I am sitting and the space through which the earth and everything else is zooming, and even the time that has elapsed since I sat down to write this morning, all of it was there at the Big Bang. If my goal is to seek religious or spiritual meaning in life or, as some might put it, to seek God, and if God is somehow synonymous with the Big Bang, then the first basic realization that grows from modern cosmology is that wherever I look I find God. God is, in a startlingly literal sense, all the raw ingredients that go into the fabric of reality.

READING THE PRAYER BOOK BY THE LIGHT OF THE BIG BANG

This realization strikes me as an entry point into the understanding, or perhaps the reunderstanding, of numerous important traditional Jewish texts. Consider, first of all, a mystical vision, described in chapter 6 of the biblical Book of Isaiah, of fiery angels with six wings each. The angels call to one another, "Holy, holy, holy is Adonai Tzevaot.[12] The whole earth is full of His glory" (Is. 6:3). This line is recited in the *Kedushah*, an important part of the repetition of the *Amidah* (the central liturgical component of every Jewish prayer service) in the daily morning and afternoon services (*shacharit* and *minchah*). As liturgy, the verse is part of a large body of text and tradition that is dismissed by many contemporary Jews as boring, meaningless, and obsolete. But our preliminary interpretation of God as being somehow associated with the singularity that stands at the root of the universe gives the line some new depth. The whole earth, meaning everything that we experience, is filled with God's glory, with God's essential presence, since all time, space, and matter emanated from the Big Bang. This is not some mystical hallucination or some New Age spiritual double talk. This is simply the reunderstanding of traditional religious language in light of modern scientific understandings (metaphors) of *what* and *how* reality is. If one way of interpreting the "glory of God" is "the presence of God the creator as reflected in all created things" then that glory does *in fact* fill the whole earth and the whole universe. Even though the earth and its contents did not exist in their present state in the first instant of the Big Bang, the primal matter and energy that make up the earth were all there. As Kohelet (that is, Ecclesiastes) said, there is indeed nothing new under the sun (Eccles. 1:9)— or anywhere else in the universe. All the basic ingredients for everything that would ever come into being were there at that first Big Bang moment.

Since first stumbling across this insight, I have found that it affects the way I hear and say these words during synagogue services. For me, the Big Bang is there every single time the congregation recites *Kedushah*. It is how I understand that particular bit of text. This realization is important because it shows how the development of new metaphors can *really* affect the meaning of our lives.

Before focusing on a second biblical-liturgical text, I must clarify a potentially serious misunderstanding that could be drawn from what I have just said. In no way do I want to suggest that our distant ancestors understood, intuited, predicted, or had revealed to them the principles of modern cosmology, physics, or any other modern scientific discipline. Both the prophet Isaiah and the Rabbis who chose his words as part of the daily liturgy lived in a world of vastly different metaphors. Their words *must* be understood as religious poetry that attempted to grasp a bit of the intense spirituality that they felt abounded in the world. If we could invent a device to carry us back through time to their era, I think our ancestors would be completely bewildered by our most patient attempts to explain the insights that have grown since Einstein's day. The poetry that they wrote and sang was a deep expression of feeling and religious belief, but it was based on *their own contemporary understandings of reality*. It could not have been otherwise! What I am doing is suggesting how we might reread this ancient poetry through the lens of *our* era's understandings of reality, so that the words speak to us with some measure of the power with which they spoke to our ancestors.

SHEMA YISRAEL AND THE BIG BANG

Let's examine a second text: In Deuteronomy, as a part of the long series of speeches that Moses makes to the Israelites before his death, we find the following: "Hear, O Israel! Adonai is our God, Adonai is One!" (Deut. 6:4). This line, known as the *Shema* (from its first Hebrew word, *shema*, meaning "hear" or "listen"), is perhaps the best-known statement of Jewish faith. Its twice-daily recitation had already become a cornerstone of Jewish religious practice long before the birth of Christianity. Generations of Jewish children have learned to recite it as part of a bedtime ritual. Jewish literature is filled with stories of martyrs who have literally breathed their last with these words on their lips. But what does the *Shema* mean? The short version of the answer is that this statement was the backbone of Judaism's claim that there is only one God. This claim, known as monotheism, flew in the face of all ancient cultures that recognized many gods in the world. *Adonai echad*, God is one, meant that God was not two, three, or more. And although later philosophers, especially those of the Middle Ages, delved deeper into the meaning of God's oneness, interpreting it as meaning that God is unique or that God is ultimately simple (not composed of parts or of any other elements whose existence is more basic), the *Shema* has represented for most Jews throughout history no more and no less than a stark declaration that we recognize only one God. The trouble is that such a declaration, although it was powerful and bold in a world in which everyone believed deeply that there were many gods, has lost some of its power in our own world, in which many people doubt that there is any God! In such an environment, sculpted as it is by our scientific sense of the world, many find little value in the time-honored recitation of God's oneness. At best, it is a valid claim that need hardly be made anymore. After all, we monotheists won! Virtually all (Western) folks now agree that there is only one God, while the polytheists of ancient Egypt, Mesopotamia, and Greece have been relegated to history. At worst, given the lack of faith in any God (be that God one or many) that has grown in our society in the modern era, the declaration of *Shema Yisrael* is meaningless.

In response to these critiques, I find a new depth of meaning in the metaphor of the Big Bang. The oneness of God can now be understood as indicating that everything, the totality of being itself, is, in a sense, God. "God is one" may now be taken to mean that "God" is a term that signifies the unity of all existence, a unity rooted in the common origin of all existence in a single point of time, space, and nascent matter. The very term *singularity,* which has become a commonplace of contemporary physics, might be seen as a modern Jewish metaphor for the traditional Jewish idea of oneness. Can we imagine a new translation of the *Shema* in a contemporary prayer book generated by the metaphors of modern science? "Listen, O Israel, Adonai is our God, Adonai, the Singularity!" This suggestion is made only partially in jest. The approach that I am proposing could, in fact, be used to generate new translations or new interpretations of many ancient liturgical texts that are currently viewed with a curious mixture of nostalgia, boredom, and incomprehension.

HAMAKOM: THE PLACE OF
THE BIG BANG

A third example will complete this brief exploration of the possible ways in which we might reinterpret our ancient textual traditions in light of the Big Bang metaphor. The Bible uses several names for God. Some seem to be borrowed by ancient Israel from the surrounding ancient Near Eastern cultures. *El*, for example, was originally the proper name of the god at the head of the Canaanite pantheon, before it (or its variant form *Elohim*) became the generic Hebrew word for "God." But one of the biblical names for God, that which is seen as God's most personal name, was the tetragrammaton, or four-letter name YHWH. Because of its tremendous power, the pronunciation of this name was eventually restricted, in the time of the Second Temple (from the end of the sixth century B.C.E. until the Temple's destruction in 70 C.E.) to one occasion each year, the climax of the Yom Kippur (Atonement Day) ritual conducted by the High Priest. After the Second Temple's destruction, however, use of "the Explicit Name" was forbidden, and in fact, Jewish scholars are no longer certain how it was pronounced. This prohibition of God's "real" name led to the development of a whole host of divine epithets in the rabbinic, or talmudic, period that ensued in the four or five centuries following the destruction of the Temple. These appellations for God are largely descriptive. They include such generic terms as "the Merciful One," "the Creator," "the Holy Blessed One," and "Master of the World." One of the most interesting rabbinic terms for God, however, is *Hamakom*, meaning "the place" (but often translated interpretively as "the omnipresent"). Although this curious term is used in a wide variety of settings throughout rabbinic literature, perhaps its best-known and most enduring use is in the traditional formula of consolation recited to mourners: *Hamakom yenachem etkhem b'tokh shaar avelei tziyon vi'Yerushalayim* (May *Hamakom* comfort you, together with all the mourners of Zion and Jerusalem). It is not completely clear how this term came to be used as a divine epithet, although one rabbinic text asks the question and suggests an answer:

> Why do we use *Hamakom* as a name for the Holy Blessed One? Because He is the Place of the world, but His world [meaning "the world"] is not His place. (*Bereshit Rabbah* 68:9)

This text suggests that the epithet results from the theological observation that God is, as it were, the place in which the world exists, the stage on which the world's pageantry is played out, yet God's existence does not happen in, and is not limited to, the world. It is hard to imagine exactly how the rabbis visualized the images evoked by such an explanation. Perhaps they imagined the entire world (meaning, essentially, the cosmos) as being contingent on God, as existing only at the behest of God. If this is the proper understanding, then it is hard for us, committed as we are to a sense that the world and the universe persist because of a complex set of natural laws, to find deep meaning in the epithet *Hamakom*. Or perhaps they imagined, more literally, that God encompasses the space in which the universe is situated, but that God is not restricted to that space; God's "space" includes all the space of the cosmos and more that is beyond the boundaries of the cosmos. This possibility seems a bit odd to us, for we have been taught that God has no substance or physical body and, therefore, that it makes no sense to speak of the physical size or extent of God. We must remember, however, that the Jewish "certainty" of God's incorporeality was a product of Jewish medieval Aristotelian thought. It was Maimonides who taught that God has no body and no semblance of a body. Based on textual evidence and also on the fact that Maimonides felt the need to teach this principle, it is quite likely that premedieval Jews felt a lot more comfortable than we do with the idea that God somehow occupies space.

This explanation of the *midrash* would also conflict with the usual modern understanding of cosmology according to which there can be no space that is outside the space of the universe. By definition, the universe is all that there is! (Note, however, that there are schools of thought in contemporary physics and cosmology that posit the existence of alternate or parallel universes. If such things do exist, then their space might indeed qualify as "space outside the space of our universe." More on this possibility in chapter 2.)

But what if we reinterpret the ancient term *Hamakom* in light of what we now understand about the Big Bang? If all matter, time, *and especially space* came into existence in a single point, a singularity, that is somehow identified with, or inextricably entwined with, God, then indeed we can refer to God as "the place," meaning the space in which the universe exists. That original singularity, of zero size, expanded into what we commonly experience as "all the space of the universe." So the ancient term for God, *Hamakom*, "the place," has a fascinating new meaning: God was the generative singularity from which all space, all *makom*, flowed. Understood this way, the name *Hamakom* would always remind us of the aspect of God that generates space.

Once again, I must emphasize that I am *not* suggesting that the Rabbis of the early centuries of the Common Era anticipated, or intuitively understood, or had a revelation about the Big Bang and the details of twentieth-century cosmology. Whatever they intended or visualized when they called God *Hamakom*, I am quite certain it was *not* the Big Bang, the unity of space and time, or the origin of the universe in a singularity. Rather, I am suggesting that contemporary Jews can "recycle" this ancient language and use the term afresh, but with new meaning. All God language is couched in metaphor. I am simply exploring a new set of God metaphors—or, more precisely, a new way of understanding ancient God metaphors—that allows us to speak about God without feeling hopelessly old-fashioned. In our era, we often feel that we can either speak about God or think scientifically about the world, but never both at the same time. The examples we have just explored are the beginnings of a system whereby Jews of the twenty-first century can integrate these two parts of themselves. In fact, Jews can be religious *and* scientific at the same time.

GOD AS BIG BANG: WHAT'S THE PAYOFF?

What is accomplished by these three reinterpretations of ancient Jewish text and language in light of the Big Bang metaphor? Do they enhance our understanding of Jewishness? I have suggested three ways in which they do:

1. "God's glory fills the whole universe" means that all "stuff" has God in it by virtue of its common origin in the Big Bang.

2. "God is One" means that the entire vast universe is a single system, all the disparate parts of which are united because of their common origin in the Big Bang.

3. We sometimes call God *Hamakom,* "the place," because all places and all spaces were originally one space, a point of zero size at the instant of the Big Bang.

Taken seriously, these and related interpretations may have a profound impact on our attitudes and our behavior. They may lead us, for example, to regard all places and things as potentially sacred, since they all share a common origin in

God. They may force us to question how things that seem radically different from (or even in stark opposition to) one another are, in fact, related to one another. Traditional Judaism has strongly opposed all forms of dualism, that is, all systems of thought that divide the cosmos into two fundamental realms—light and dark, good and evil. Throughout Jewish history, we find numerous polemics against such dualism, with rabbis and philosophers insisting that God alone is the source of all things, including light *and* dark, good *and* evil, the pure *and* the impure. Nevertheless, we tend to slip periodically into the conclusion that there are forces in the universe that are so malevolent that they could never have originated with God. The textual reinterpretation that I am suggesting here can refocus our attention on this ancient question of whether the world constitutes a single system or two distinct realms, and this refocusing can have significant benefits. In a world racked by hatred and hostility, the recognition that all peoples and all places share a common origin could curb the righteous certainty with which humans demonize and dehumanize—and then find it easy to destroy—those who are different.

Another benefit of thinking of God as the Big Bang is in what it suggests about our ability to understand God fully. In Exodus, we read that Moses, after the incident of the Golden Calf, asks to see God's glory. God responds that Moses may see God's goodness, but not God's "face." God says, "You may not [or cannot] see My face, for no human can see Me and live" (Ex. 33:20). There is a fundamental limit in the direct knowledge of God beyond which humans cannot or may not go. Similarly, in the end of the Book of Job, God tells Job that he cannot possibly understand the divine realm (and, presumably, its logic and its justice) because he, as a human being, was not present at the creation, did not see God measure out the dimensions of the earth, and so on (Job 38:1–40:2). I read this as a poetic way of saying, once again, that there is an unbridgeable

chasm that ultimately separates us from full and direct knowledge of God. This response is deeply troubling to a species like
ours that seems by its nature always to seek greater and deeper
understanding of the world. We have an insatiable appetite for
knowledge and understanding and cannot accept the idea that
there are things that we just cannot know. The response makes
us feel like children whose parents tell them, "You can't understand this. You're too little." How frustrating!

In physics and cosmology, however, we are told that the
absolute limit of knowledge is at the Big Bang. All knowledge
is associated with some sort of signal, some energy that travels
from place to place. If I see something, it is because light rays
have traveled from the object I see to my eye. Thus, if we gaze
out into space with the naked eye or with more and more powerful telescopes, we see farther and farther out. As the distance
between us and the object of our astronomical observation
increases, we are actually looking farther and farther back in
time, for the starlight that reaches earth today left the star that
emitted it long, long ago. Thus, if we look at a star that is
10,000 light-years away (the distance that is traveled by light in
10,000 years), we are not seeing what the star looks like now,
but rather what it looked like 10,000 years ago, when the light
rays entering our telescope first left the star. If we were to look
farther and farther away, and farther and farther back in time,
we would eventually (assuming unlimited improvement in telescope technology) see back almost to the Big Bang. It is clear
that we would never be able to see anything farther than the Big
Bang, since all the light rays, and thus all the information,
started then! But why can't we see the Big Bang itself? The reason is that in the first, very short period after the Big Bang, the
explosion was still so dense and had such a tremendously
strong gravitational attraction that no energy, no electrons or
photons, could escape. It took a while (perhaps only a fraction
of a second, but that is like an eon when we are talking about

the Big Bang) for the whole thing to expand and cool enough so that its gravitational field weakened enough for the first rays of light to escape. Thus, we can see neither the Big Bang itself nor, obviously, anything before it. It is the absolute limit of our knowledge, not because we aren't "smart enough," or because we are technologically limited, or because we are "merely" human, but because, by definition, no knowledge could ever reach us.

If we now return to the idea of God as Big Bang, we see that God's statement to Job that the divine realm is simply beyond Job's comprehension can be taken not as a patronizing divine version of "You're too young to understand" but rather as an expression of a deep physical truth about the universe: No information can be acquired, nor any observation made, about the Big Bang—or God.

This idea that God's essential self is utterly hidden and that only the effects of God's presence can be detected is familiar to Jewish tradition. First of all, if we look again at Moses's exchange with God after the incident of the Golden Calf, we find God offering to "make all My goodness pass before you" (Ex. 33:19) and agreeing to allow Moses to "see what comes after Me"[13] (Ex. 33:23). These verses are often understood to mean that although no information is available about God's essence, we can know a great deal about God's effect on the universe. A second echo comes from the kabbalistic, or mystical, idea that God's inner essence, called *En Sof,* is fundamentally unknowable, although God's emanations, the *sefirot,* can be known in some measure. (This idea will be examined in some detail in chapter 4.)

A FEW TROUBLING QUESTIONS

These are some of the benefits and advantages of the new metaphor that I am proposing. As a metaphor for God, the Big

Bang makes several aspects of traditional Jewish thought and belief easier for me to understand and accept. But the idea raises some thorny problems as well. First of all, the Big Bang was almost certainly a unique, onetime event.[14] Thus it suggests that God's input into or involvement with the universe was a one-time event; that is, God had everything to do with the initial setting into motion of the creative processes that would eventually result in the universe that we experience, but has had no additional input or influence since. In theological terms, such a system is known as *deism,* and is often described by reference to the metaphor of God as the watchmaker. If the universe is conceived of (as it was by many thinkers in the generations following Newton's revolution in physics) as a huge watch mechanism, then God's role was simply to build the watch and wind it up. God then sits back and has no further involvement as the universe ticks away the eons. This theory raises obvious religious dilemmas. If God was involved in a crucial but merely momentary way at the very beginning of creation, then how (and, for that matter, why) ought we to have a relationship with God in any subsequent age? Furthermore, why would a God who has no involvement in the universe after its initial creation be worthy of worship? And how are we to understand the belief, central to Judaism and common in many other religious traditions, that God acts *in history*, revealing divine will and intervening in the affairs of the world?

Other problems flow from the apparently deistic nature of the Big Bang metaphor. At its core, Judaism believes in a God who cares, who loves justice, who chooses to enter into a covenantal relationship with the people of Israel, and who responds to the quality of human behavior. It is hard to imagine the Big Bang doing any of these things. For aside from the fact that the Big Bang was the initial cosmic "kick in the pants" that started the universe off but that has not exerted active influence since that first moment, it is also fairly obvious to me that the Big Bang was not a conscious, sentient, moral entity. It was simply a unique, immensely powerful, and tremendously creative natural phenomenon. It did not "consider" what it was setting in motion, nor did it set moral standards for the beings who would eventually evolve in the universe it was creating, any more than a hurricane "intends" to kill the inhabitants of a seaside village.

Do these objections constitute fatal flaws for my approach? Perhaps not. I have pointed out before that whenever we think or speak about God, by necessity we think and speak in metaphorical terms. And any metaphor that we use, no matter how helpful it is in giving us a sense of God's essence, is incomplete and imperfect. If you push any metaphor for God far enough it will collapse. This is true with all traditional God metaphors. For example, traditional religious language often refers to God as father. The metaphor is highly instructive. It tells us that, like our fathers, God cares about our development, looks out for our welfare, protects us, and so on. For traditional societies the image of father also combined a sense of overwhelming love with one of stern judgment. But is God completely fatherlike? Hardly! Fathers usually age and die long before their children, often becoming feeble and childlike, in need of their children's care, before dying. Is this part of what we intend when we refer to God as father? Most theologians would say it is not. Similarly, traditional literature refers to God as a shepherd (see Ps. 23, which begins, "Adonai is my Shepherd, I shall not want"). Again, the image is useful. It implies caring and protection and a thorough dependence of the "sheep" on the shepherd. But in most agrarian societies, shepherding is not done solely for the benefit of the sheep. The shepherd cares for the flock for the most selfish reasons. Generally, the sheep are shorn, for the shepherd and his people need the wool to keep warm. And occasionally, the shepherd also slaughters sheep to eat. Is this what the psalmist had in mind?

Certainly not! The point is that these and all other metaphors for God provide useful imagery, but they are not perfect. Rather, we accept each of them as a partial description, and we hope that by using them all in combination, we will move incrementally toward a more and more complete description of God. In this respect, religious human beings are somewhat like the five blind men who encounter an elephant. The old story judges them to be fools, for after their research they claim, respectively, that the elephant is like a spear (for the one who touched a tusk), a water hose (for the one who touched the trunk), a wall (for the one who touched the beast's side), a huge palm leaf (for the one who touched an ear), and a rope (for the one who touched the tail). Had they been wise, these five would have realized that each of them had perceived just one element of elephantness, and they would have combined their varied perspectives. They still would not have grasped the full essence of the animal, but they would have been much closer to it. So it is with God metaphors. In the previous paragraph, I noted that the Big Bang counts among its characteristics *uniqueness, immense power,* and *tremendous creativity.* These are all characteristics that my Jewish mind and imagination associate directly with God. For me, such appropriate associations make the Big Bang a valuable, if incomplete and imperfect, metaphor for God.

2
QUANTUM MECHANICS
God in the (Subatomic) Details

In the last chapter, we focused primarily on one important element of the Big Bang as the central "cosmogonic myth"[1] of our time, namely, the idea that all matter, all time, and all space, which we experience as constituting the universe, were originally intertwined and unified. We turn now to another important feature of the Big Bang model, which is that the crucial first instant of the creation of the universe occurred in an unimaginably tiny area. Although, as I mentioned earlier, the Big Bang itself began with a point of "zero size," its importance did not end there but continued for at least the first infinitesimal fraction of a second. During that time, the whole universe had grown to a nonzero size, but its size was, nevertheless, still quite small. How small? Physicists speak of the Planck time or Planck epoch (named for German physicist Max Planck, who pioneered much of quantum mechanics), which constituted the first 10^{-43} seconds (that is, the first 0.0000000000000000000000000000000000000000001 seconds) after the Big Bang, when the entire universe was far smaller than a single proton! At such a tiny scale, the "rules" by which things function are very different from the rules with which we are familiar in our day-to-day lives. On the scale of the very, very, very small, the world functions according to the rules of quantum mechanics. These very different rules are another of the innovations of modern physics that have fundamentally and radically changed the way we think about reality. In this chapter, I explore these rules and consider their religious implications.

QUANTUM MECHANICS: THE BASIC IDEA

The German physicist Max Planck first suggested in 1900 that electromagnetic waves cannot be emitted at any arbitrary rate but only in discrete "packages" called quanta (quanta is the plural form of quantum). Each quantum has a certain amount of energy, and the higher the frequency of the wave, the higher the energy. (The frequency of the wave is the number of wave crests or troughs that pass any given point in a specified period of time. See figure 1.1, p. 6.) Then in 1926, another German physicist, Werner Heisenberg, built upon Planck's insight to develop his *uncertainty principle*, according to which one cannot know both the exact position and the exact momentum (speed and direction) of a particle at the same time. Why not? The reason is simple: If you want to measure the position and velocity of a particle, you have to see it by shining a light on it. The light might be visible, or it might be a radar pulse, an x-ray beam, or any other form of electromagnetic radiation. But the maximum accuracy of the measurement of the particle's position will be limited by the wavelength of the light. You can't pin down the position of the particle more precisely than your shortest "ruler." This is analogous to any measurement. If your ruler is broken down to sixteenths of an inch, then you won't be able to measure precisely the difference between two lines that differ from one another by only 1/32 of an inch. If your digital scale reads out in pounds, you won't be able to detect the difference between the weights of two objects that are within two ounces of each other, and so on. When it comes to light, the wavelength is the equivalent of the marks on a ruler. So the obvious way to measure a particle's position more accurately is to use shorter and shorter wavelengths of light, that is, a "ruler" with smaller and smaller divisions between its marks. But there is an inverse relationship between wavelength and frequency. In other words, in any electromagnetic radiation (such as visible light, infrared radiation, cosmic rays, microwaves), the shorter the wavelength, the higher the frequency. And Planck's theory says that the shorter the wavelength, or the higher the frequency, the more energy is packed into a single quantum. To measure the position of a particle, you have to "bounce" the quantum of light off the particle—that's what seeing is all about. When we see a thing, it's because light has bounced off it and been reflected back to our eye; likewise, a radar antenna "sees" an object because some of the radar energy has bounced off the object and returned to the antenna. Inevitably, the energy of the quantum of light hitting the particle will disturb the particle—move it a bit, or change its position or velocity. Here is the uncertainty paradox: The more precisely you try to measure the position, that is, the shorter a wavelength you use, the higher the energy of the quantum and the more it will jostle the particle. So the more precise the measurement of position, the less precise the measurement of velocity. These insights led Heisenberg, together with physicists Erwin Schrödinger and Paul Dirac, to develop *quantum mechanics* in the 1920s.

Quantum mechanics does not assign a precise position to a particle and give up on its velocity, or vice versa. Rather it assigns a *quantum state* to a particle, which is a combination of position and velocity. But because of the uncertainty principle, a particle's quantum state does not give a single precise description of its position-plus-velocity, but rather assigns a calculable probability to any given position-plus-velocity. Thus, for example, prequantum pictures portrayed an atom as being a nucleus surrounded by a given number of electrons, each in a particular position, not unlike the solar system, with the sun as the nucleus and the planets as the electrons. Quantum mechanics, however, leads to a picture in which the nucleus is surrounded by a "cloud" of electrons, each of which has a certain probability of being at a given spot at any given moment, but the precise position and velocity of any of which can *never* be determined. In other words, on the tiniest subatomic level, we simply cannot know where a particle is and where and how fast it is moving. This leads to a sense of inevitable uncertainty, or randomness, at the core of reality. It was against this sense of randomness that Einstein rebelled in his famous assertion that "God does not play dice" with the universe.[2] In so saying, Einstein was betraying a sympathy with the scientific theory of *determinism*.

THE RISE AND FALL OF DETERMINISM

Determinism, which was best articulated by the late-eighteenth-century French mathematician Pierre de Laplace, holds that the universe functions in completely predictable ways, such that if we could know the precise position and velocity of every particle in the universe at any given instant, we could extrapolate forward or backward in time to find the state of the universe at any other instant in its history, whether past or future. Hence the name *determinism*: The position of the system at any one moment will determine its position at any and all other moments. This view of the world, rooted firmly in the physics of Sir Isaac Newton (1642–1727), sees reality as being 100 percent law abiding. Immutable laws govern how any given situation must develop. If I drop a shoe out a window and I know the exact height of the window, I can predict exactly where the shoe will be at every instant of its short trip to the ground. The laws require it. If I fire a cannonball on a battlefield, I can predict exactly how far it will travel, how high, and where and when it will land. The laws require it.

Quantum mechanics undermined all the certainty that the determinists had brought to the world. It claimed that, although on the macroscopic level of falling shoes and whizzing cannonballs, the world is roughly deterministic, on the subatomic level it is governed largely by chance, randomness, probability, and uncertainty. How disturbing this notion must have been to a world that had completely embraced the Newtonian picture of a law-abiding universe!

You might ask: Is the quantum universe really not law abiding? Isn't it just our inability to detect precisely a particle's position and velocity that makes the world *seem* uncertain? After all, the uncertainty in a particle's position and velocity develops when we shine a light on it to see it. Isn't it possible that the particle had a precise position until we tried to see it, and that it was just our desire to see it (and the accompanying necessity of shining a light on it) that led to the uncertainty? Here there seems to be some disagreement. Stephen Hawking writes:

> We could still imagine that there is a set of laws that determines events completely for some supernatural being, who could observe the present state of the universe without disturbing it. However, such models of the universe are not of much interest to us ordinary mortals.[3]

This suggests that reality is not uncertain, but that only our ability to know about reality is uncertain. Our finite ability, our humanness, introduces uncertainty into our perception, or measurement, of what might theoretically be a deterministic universe. But this view is not shared by all. An alternative position is expressed succinctly by Timothy Ferris:

> The indeterminacy principle is often discussed as if it represented the difficulty of accurately *measuring* the locations and trajectories of particles. But the point is not that it is hard to find out just where, say, an electron is, but that the electron actually *has* no exact location.[4]

Now as disturbing as it might be to realize that no matter how sophisticated our measurement techniques ever become, we will *never* be able to determine the exact position and velocity of subatomic particles, I think it is far more disturbing to imagine that this indeterminacy is not a function of our human technological limitations but a characteristic of the nature of particles themselves! The approach described by Ferris suggests that the particle *has no precise state*. It is unknowable, by us and even by Hawking's imagined supernatural being. The precise state simply does not exist.

UNCERTAINTY AND GOD

What does this disturbing insight into the quantum nature of reality mean for Jewish thought and belief? Our traditional notions of God, going all the way back to the Bible, teach us that God's knowledge is limitless and that our own is very, very limited. After suffering all manner of pain, affliction, loss, and sorrow for no apparent reason, the hero of the biblical Book of Job finally asks God for a bit of an explanation. The divine voice responds (the way the scene has always played in my head includes a hefty measure of divine impatience, even irritation in the response) as follows:

Who is this who darkens counsel, speaking without knowledge? ... Where were you when I laid the earth's foundations? Speak if you have understanding. Do you know who fixed its dimensions or who measured it with a line? ... Have you ever commanded the day to break? Assigned the dawn its place? ... Which path leads to where light dwells, and where is the place of darkness, that you may take it to its domain and know the way to its home?... By what path is the west wind dispersed, the east wind scattered over the earth? ... Do you know the laws of heaven or impose its authority on earth? (Job 38: 2–33)

This answer, and many other similar statements throughout Jewish literary history, clearly sets out the difference between God and humankind. God has ultimate and complete knowledge of the world; we do not. This simple statement has had a profound impact on how we think about God, how we pray, and how we react to the events of the world. On a day-to-day level, the colloquial use of expressions such as "God knows" to mean "I don't know," or "God willing" to mean, "I intend to do such and such, but whether I will actually end up doing so is something I cannot guarantee for certain," indicates the popular effect of such thinking about the vast, unbridgeable chasm between our knowledge and God's knowledge. On a more literary level, our liturgy is filled with humble human acknowledgments of God's unlimited knowledge and the vast power that such knowledge confers on God. A powerful example comes from the confession recited again and again during the daylong liturgy for Yom Kippur, the Day of Atonement. In part it reads:

You know about malicious sins and accidental misdeeds. Whether committed willingly or under duress, in the open or in secret, they are open and known to You … You know the secrets of the world, and the hidden secrets of all life … There is no thing that is concealed from you.[5]

This traditional attitude has led to an entire system of assumptions. God is great, powerful, and all-knowing. We are small, insignificant, powerless, and (relatively speaking) ignorant. These assumptions create a relationship of dependence on God, and that dependence leads, among other things, to great disappointment and even anger when God "doesn't come through for us." On the other hand, the perceived disparity between our knowledge and God's knowledge sometimes brings great comfort, as when a tragic and inexplicable death occurs and the mourners find solace in the thought that, even though they don't understand why this tragedy has occurred, God must understand it as part of some great plan. In such a case, the notion that there is a logic and a predictability to the universe, *even if we cannot know it,* brings comfort.

In light of this history, we begin to realize what a revolutionary effect quantum theory must have on Jewish life! If, at its core, reality is essentially unknowable, even to God, if there is indeed a significant effect of randomness or chance in the universe, then our traditional notions of God are taken down a peg or two, along with many of our assumptions about our relationship to God, the protector, the one to whom we can call out in need, the one whose knowledge is perfect. If, like us, God *cannot* know everything—because everything simply cannot be known—then the chasm between God and us, the gulf that separates divine knowledge from human knowledge, shrinks from being absolute and unbridgeable to being just very, very large and only practically unbridgeable. That shift in status may, at first glance, seem a picayune semantic difference, but it is much more than that. Once there are basic characteristics of reality that God simply cannot know, then we and God becomes players in the same arena. Once that happens, then even if God still knows much, much, much more than we do, we have a sense that we are on more of an equal footing. This is roughly analogous to the shift that occurs when a child realizes that her parents are very, very smart but are not omniscient. With the dawning of that realization, the child can begin to imagine that someday there might be things that she knows as well as, or even better than, her parents. That day may still be so far off as to be practically unimaginable, but it is there all the same. Similarly, once we sense that God is fundamentally limited in knowledge just as we are, then the *difference* between us shrinks by a tiny, but significant, amount. We may no longer feel that we stand before God as humble supplicants who plead, "You know everything and we know nothing." If God is no longer understood as knowing everything, because there are things in the universe that are, by definition, unknowable, then our approach to prayer must change. Prayer can no longer be seen as the appeal to the ultimate authority, but instead will begin to be seen as, among other things, the appeal to a very powerful presence, but one that, in certain circumstances, is no more knowledgeable about, or in control of, the world than we are. This shift ought to change our expectations with regard to prayer, and with changed, more realistic, expectations will come less disappointment. If the world is a puppet theater and God is the puppet-master, then I can reasonably be disappointed and even angry, when I pray for something and it doesn't come to pass. But if the puppet-master is seen as no longer having complete control over or knowledge of the puppets, if, in fact, the puppets sometimes do things spontaneously that cannot be known or controlled by *anyone*, then my requests to the puppet-master will take on a different tone. We will consider at another point where such developments leave prayer.

THE COSMIC ROLE OF CHANCE

In a related development, the quantum revolution will also require us to formulate a new attitude toward chance. Rather than being the "noise" in the system, that is, the occasional accidental occurrence that throws a monkey wrench into an otherwise well-oiled and precisely driven divine universe, chance in a postquantum age must be seen as an important element of the core of reality. How can such an unsettling idea find a home in the repertoire of Jewish symbols and metaphors? Isn't it a threat to much of what we have taught over the centuries about God's ultimate control? Perhaps not. Consider two images. The first is the dreidel of Hanukkah. Perhaps more than at any other time in the Jewish year, we focus during Hanukkah on miracles. A miracle may be understood as a divine intervention in the course of nature and history. It accomplishes something that, without the miraculous intervention, would be impossible. Note that this is a much stronger definition than the one that we normally use when we call an event "miraculous." When we say that the birth of a baby, or the outstanding performance of the 1969 New York Mets, is "a miracle," we mean that the event is highly unlikely to have occurred and wonderful, and we marvel at the world that could bring such a thing about. On the other hand, a *real* miracle (the splitting of the Red Sea) is *impossible* and requires a temporary divine suspension of the laws of nature. We may argue about what the Hanukkah miracle really was: Some may cite the talmudic tale of the one-day jar of oil that miraculously burned for eight days, while others, rejecting the story as fiction, may claim that the "real" miracle was the perseverance and survival of the Jewish people despite overwhelming military, cultural, and spiritual odds. But all agree that the holiday is a time to celebrate miracles.

A part of the celebration involves playing with a dreidel, a four-sided top inscribed with the Hebrew letters *nun, gimmel, hay,* and *shin.* Our tradition understands these letters as standing for the Hebrew statement *Nes gadol haya sham,* or "A great miracle happened there."[6] But how curious that the very toy that reminds us of God's intervention is governed by the principles of chance! When I spin the dreidel, I do not know whether I will get a *nun,* a *gimmel,* a *hay,* or a *shin.* Consequently, I do not know how my status in the game will be affected. Will I be rewarded, punished, or left alone? The whole point of the game, and the source of its excitement, is that I do not know! Most remarkable, however, is the fact that I have never heard anyone imply that God knows how the dreidel will land! Unlike the situation of a grave illness, when one would not be surprised to hear a physician or a family member say, "We've done all we can. Now the outcome is in God's hands," people who play dreidel at Hanukkah seem to believe that the results of the spin will be governed by chance alone, over which no one, not even God, has control. The game is a gambling game, no different in its underlying mechanism from a dice game or a roulette wheel. And although we might not be surprised to hear a desperate gambler in a casino utter a fervent prayer before tossing the dice, dreidel players generally do not pray to God to affect their spin favorably!

Now you may protest that such a dreidel prayer would be foolish and offensive: To request God's providence regarding a simple child's game, the outcome of which will only affect how many nuts, or M&Ms, or—in a really high-stakes dreidel match—nickels I will win seems like a cheapening of religion and faith. How dare we compare such frivolity to the seriousness of a couple whose genes dictate that, in every pregnancy, there is a one-in-four chance that their baby will have a serious birth defect! For them to pray is understandable, but for a dreidel spinner to pray for a *gimmel* would be almost a *chillul* hashem—a desecration of God's name. My point, however, is that the deep understanding, available even to children, that the outcome of the dreidel spin is really a random event governed by chance may provide us with an important model for the world in general, and the extent to which it is governed by chance on a quantum level.

A second image that may aid in incorporating ideas of chance and probability into the Jewish metaphor system is far more sober than the simple children's game of dreidel. It comes from the Torah, from the Book of Leviticus, chapter 16, the morning Torah reading for Yom Kippur, which describes the ancient Atonement Day ritual. The high priest was instructed to use two goats for the ritual. He would sacrifice one goat to God on the altar and would symbolically transfer all the sins and guilt of the entire community onto the other goat before driving it out into the wilderness, where it would die. Thus would the people be cleansed of their sins. This latter goat was the original "scapegoat." But unlike its modern human namesakes who are blamed for the troubles of a family or a nation, no psychologist could predict which one of the two goats chosen by Aaron would become the scapegoat, for the Torah commands that the decision as to which goat would be ritually slaughtered and which would be driven away laden with guilt should be made by lottery. Leviticus 16:7–8 sets out the procedure:

> [Aaron] shall take the two goats and place them before the Eternal, at the entrance to the Tent of Meeting. Then Aaron shall cast upon the two goats lots—one lot for the Eternal, and one lot for Azazel.

How did the ancient Israelites understand this process of casting lots? According to most biblical scholars, the procedure was seen as a way of determining God's will. Other peoples made decisions by reading natural signs and omens through techniques such as hydromancy (divination by the observation of water) and hepatoscopy (divination by inspection of the livers of animals). These methods were all rejected by the Bible, however, in favor of the casting of lots. The modern biblical scholar Yehezkel Kaufman notes that

> It is no accident that the religion of YHWH preferred lot oracles to all other manner of augury. They are the simplest, most unsophisticated method of decision-making. They address God rather than nature, and express complete reliance upon his decision rather than upon a science of omens.[7]

Kaufman is quite certain that, for the ancient Israelite, reliance upon the lottery ensured that the decision would result in a pure reflection of God's will, unadulterated by any "natural" influences. For us, on the other hand, the whole province of probability is governed by the notion that a lottery is *fair* because it is controlled purely by chance. We accept the coin toss, the short straw, or the piece of paper picked out of a hat as ways of choosing people or making decisions precisely because we believe that such procedures favor no one, neither the righteous, pious person nor the wicked, undeserving one. This understanding, reinforced by endless sessions of meticulous coin tossing in junior high school math classes the world over, leads us to a very different perception of the Atonement Day ritual from that of our ancestors. The fate of the goats and, in a sense, of the entire people, is in fact decided by chance.

Albert Einstein's most famous insight is certainly his formula for general relativity: $E = mc^2$. But his next-most-famous insight may well be his comment that "God does not play dice" with the universe.[8] Einstein's insistence on this position seems to reflect an ancient Jewish belief that the decision about which goat was to be sacrificed and which driven away, a decision that would have significant impact on the spiritual if not physical well-being of the people and their relationship to God, could *not* be left to mere chance, but must be in the controlling hands of a caring God. I am suggesting that, if we take the probabilistic nature of quantum theory *seriously*, we must be open to the possibility that God *does* play dice (or perhaps dreidel) with the universe. In other words, there are elements of causality in the world that are governed not by a guiding hand that rewards good, punishes evil, and makes decisions with an eye on the "big picture," but by pure chance.

Yet the notion that God would "play dice" is offensive, because it imagines God giving up control of, and thus responsibility for, the world; it suggests that God *could* control matters but somehow occasionally becomes capricious, preferring a toss of the dice to a decision rooted in justice or compassion. Capriciousness is not a quality one wishes to find in one's deity. But if we imagine that the dice toss or dreidel spin does not reflect a conscious abdication of divine responsibility, but rather an important indeterministic element of the underlying mechanism of reality, then the fact that God sometimes, or often, leaves things to chance may be less disturbing. This realization requires that we adjust our thinking about God and allow for situations in which God does not control every outcome, because the nature of the universe makes such control *impossible*, even for God. As was the case with the uncertainty principle, we see that the centrality of randomness in quantum mechanics challenges us again to rethink God's omnipotence.

A final thought about chance: On a human level, we sometimes make decisions based on chance in order to make clear that we are *not* favoring anyone. If there is one last candy in the box and all my children want it or if some onerous household task needs doing and none of them want to do it, I may decide by flipping a coin or choosing straws *precisely* so that no one can claim that there was any discrimination in the decision-making process. It's the only "fair" way. I wonder if the same logic might be incorporated into our thinking about God and probabilistic decisions. Are there situations in which the only way that God can render an unbiased, a just decision is through the toss of the cosmic dice?

THE ROLE OF THE OBSERVER

The probabilistic nature of a quantum system raises other thorny problems. One of the most important concerns the role and importance of observation and observers in quantum systems. If we imagine a very simple system, say a system consisting of just a single particle, quantum theory tells us that we cannot know its precise position, momentum, or other characteristics, but we can only calculate probabilities for each value. These probabilities, taken all together, constitute something known as the *wave function* of the particle. So the wave function might determine that there is a particular probability that the particle is in location X, a different particular probability that it is in location Y, and yet another probability that it is in location Z, and so on. However when we *look* at the particle (in other words, when we *measure* its quantifiable characteristics), we see it in a definite spot, with a definite momentum, and so on. What is the relationship between the system, which is only probabilistic, and our observation of it, which is definite? The first response, known as the Copenhagen interpretation of quantum theory (so called because of its development by Niels Bohr and his colleagues at the University Institute for Theoretical Physics in Copenhagen), suggests that the act of observing (or measuring or becoming conscious of—these all amount to the same thing) a quantum phenomenon plays a critical role in *creating* or *determining* the phenomenon. In the language of the quantum theorists, the observation of the system collapses the wave function of the system and yields either one outcome or the other.

This assertion was attacked by Erwin Schrödinger in 1935 in the famous thought experiment[9] known as Schrödinger's cat. The experiment involves placing a live cat into a sealed box in which there is a quantity of a radioactive element, a Geiger counter, a mechanism attached to the Geiger counter linking it to a hammer, and a sealed glass flask containing deadly poison fumes. When we define an element as radioactive, we mean that the nuclei of its atoms decay, or break apart. This process releases radiation, which is detectable with a Geiger counter. The setup is such that when an atom of the radioactive material decays, the decay is detected by the Geiger counter, which activates the mechanism that drops the hammer onto the flask, which breaks the flask, which releases the fumes, which instantly kill the cat. A simple enough design, if perhaps somewhat cruel and laughably Rube Goldbergian. But now quantum theory steps in, for the question of whether any particular atomic nucleus will decay in any given period of time is a quantum phenomenon, governed by probabilities. If we assume that the type of radioactive material in the box is such that quantum mechanics assigns a 50 percent probability to the decay of one nucleus every hour, then one hour after the start of the experiment there is a 50 percent chance that a nucleus has decayed. Paradoxically, according to many standard interpretations of quantum theory, at the end of the first hour of the experiment there is an equal probability of either of two quantum states, namely, the quantum state of a dead cat and the quantum state of a live cat. One description of this bizarre situation is as follows:

> Quantum theory ... would predict that exactly one hour after the experiment began the box would contain a cat

that is neither wholly alive nor wholly dead, but a mixture of the two states, a superposition of the two wave functions.[10]

Another explanation seems to make no more sense:

Question: Right before we open the box, is the cat dead or alive? The Copenhagen interpretation answers that until we open the box and observe it, the cat is neither dead *nor* alive but exists in a superposed state of dead/alive.[11]

No matter how they are described, the results of this thought experiment violate our everyday sense of what must be. We "know" that the cat is either dead or alive, and the fact that we can't be sure whether it is dead or alive until we open the box reflects only our lack of information, not a lack of certainty in the poor animal's "real" state! Obviously, this quantum theory must be flawed. This conclusion was exactly the goal desired by Schrödinger. He hoped to undermine the Copenhagen interpretation by showing that, when quantum effects were magnified to a macroscopic scale, they yielded an absurd—and thus an untenable—picture of reality.

Is it in fact possible that our *consciousness* has an impact on physical reality? According to some interpretations of the Copenhagen interpretation, the answer is no. Rather,

In the Copenhagen view, the Schrödinger wave does not represent the *particle itself*, but *what we know* about it. Through the quantum theory, nature teaches us a lesson in philosophy. We only *pretend* that science is about nature itself—in reality, science can only depict what we *know* about nature, and in a probabilistic theory, we can't know everything.[12]

This seems to accord with our practical, everyday experience. Surprisingly, however, later versions of the Copenhagen interpretation are far bolder. The eminent physicist John Wheeler and his colleagues at Princeton have adopted a far stronger stance, according to which

> human consciousness actually *creates* reality by observing it! The big bang created our universe in some sense *because* ten billion years later there would be human beings with minds that could decipher the clues that point back to the cosmic explosion. *No mind, no universe.*[13]

Many theorists reject this interpretation, and we will presently explore an alternative to it. But before we do, it is worth asking what the philosophical or theological ramifications of the Copenhagen interpretation would be, for even if it ends up being rejected by most physicists (and it has not yet been unanimously rejected) it has been espoused by enough serious thinkers in the last seventy years to warrant some serious thought.

JEWISH CONSCIOUSNESS
IN COPENHAGEN

One of the primary features of our humanness is our conscious awareness of the world about us. This feature has received significant attention in Jewish thought over the centuries, especially in rabbinic, or talmudic, Judaism. The rabbis saw human consciousness as an ideal state, while unconsciousness was seen as a threat to be warded off wherever possible. The two best examples of this rabbinic view are the development of the blessing (*berakhah*, plural *berakhot*) and the idea of *kavannah*, or "intention." The blessing, or *berakhah*, is a bit of religious behavior "invented" by the Rabbis and given great importance by them. It is a simple and brief verbal statement made generally before (although occasionally after) performing various normal actions in daily life. Among these actions, the most common include eating and drinking. There are different blessings to be recited before eating at least five different categories of foods, as well as a "meta-*berakhah*," *Hamotzi*, for bread, which, when recited before eating a meal of which bread is a part, covers all the other categories of food eaten at that meal. There are also blessings recited after eating. In addition, there are blessings to be said after urinating or defecating, upon seeing a rainbow, upon seeing the ocean, upon seeing a scholar, upon seeing a large crowd of people, upon hearing good news or bad news, and so on and on. Most of these *berakhot* are "one-liners," consisting of an introductory formula, *Baruch Ata Adonai, Eloheynu Melekh ha-olam* (Blessed are You, Eternal God, Ruler of the Universe), followed by a short ending specific to the action being performed ("who brings forth bread from the earth," "who creates the fruit of the tree," and so on). So important was this simple bit of religious verbiage that the Rabbis suggested that every Jew should recite at least one hundred blessings every day.[14]

What is the purpose of this constant recitation? Many people think of blessings as serving the purpose of giving thanks. Although there are specific blessings that express human gratitude for divine gifts, most blessings say nothing about thanksgiving. Rather, the purpose is simple but profound: The recitation of a blessing raises the level of human consciousness regarding an action that is so common that we would normally pay little or no attention to it. For example, when it comes to eating or drinking, we participate in these basic biological behaviors so often, in fact every day of our lives, that it is easy to do so without any awareness. Similar nonawareness normally accompanies urination and defecation. The recitation of a *berakhah* on each and every one of these occasions requires us to pause and pay at least minimal attention to a "normal" human action, placing it in the larger context of a highly complex world. (The problem is that once the recitation of *berakhot* becomes a common part of life, the recitation tends to be so routine and habitual that it loses much of its power to raise awareness—but that is another issue.) The system does not allow us to nibble or snack absent-mindedly or to do anything else in that manner. In fact, absent-mindedness is precisely the enemy that the *berakhah* was designed to fight.

A similar purpose is evident in numerous talmudic discussions about the need for *kavannah* in the performance of religious obligations *(mitzvot)*. The word *kavannah* (plural *kavannot*) which comes from the root word meaning "direction," describes a state of awareness and intention. The Rabbis prescribe numerous *mitzvot* that must be performed at various times. Many of these are biblical in origin, while some are rabbinic innovations or modifications. The Rabbis were apparently concerned, especially when it came to *mitzvot* performed frequently (such as obligatory daily prayer) about the possibility that people would fulfill these requirements in a routine and habitual manner, without paying attention. So they discuss, in several parts of the Talmud, which *mitzvot* are not considered to have been properly fulfilled *unless* they are done with *kavannah*. These discussions reveal a view that performing such a symbolic act without mental focus, without intention, is worthless and meaningless. Ultimately, however, the Rabbis decided that only a specific few *mitzvot* require real concentration. This may reveal a rabbinic concession to the overwhelming human tendency to perform repetitive behaviors without paying attention, but the decision is clearly one with which the Rabbis were not thrilled.

Later on in Jewish history, the recitation of *berakhot* as a consciousness-raising device and the question of *kavannah* come together. Among kabbalists, or Jewish mystics, in the medieval period it became common to compose short introductory meditations or reflections to be recited before performing *mitzvot*, even though the *mitzvot* involved already had prescribed blessings. So, for example, the Torah commands that we eat *matzah* (unleavened bread) on Passover. This *mitzvah*, which takes place shortly before dinner is served at the Passover seder, is preceded by a *berakhah*, or rather, by two different *berakhot*: the first is the usual blessing before eating bread ("who brings forth bread from the earth"), and the second is the specific blessing for the *mitzvah* of eating *matzah* ("who sanctified us with *mitzvot* and commanded us about eating *matzah*"). One would imagine that the blessings would suffice to raise our consciousness of the importance of the action we are about to perform. But Haggadot edited with even the slightest kabbalistic influence add a *kavannah*, or preparatory meditation, to be recited in a whisper just before reciting these two blessings. Typical is the following *kavannah* from a Haggadah associated with the teachings of the Sefas Emes, a nineteenth-century Hasidic leader:

> Behold, I am prepared and ready to fulfill the mitzvah of eating *matzah*. For the sake of the unification of the Holy One, Blessed is He, and His Presence, through Him Who is hidden and inscrutable, [I pray] in the name of all Israel. May the pleasantness of my Lord, our God, be upon us. May He establish our handiwork for us; our handiwork may He establish.[15]

Similar *kavannot* accompany most of the blessings in the book. Their purpose is clear: to make the person who is about to perform a ritual obligation acutely aware of him- or herself, and of the importance of the ritual action about to be performed and its impact on the relationship between human beings and God. What is the explanation for this deep concern with awareness and consciousness? It may be understood as a part of the belief that human beings are created in the image of God (see Gen. 1:26ff). One of the few claims about God that seems unassailable, based on traditional Jewish texts and interpretations, is that God is aware and conscious. God is not some automatic force or being that influences the universe without intention, will, or awareness, but is rather deliberate and conscious in affecting reality. Just a few biblical examples will suffice to make this point clear. God's deliberative statement to self before creating human beings—"Let us make humans in our image, after our likeness"[16]—clearly indicates intention and awareness, as does God's repeated notice upon creating something that the created thing is good (Gen. 1:4, 10, 12, 18, 31). God's awareness does not cease with creation, however. In contemplating whether the sin of Sodom and Gomorrah is sufficiently egregious to warrant the destruction of these cities, God says, "I will go down to see whether they have acted altogether according to the outcry that has reached me" (Gen. 18:21). And when Moses first meets God at the burning bush, the divine voice says to him, "I have marked well the plight of My people in Egypt" (Ex. 3:7). If God is aware, then is not human awareness a part of the *imitatio dei*, or imitation of God, that is required of a species created in the divine image?

CONSCIOUSNESS AND CREATION

What does all this have to do with modern Jewish metaphors and the Copenhagen interpretation of quantum theory? We started out with the observation that many contemporary Jews who accept the basic propositions of modern cosmology and physics as the foundation stones of their world have serious difficulties with the traditional notion of a God who preceded creation and who thought and spoke the world into existence. Haven't we slipped right back into such old and outmoded metaphors in the foregoing discussion of God's awareness? Not quite. True, the notion of a conscious, thinking, speaking God sounds quite traditional. But the essential point here is that it is *our* consciousness that makes us like God. By making this claim, I am saying that consciousness is a divine attribute and that an important part of the system of metaphors by which we attempt to describe God is *awareness*. If we can de-anthropomorphize our thinking about God and stop thinking about God in human images, then we can understand this claim as being the equivalent of saying that *consciousness is a crucial creative, or Godlike, attribute*. Thus, when human beings seek to be conscious and aware, as opposed to absent-minded, we are fulfilling our destiny as partners with God in the work of creation. This ancient rabbinic notion of human partnership with God is rooted in the initial divine mandate to us to "[b]e fruitful and multiply, fill up the earth [with more life] and subdue it" (Gen. 1:28). It portrays humans as having a privileged position in the created world by virtue of our ability to improve, repair, or complete the work of creation.[17] Now, in addition to all the human activities that have been defined in the past as the fulfillment of this destiny, the Copenhagen interpretation of quantum theory suggests that our conscious *observation* of quantum phenomena plays a significant role in creating those phenomena! My son Lev recently told me an old joke about the seventeenth-century French philosopher René Descartes, the one who claimed, "*Cogito ergo sum*," meaning "I think, therefore I am." It seems he was in an airliner and was asked by a flight attendant if he would care for a drink. "I think not," Descartes replied—and instantly disappeared! The logic of the joke might be applied to the statement quoted above in describing the "strong" version of the Copenhagen interpretation favored by John Wheeler and company at Princeton: "The human consciousness actually *creates* reality by observing it…. *No mind, no universe*."[18] That is, our consciousness of the universe is a *necessary* component of its continued existence! If that is so, then the religious requirement for us to fill our days with the recitation of little consciousness-raising formulae (that is, *berakhot*) seeks far more than pious mumbling. Done correctly, the recitation is nothing less than the exercise of a willful creativeness. To say a *berakhah*, thereby creating awareness, is to create a world. "Blessed is the One who spoke and created the world."[19] I would think that such an understanding, if we took it seriously, might lead far more of us to recite *berakhot* over a far wider variety of activities than we do now.

But certainly an important objection will be raised: The wave-function-collapsing effect of human observation is important only on a quantum—that is, subatomic—level. On a macroscopic level—a large, observable, everyday level—such effects are completely unimportant. The entire continent of Antarctica was there for eons even without being observed by humans. So this nonsense about the cosmic impact of conscious human observation is a fascinating bit of science trivia but of little real importance. I offer this response: The quantum world is what we find when we break down the classical everyday world into its tiniest pieces. It is not a different world or a different reality. It is the world in which we live, albeit on a scale very different from the one to which we are accustomed. This means that the rules of the quantum world are the rules of our world, even if we have not been accustomed to thinking in terms of those rules for most of our history as thinking beings. Once we incorporate these rules into the way we think about "how the world works," they must find some expression in the metaphors by which we describe the experience of humanness. Once we integrate into our mental picture of the world the idea that awareness, observation, or measurement of a phenomenon by a human being can have a real creative effect on that phenomenon, however limited the range of situations in which such an effect might "really" be observed, our sense of the relationship between awareness or consciousness and the "real world" will be forever altered. In a sense, I am reframing the thought experiment of Schrödinger's cat as a parable, in a traditional religious sense. It is a story, a scenario, a *midrash* that we can imagine happening (even if we never actually observe it), and the imagining of it fundamentally changes our view of the world. It is in this sense that the Copenhagen interpretation can lend new meaning to traditional Jewish teachings about awareness, consciousness, and *kavannah*.

NOT ALL ROADS LEAD TO COPENHAGEN

I said earlier that the Copenhagen interpretation, although not conclusively rejected, is far from being the only view of quantum theory. What are the alternatives?

One of the most fascinating alternative candidates for a comprehensive interpretation of quantum theory is the many worlds interpretation. (This interpretation goes by several names. Murray Gell-Mann prefers to call it the many histories interpretation, while others, including Fred Alan Wolf, think of it as the parallel universes interpretation.) The approach was first suggested by Hugh Everett III, a Princeton graduate student in physics who studied under John Wheeler in the late 1950s. It radically redefines the terms in which we think of the quantum world. Whereas the Copenhagen interpretation describes a wave function that assigns specific probabilities to each of the possible states of a quantum system, the many worlds interpretation claims that the system *actually exists* in all its possible states at any given moment, but that each possible state of the system exists in a separate universe. Thus, all the possible quantum states of the system, taken together, create what we normally (that is, in our everyday, classical, common-sense lives) think of as a single universe but what is, on a quantum level, an infinitely large bundle of parallel universes that usually do not interact with one another.[20] Now in the

Copenhagen interpretation, the role of the observer, who stands outside the quantum system, is critical. The quantum system goes merrily on its way, with no particular state but only a wave function that describes the probabilities of each of its possible states, until an outside observer comes along and makes an observation or a measurement. This external act collapses the wave function and creates a particular state. The many worlds interpretation objects that there is no such thing as an "outside" observer. Any observer, by definition, is part of the system that he or she observes. Thus, the many worlds interpretation pictures each possible state of the quantum system as being *real*, that is, as actually existing, together with the observer who observes it, in its own unique universe. Physicist Frank Tipler describes this strange and thoroughly counterintuitive situation as applied to Schrödinger's cat:

> According to the Many-Worlds Interpretation there is no reduction [i.e., collapse] of the wave function at all. That is, after one hour in the steel chamber, the cat really is in the quantum state "dead cat plus live cat." The Many-Worlds Interpretation resolves the obvious inconsistency with observation by saying that the radioactive decay of the atom has forced the cat and all the other pieces of equipment to split into two different worlds: the cat is alive in one of these worlds and dead in the other. If we now try to see whether the cat is alive or dead, then we also split into two. In one world, we see the cat dead, and in the other we see the cat alive.[21]

In other words, the quantum system exists simultaneously in every one of its possible states, although no two of these states coexist in the same universe. Rather, each possible state exists in its own universe. As soon as I observe, measure, or become conscious of a quantum system, my self splits into as many parallel selves as there are possible states of the system I have observed. That is, each observation of the system *creates* a huge number of new observers. Each of these observers is only aware of the universe in which he or she exists. Each perceives his or hers as the *only* state (and may not even think of the possibility of other states).

What effect would the many worlds interpretation have on Jewish thinking and lives if we were to take it seriously?[22] How would it affect the metaphors by which Jewish identity is constructed? The most important impact, I think, would be on notions of history and the role it plays in Judaism. The fundamental image of the many worlds interpretation is that of a "branching tree" of histories, where each quantum event multiplies the number of branches. But unlike the version of branching paths portrayed in Robert Frost's famous poem "The Road Not Taken,"[23] in this view of quantum theory we do not choose to follow one path and not the other when the two paths diverge. Rather, at each quantum event, the whole universe splits in two (or in as many pieces as there are possible outcomes of the event). Both branches are created, and I, the conscious observer, having split in two along with the rest of the universe, take *both* paths. Each "copy" of my conscious self takes one path, such that each possible path is followed by one copy of me. Each of these branches, with its own copy of "me," exists in a different parallel universe. Thus, the series of branches and paths that *I* am conscious of, that have led *me* to this particular point in my life and the life of the world, is not the only series of branches and paths that existed (or exists). Things could have gone differently and in fact *did* go differently in different universes. Every possible outcome that could have occurred did occur.

Our consciousness of this notion that things could have been different, had we taken different branches, is a central theme of the most powerful Jewish celebration of history, the

Passover seder. Immediately following the Four Questions, just moments after the start of the seder, we recite a passage known by its opening words, *Avadim hayinu*:

> We were slaves to Pharaoh in Egypt, and the Eternal our God brought us out from there with a strong hand and an outstretched arm. And if the Holy Blessed One had *not* brought our ancestors out of Egypt, then we, our children and our grandchildren would [still] be enslaved to Pharaoh in Egypt.

This passage is a clear expression of our awareness that our current situation is a result of the vast number of paths that the Jewish people has taken and, obviously, of the even greater number we have not taken. We would have been a very different people had we lived in the universe in which Moses never led us out of slavery. We are who we are *because* of the countless branchings of history.

Later in the seder, we come to one of my favorite songs in the entire evening, *Dayenu*. Here, again, we see some awareness of the importance of the branchings that fill our history, but the text reaches a different conclusion from that reached in *Avadim hayinu*. The song explores how we would have reacted to a different series of branchings: If we had been taken out of Egypt but judgment had not been executed upon our enemies, or if we had been led safely through the split-open sea but our enemies had not been drowned in it, or if we had been brought to Mount Sinai but had not been given the Torah, then what? Whereas *Avadim hayinu* concludes that if our history had taken a slightly different path, we would still be slaves, *Dayenu* concludes that even if we had taken a different path at any of these junctures, then—*Dayenu!*—it would have been enough for us. This claim of sufficiency certainly cannot mean that any one of these steps would have really been enough. Only in the universe that we remember experiencing, in which *all* the requisite branches *were* taken, would we have experienced a full redemption. Anything less would have been a failed, or at best a partial, redemption. So what is the meaning of *Dayenu*? What does it mean to say that it would have been enough? I believe it means that we realize, given the tremendous number of possible universes, or possible branchings of history, that even a small piece of the "correct" path—the path that would ultimately lead us to develop a sense of peoplehood and relationship with God—was remarkable enough to deserve our attention, our thanks, and our appreciation. Once we are aware of the countless possible paths that we *could* have taken, we must surely marvel at each branching that led us closer to our goal, even if a particular path was cut short at the next branching point. Furthermore, this awareness leads us to realize that even the series of paths that we are aware of having taken has not been perfect. In a slightly different set of branches, for example, we never built the Golden Calf. In another, we arrived in Canaan in a matter of months instead of forty years after leaving Egypt. So *Dayenu* teaches us to be aware of and grateful for each part of the path we did take.

Our consciousness of, and gratitude for, the particular set of branches that we *did* experience finds perhaps its most beautiful expression earlier in the Haggadah of Passover in a *berakhah* recited at the beginning of each holiday and on numerous other occasions, namely the *Shehechiyanu*. The blessing says, "Blessed are You, Eternal our God, Sovereign of the Universe, who has given us life, sustained us, and brought us to this time." The traditional interpretation has seen the flow of time as a single path. The blessing acknowledges our debt to God for having kept us alive long enough to get this far along. It is as if we are saying, "Thank God we made it through another year." This is not a trivial or meaningless sentiment by any means. Especially for those of advanced age, or for those in poor health, the very fact of having survived to see another festival or joyous occasion is a wonderful thing, appropriately savored. The many worlds interpretation, however, suggests an additional, alternative understanding of the blessing's meaning. Rather than seeing life as a single path and being grateful for how far along it we have come, we now see history, and time itself, as a vast series of branching-off points. Each time we come to such a point, we go off along all the possible branches, and each leads to a different reality as the paths diverge. We are aware, however, of only the particular set of branches that have brought us to this time and place. This *berakhah* raises our awareness that we could have survived this long, but on a completely different set of branches, in a completely different universe, in which our lives would have been completely different. The blessing acknowledges not that we have stayed alive long enough to get this far, but that we have gotten *laz'man hazeh*, to *this particular* time, and not to another time in another universe. In other words, the blessing is not responding to the duration of my life, but to the particular set of paths and branches that have brought me to this universe, this moment. As such, it makes me aware of the unique, complex set of choices and paths that have produced what I now experience as "reality."

Of course, to be consistent with the theory requires awareness of the fact that the other copies of "me" that exist in the other universes (all those, at least, who have survived this far) may also be saying *Shehechiyanu*, each in his own universe. I might wonder how each of these versions of me is faring, but I cannot know. I also cannot assume that the outcomes of the historical path in my universe are the best possible outcomes. In fact, I can easily imagine better outcomes—histories without a Holocaust, or without ongoing, chronic violence in the Middle East, for example. But the recitation of *Shehechiyanu* does not require the assumption that this is the best of all possible worlds. Rather, it requires only an awareness that this particular universe, with all its flaws and failures, still contains wonders sufficient to amaze me. *Dayenu!*

SPELUNKING IN PARALLEL UNIVERSES: THE WORLD OF *MIDRASH*

Now I want to explore another way in which the parallel universes or many worlds idea might enrich our contemporary understanding of what Jewishness is all about. It involves a peculiar genre of traditional Jewish literature called *midrash* (plural *midrashim*). *Midrash* is a tool developed by the Rabbis of the talmudic period to explore the deeper meaning of our sacred texts and to expound upon and teach their own philosophical and theological views. It may be described as a method by which stories are spun to fill apparent gaps in, and answer questions arising from, biblical texts. A typical and well-known example is the following *midrash* on a single verse in Genesis 22, the chapter known as the Binding of Isaac. In the biblical text, Abraham has been told by God to take his son Isaac to the land of Moriah and sacrifice him there. Immediately, Abraham prepares for the journey and sets out, taking Isaac, two servants, and a donkey. Then the biblical text tells us:

> On the third day [of the journey] Abraham looked up and saw the place from afar. Abraham said to his two [servant] boys, "Sit here with the donkey. The lad [Isaac] and I will go there, we will prostrate ourselves, and we will return to you." (Gen. 22:4–5)

The *midrash* starts by quoting a section of the biblical text, then adds a few details, as follows:

"... and saw the place from afar ..." How was it visible from afar? This teaches that this was originally a low place. But when the Holy Blessed One declared that the divine Presence would dwell there and that it would become a sanctuary, the place said, "It is not the custom of a ruler to dwell in a valley, but rather in a high place that is exalted, beautified and visible to all." The Holy Blessed One immediately hinted to the land surrounding the valley that it should all contract into a single place to form a spot for the divine Presence. Abraham said to Isaac, "Do you see what I see?" He responded, "I see a beautiful and glorious mountain with a cloud bound round it." He [Abraham] said to his servants, "Do you see anything?" They said to him, "All we see is desert." He said to them, "A people that resembles a donkey! Just as the donkey sees without understanding, so too is it with you! 'Sit here with the donkey.'"[24]

This *midrash* serves several different functions. It explains how Abraham was able to see the place from far away, what he saw, and how he was able to identify it as the correct place (since God had not told him in advance to which particular spot he should go). It provides a linkage between verse 4 (up to "the place from afar") and verse 5 ("Abraham said"). And it allows the Rabbis an opportunity for some rather ethnocentric bashing of other groups in its likening of the servant boys (who are unidentified in the Bible but whom other midrashic sources identify as Abraham's steward Eliezer and Isaac's half-brother Ishmael) to donkeys. As such, the *midrash* does a good job of filling some gaps, answering some questions, and expressing a piece of the rabbinic agenda (in this particular case, an element of the socio-ethno-political agenda). Part of its success as a *midrash* also comes from the fact that it fits well into the framework of the extant biblical text. We could imagine a different version of the Bible with this *midrash* included, and we would not be aware of the "seams" that separated it from the Genesis material. This is a common feature of many *midrashim*. In fact, there are some well-known stories that many people assume to be in the Bible but are actually *midrashim*. Two good examples are the story of Abraham breaking the idols in his father's shop and the story about baby Moses in Pharaoh's home being given the choice between a pile of glittering jewels and a pile of burning coals. Neither story is in the Bible, but both are so well known, so often told, and so comfortably situated in the biblical narrative that many people grow up thinking they are from the biblical text.

There is another sort of *midrash*, however, that is so out of place in the narrative flow of the biblical text as to seem absurd. A good example of this type of *midrash*, also connected to the Binding of Isaac, is a whole group of *midrashim* in which Abraham goes through with the sacrifice, slaying his son despite the angel's countermanding warning, "Do not raise your hand against the boy! Do not do anything to him!" (Gen. 22:12). Upon reading or hearing of such *midrashim*, many people familiar with the biblical story react with a mixture of confusion, disbelief, and derision. Where do the Rabbis get this stuff? Who authorized them to take such bizarre liberties with the sacred text, actually changing the *outcome* of the story? Do they expect us to take this seriously? After all, the biblical story, as wrenching and morally challenging as it is, *does* have its own logic! By the end we learn (perhaps) that God never intended for Abraham to kill his son, but only wanted to assess his *willingness* to do so. The story as told in Genesis is still full of serious problems: What kind of a God would conduct such a cruel test? What kind of relationship could Abraham have with God, or could Isaac have with Abraham, after the event? But at least all turns out well (sort of) in the end. These *midrashim* that have Abraham killing his son fly in the face of all we've been taught about the sanctity of human life and the prohibition of human sacrifice. And how do these stories deal with the subsequent chapters of Genesis, in which Isaac appears alive and well? Most of the *midrashim* in question have Isaac miraculously resurrected immediately after being slaughtered.[25]

In response to these questions, I want to propose that this sort of *midrash,* in which a "what if?" scenario that differs radically from the plot of the biblical story is sketched out, is an important exercise in the process by which a people creates its consciousness of its own identity. How? Imagine that your life is an exploration of an endless, labyrinthine series of caves and tunnels which you explore with an endless supply of companions. At every point in the exploration where a branching occurs in the tunnels, different members of the group choose to go on different paths. At each branching, you and your party bid a sad farewell to the other groups that have decided to take other paths, for you will probably never see them again. The rule of this spelunking expedition is that once you choose a path, you will never be able to explore the other path, the one you chose not to take. Given this description, it is clear that where you are in life, and who is in your traveling party, is the product of all the decisions you and the other explorers have ever made. Now imagine further that this expedition has been going on for generations, even centuries. We have all been born to parents who were born to parents who were born to parents who were already all born on the expedition. Now "reality" as we know it has an additional element, namely, our memory of which turns, which paths, and which choices our group took at every juncture. Given this scenario, we are only aware of, and *can* only be aware of, one reality, that being the one that has resulted from all the decisions *we* have made plus the memories that *we* have preserved and studied about our trip. We *know* that there are other realities, since for as long as anyone can remember we've been coming to branching points in the cave system and saying tearful goodbyes to other subgroups who decide to take other branches. But knowing that the other realities are out there doesn't change the fact that we can only experience this one. This is a one-way expedition.

But now we find a way in which we *can* explore the other caves and tunnels, the other realities. We sometimes sit around and play an imagination game, like this: "What do you think would have happened if great-great-grandmother had taken the right fork rather than the left? The left, the one she took, was brightly lit, but the right-hand fork was dark. What would have happened to us, how would we have developed differently, if we had gone along in darkness?" Of course the historians among us scoff at this silly what-iffing. They say that it's a waste of time, since we can never really *know* what the other tunnels are like. But the more imaginative among us realize that reality is constructed, at least in part, by what we *imagine* to have occurred in our past, what we *remember* having done, regardless of whether there is any "hard historical evidence" for our imaginings or our memories. And since a large part of the meaning in our lives comes from our collective memories of what has happened to us over the generations, our imagining of other tunnels can be critically important to our sense of who we are.

This rather elaborate metaphor of spelunking is a good description, I think, of the process by which religious communities construct meaning in their lives. And the sort of "contrary to fact" *midrashim* that I mentioned above, in which, for example, Abraham really *does* sacrifice Isaac, is a way (perhaps the only way) for us to explore how our lives might have been different had we taken a different path at some crucial branching point in the past. Such explorations, by allowing us to "tour" other realities that are the products of choices that we did not make, can help us understand what our lives are all about in the reality that we do inhabit. This is what is happening in the Passover seder. By asking what would have happened if we had not escaped Egyptian bondage, we are trying to understand better what it means to be free, or to be grateful, or to be aware of the extent to which we are—or are not—free.

The many worlds interpretation of quantum theory seems to me to be a very fitting metaphor for the sense that the reality that we know is only one of a large number of possible realities. Each is the unique product, for those who inhabit it, of the choices they have made (and those that have been made for them). *Midrash* can be seen as a way of exploring the other realities, the universes that we do *not* inhabit.

But the exploration via imagination of other realities, other universes, can have an even more profound effect. It can actually change our sense of who we are. Here is an example of how this happens. At some point in the early Middle Ages, a *midrash* was developed about a woman named Lilith, who preceded Eve. I say "developed" because it is not clear how early the initial story of Lilith was told, but by the early Middle Ages[26] the *midrash* had been fairly well fleshed out. This woman, created simultaneously with Adam on the sixth day of creation (as opposed to Eve, who was created later out of Adam's rib in the Garden—see Genesis chapters 1 and 2) quarreled with Adam over who would lie on top when they made love. This argument may be taken on a literal level, or it may be understood as a symbolic statement of a more fundamental disagreement over issues of inferiority and superiority, authority and submission, and the general contours of the relationship between them and the power dynamics that characterized it. According to the *midrash*, Adam absolutely refused to allow Lilith to be on top, so she left him and ran away to the bottom of the sea. Numerous pleas for her to return, made by various heavenly emissaries, went unheeded, and in the end the *midrash* portrays her as a demonic creature who threatens the health of newborn babies. In response to Adam's loneliness after Lilith's departure, Eve was created.

The details of this story seem to the reader of the Bible to be completely unjustified fiction. There is not the slightest hint in the text of Genesis 1 and 2 that such a thing could have happened. Unlike the case of the Abraham *midrash* cited above, in which the details supplied in the *midrash* could conceivably fit into the story of Genesis 22, the Lilith narrative seems wholly incompatible with the Genesis creation story. The only way to justify taking it seriously is to see it as a "what if" tale that admits that this is not what *did* happen but then goes on to imagine how life would be if it *had* happened. In this respect it is a good example of the metaphorical use of the parallel universes interpretation. It imagines what would have happened if the reality that we experience had taken a different path through the maze of branching points as the tree of history developed. In this case, the impact of such a journey of imagination is profound. In the last three decades or so, Jewish feminists have searched for textual roots for their developing sense of the changing role and status of women in Jewish life. Often the search has led to the Lilith story. The text provides an ancient model of a woman refusing to accept a subordinate role and opting for independence. The importance of this model can be seen in the use of the name Lilith for what has been since 1976 the most important magazine of American Jewish feminism.

You may object that this case stretches the many worlds metaphor much too far, since the alternative reality of the Lilith story is an alternative to a "reality" (the narratives of Genesis 1 and 2) that, in the view of most moderns, is itself not real but a fiction in its own right. What sense is there in referring to this story as an alternative *reality* when neither it nor the original story is real at all? After all, we don't believe that man and woman were created in an instant on the sixth day of creation, or that woman was created from a rib removed surgically from a man! The question and my response to it come perilously close to the very marshy and treacherous ground of determining the nature of reality. I shall try to respond without sinking into that swamp. The parallel universes (or many worlds) theory suggests that there are, in fact, a vast number of alternatives to the "reality" that we experience. In discussing the independence of these universes from one another, author Fred Alan Wolf cites the work of a major proponent of the many worlds interpretation, physicist Bryce DeWitt:

> In DeWitt's view ... a branch contained both an object or universe and an observer of that object or universe. In each branch, *there was a fundamental unattainability of information about the other branches.*[27]

But the unattainability of information from other branches does not mean that our powers of thought and imagination are imprisoned in one branch with no access to any other. Two pages after the passage I have just quoted, Wolf writes:

> Quantum physics appears to be telling us that what we choose to observe alters, and even creates, what we observe. Thus in a quantum world view, we have choice—something I see as synonymous with consciousness. In other words, to have consciousness there must be choice.
>
> But how can choice manifest? There must be mind. In other words, it is self-consistent to have choice if there is mind, and choice then exists in the mind. Mind, I believe, exists as fleeting energy in parallel universes. The universe we perceive consists of the overlap of these fleeting flashes of energy. The patterns create mind as surely as they create matter. Both the existence of matter and the perception of it are the same thing.[28]

This rather extreme position seems to suggest that what we perceive and experience as the real world is largely a product of our consciousness. In other words, we construct what appears to us to be a concrete and integrated reality by how and what we choose to perceive and to be aware of. As Wolf describes it, this is an outrageous idea, and one that clearly violates our practical experience that there is only one reality, which we may not be entirely aware of, but which chugs along merrily regardless of our level of perception. His position defies what we have come to think of over the course of many centuries as "logical," but there it is, all the same!

In my Lilith example, I am proposing something much less radical and outrageous, since I am not suggesting that the Genesis account of Adam and Eve represents historical reality at all. Indeed, to make such a claim would fly in the face of what I have said elsewhere about rethinking Jewish notions of creation in light of Big Bang cosmology, evolution, and so on. But if I am not claiming the exalted status of physical historicity for Adam and Eve, then why do I bring the story up and refer to it as a "reality," to which the Lilith story could be an "alternative"? The Adam and Eve story is real in that it is a narrative construction, a story, that generates a great deal of social reality in human life. About this there can be no argument. By telling a story like that of Adam and Eve, Jews, and other peoples as well, have created a reality that has shaped much of the intricate system of relationships and hierarchies on which our lives—our very *real* lives—have been based. The tale of Adam and Eve, for example, has quite a lot to say about the relationship between men and women. Men precede women, both chronologically and in their position of power in public life. Men see women as temptresses whose poor judgment leads society to ruin. Men are, in the hierarchy of life, superior to women. Now liberal moderns may disagree with these statements (I certainly do), but they can hardly deny that, for most of human history through which Jews have lived (and surely many other eras as well), they have been true. The telling of the story of Adam and Eve helped construct that reality. Did the story *cause* the gender hierarchies that have characterized our life until the last few decades? Certainly not, at least not all by itself. But it was surely an important element in the foundation that supported the reality. The story essentially claims that the hierarchical situation in which we find ourselves was deliberately planned this way, from the beginning. It was, if you will, God's original plan, and therefore ideal. To say so means that the situation is in no way a problem that needs to be fixed, any more than that we are bipeds or need to ingest certain nutrients that our bodies cannot synthesize is a problem that needs fixing. These are simply the way things are, and the way they've always been and will always be. In a word: reality. So although I do not claim that the Adam and Eve story tells the physical history of how human males and females came to be, I am completely comfortable with the claim that the story does represent a human construction of reality. The story is an example of how humans construct social reality through narrative. This sort of reality does not just "happen." It is clearly created over centuries of human social development, as the result of eons of storytelling. In this respect, the reality of the hierarchical relations between men and women in our society has, in fact, been *created* by our consciousness, our choice of awareness. That being so, the Lilith *midrash* can legitimately be seen as an alternative path, a different reality. So you see that this claim is far less outrageous, far less counterintuitive, than that of the many worlds theory, which claims that the reality of the physical universe is also a result of our consciousness.

MANY WORLDS CAN
HAVE MANY TRUTHS

What is the effect of thinking about reality and history this way? What difference does it make if we reunderstand our

Jewish lives with the addition of the many worlds metaphor?[29]
The difference is enormous. According to the old way of thinking about reality, we knew that there was, and *could only be*,
one reality. To imagine other realities was to play the "what if"
game, for which historians have so little patience, to fantasize,
to be immature, to waste time. This understanding led inex-
orably to a worldview that recognized the status quo as the only
acceptable, or imaginable, version of the world. This is the way
things are. Such a worldview tends to invalidate, or delegit-
imize, all imaginings of reality that do not correspond with the
way things actually are. Once we think seriously about many
worlds/parallel universes, however, our entire attitude changes.
This is *not* the only possible version of reality, nor is it even the
only one that *really* exists! It happens to be the one in which we
find ourselves at the moment, but we could have just as easily
found ourselves in an endless number of alternative realities,
which exist right alongside our current reality. This realization
changes our whole view of realities, choices, and worldviews
other than our own. It makes us see that although we may
endorse, support, and participate in our reality deeply and fully,
it makes sense for others to believe in and live out other realities. It weakens the certainty with which we say that they, those
"others," are *wrong*. In a world that incorporates the parallel
universe metaphor, my being *right* does not require everyone
else to be *wrong*. In parallel universes there can be parallel
truths, each of which is singular and ultimate in its own universe, without diminishing the truth of the others, in their
respective universes.

The impact of this idea that there can be parallel, ultimate
truths is perhaps best seen in its effect on the idea of the chosen
people. As Jews, we have traditionally cherished the notion that
God chose us and made us the divine favorite. The language of
the blessing recited in synagogues before the reading of the
Torah sums it up: "Blessed are You, Eternal God, Ruler of the

Universe, Who chose us from among all peoples and gave us His Torah. Blessed are you Eternal God, Giver of the Torah."

Similar sentiments can be found in the blessing immediately preceding the recitation of *Shema Yisrael* in the morning service, in the Kiddush, or sanctification blessing, recited over wine on Friday evening, and elsewhere. These assertions of chosenness give us a sense of special purpose and status, and foster in us a sense of special responsibility toward the world. They reinforce communal cohesion and loyalty and can be used to create a sense of communal responsibility, a sense that we are obligated to repair the world's flaws. So far so good. But the same ideas can lead to ethnocentric chauvinism and the disparagement of all others. I am deeply disturbed by the arrogant sense of superiority that sometimes results from our belief that we are the chosen people, and I am not alone in my discomfort. One of the prominent features of Reconstructionist Judaism, a movement founded in the first part of the twentieth century by the great American rabbi Mordecai M. Kaplan, is its rejection of chosenness. In one of numerous passages devoted to the subject, Kaplan wrote:

> But nowadays ... the doctrine of Israel's election, in its traditional sense, cannot be expected to make the slightest difference in the behavior or outlook of the Jew. From an ethical standpoint, it is deemed inadvisable, to say the least, to keep alive ideas of race or national superiority, inasmuch as they are known to exercise a divisive influence, generating suspicion and hatred.[30]

Similar objections are common in a wide range of modern Jewish writings from many philosophical viewpoints. Each modern objection to the chosen people idea carries with it its own solution. So, for example, the authors of the Reconstructionist prayer book rewrote the offensive phrase from the blessing before the reading of the Torah; the new version says that God "drew us near to His service." This rewrite allows Jews to feel embraced by God without requiring us to feel that we are *more* chosen than other peoples. God could be imagined as having drawn many groups to divine service. Another creative reinterpretation of chosenness involves a play on words by which the chosen people becomes a choosing people. This interpretation suggests that it is not that we are God's favorites but rather that *our* faith and belief lead us to seek God and to seek to do God's will. Such a rereading is not unlike that of the Reconstructionists: If we can choose God, then other peoples can do so as well. Another makeover of the offensive notion allows us to be chosen, but instead of being selected out for special treats and favors, it sees us as being chosen for the special responsibility of repairing the world's flaws and imperfections. And in a sober, theological twist that sounds as if it has been profoundly influenced by Christian faith, some have even suggested that we Jews are chosen for special suffering. Again, this relieves the modern discomfort with the idea of chosenness by making it an unpleasant burden rather than a proud and uplifting badge of honor.

If we incorporate ideas from quantum theory into our repertoire of metaphors, however, and take them seriously, much of the discomfort of the chosen people idea disappears. We are indeed chosen and special, the elect of God, in the version of reality that our community's consciousness creates. But we are also well aware that there are endless other realities, created by other communities' consciousnesses, in which *they* are chosen. In some they are chosen instead of us, while in others they and we are both chosen. Note that I am taking some liberties here, by combining the Copenhagen idea that reality is to some degree an effect of consciousness with the parallel universes idea that no one reality has any privileged status over any other. With this "mixed metaphor" in hand, we see that no one universe can claim to be *the* real one; each can only claim to be *a* real one, created by its inhabitants' consciousness. So, in our people's version of reality, for example, Isaac was the favorite of Abraham's sons and was chosen by God to be the continuation of the covenantal line. But in the Muslim version of reality, Ishmael was the favorite, chosen one. Our chosenness does not require the negation of their chosenness.

MAKING PEACE IN PARALLEL UNIVERSES

The inability of any single universe or reality to claim privileged status as *the* real universe is a crucial element in the development of this metaphor. We cannot avoid or deny the fact that the realities created by peoples' consciousnesses are not only flights of imagination, to be used for stories, rituals, and other benign cultural expressions. In fact, the reality that a people experiences leads to its creation of social and political theory and policy. Many a war has been fought, many a people enslaved and oppressed and even slaughtered, as the direct result of the "realities" experienced by one group or another. Any set of religious metaphors needs a safety mechanism to prevent its adherents from claiming a privileged status, which it can then use to justify the destruction or persecution of others. We live in an era that has witnessed a long series of genocidal horrors, including the murder of six million Jews in the Holocaust, but not limited to that tragedy (by such limitation, Jews commit a serious error of making their reality absolute). In such an era I believe that incorporating such a safety mechanism must be an absolute moral requirement of any system of religious, social, or political thought. The combination of the parallel universes notion of parallel realities with the Copenhagen notion of the importance of consciousness as a creative force may provide such a safety mechanism. It allows us to construct our identity and our Jewish lives based on a set of historical and current realities, but cautions us to remember that every other group has the same right and the same ability to construct reality. In the labyrinth-of-caves analogy, this principle is expressed as follows: No spelunker may do anything to prevent a fellow spelunker from freely choosing his or her own path.

The use of the parallel universes idea raises a problem, however, that requires further thought. In the quantum theory of parallel universes, there is no possibility of exchanging information between one universe and another. Once a branching point is passed, the two resultant branches are isolated from each other. In our human-scale world, on the other hand, we share our world with many other individuals and groups, all of whom, according to this interpretation, have their own realities. There is *constant* interplay among all the parallel universes. Is it a false solution to the problem of chosenness to suggest that each community creates a reality in which it is *the* chosen group, if the communities still have to live together, interact, and share a world?

The answer seems to depend on whether we and another group experience parallel realities in the present, or only in the past. It is quite common in our experience to find that two individuals who share a common present have different memories of the past. Family members, for example, who reminisce about a given period—say, "when the kids were little" or "the summer we spent on the Cape"—will often have clear but different memories of that period. It is as if they lived different versions of the events in question. We are accustomed to explaining the differences between the two versions of remembered reality as the result of different points of view. But we might just as well think of them as resulting from different choices made in the "spelunking expedition" that I described. The only modification that needs to be made to the metaphor is that, by definition, if I can discuss the past with someone else, it means that I am sharing the present with that person. But everyday experience makes it clear that my sharing the present with her does *not* require that we shared a common past, even if we have lived together all our lives. It seems that, in the constant branching of universes as we live and make choices, often branching paths that have diverged for a short time, or for a very long time, reconverge. If my path and that of another person (or my group's path and the path of another's group) have diverged in the past but have now reconverged, it would make no sense for me to say that my version of the past was better or more valid. No one reality is privileged over all others.

There is another important observation to be made about the branching process. Sometimes the creation of new parallel universes is the result of an active, conscious choice. But often the choices that generate branching points are *not* conscious or deliberate. They are subtle choices made without thinking, choices that we make never anticipating that they could generate new universes. (The tremendous power of negligibly trivial choices to result in whole new universes is related to another idea in physics, the butterfly effect, which I explore at length in chapter 3.) This observation is important because without it we would all be "culpable" and responsible for the universes in which we live or have lived. This might very well lead to the common practice of blaming victims for being victimized. The practice might make sense if every universe through which we lived were solely the result of conscious and active choices. But many of the choices are not conscious. Furthermore, it is a central tenet in quantum theory that branching-off-point decisions are often the result of chance. Schrödinger's cat does not choose to end up dead or alive—the choice is governed by chance and probability. Despite Einstein's discomfort with the notion, the choice is sometimes the result of a roll of the cosmic dice.

QUANTUM THINGS JUST HAPPEN

In chapter 1, we struggled with the idea that the event that gave birth to the universe, the Big Bang, may not be susceptible to certain kinds of questions. Specifically, it makes no sense to ask what caused the Big Bang, or what came before it. The frustration generated by the illegitimacy of such basic questions may be addressed in part by quantum mechanics. In the classic, that is, nonquantum, world, deterministic causality plays a major role in the way we imagine the world. By this I mean that our understanding of how the world functions is overwhelmingly shaped by the notion that every phenomenon in the world, every event of any kind, can be seen as an *effect* that has a preceding *cause*. Things don't "just happen"—they are caused by things that come before them. Aristotle reasoned that if each event was an effect with a preceding cause, then its cause was also an effect with a preceding cause, which was also an effect with a preceding cause, and so on. But Aristotle also objected strenuously to the idea that there could be any infinite chain— of anything. No object or quantity could go on forever. Thus he proposed an initial event at the beginning of the universe that has come to be described as the prime mover or the uncaused cause, a force of some sort that is the cause of things that follow it, but which does not itself have a preceding cause. This line of reasoning has profoundly influenced many philosophers in their search for a creator of the universe. If all things are caused, and if the universe exists, but if it is absurd to imagine an infinite chain of effects and causes, then there must have been some initial cause that was not itself caused. Call it God. It is not hard to see how this logic brings us right back to Paul Davies's imagined debate about God and the Big Bang. Once again, we have stumbled back into arguing about the chicken and the egg, and such arguments, once they get hold of us, never let us go. But what if we could imagine an initial logic other than that of deterministic causality? What would happen to our thinking about origins if we incorporated into our view of the world some aspect of physical reality that would not *need* to be caused, but that could just pop from nonexistence into existence without a deterministic cause? This is precisely what is suggested by Paul Davies in a couple of passages about quantum mechanics and the Heisenberg uncertainty principle:

> [T]he essence of the origin problem is that the big bang seems to be an event without a physical cause. This is usually regarded as contradicting the laws of physics. There is, however, a tiny loophole. This loophole is called quantum mechanics.... [T]he application of quantum mechanics is normally restricted to atoms, molecules, and subatomic particles. Quantum effects are usually negligible for macroscopic objects. Recall that at the heart of quantum physics lies Heisenberg's uncertainty principle, which states that all measurable quantities (e.g., position, momentum, energy) are subject to unpredictable fluctuations in their values. This unpredictability implies that the microworld is indeterministic: to use Einstein's picturesque phraseology, God plays dice with the universe. Therefore, quantum events are not determined absolutely by preceding causes. Although the probability of a given event (e.g., the radioactive decay of an atomic nucleus) is fixed by the theory, the actual outcome of a particular quantum process is unknown and, even in principle, unknowable.
>
> By weakening the link between cause and effect, quantum mechanics provides a subtle way for us to circumvent the origin-of-the-universe problem. If a way can be found to permit the universe to come into existence from nothing as the result of a quantum fluctuation, then no laws of physics would be violated. In other

words, viewed through the eyes of a quantum physicist,
the spontaneous appearance of a universe is not such a
surprise, because physical objects are spontaneously
appearing all the time—without well-defined causes—
in the quantum microworld. The quantum physicist
need no more appeal to a supernatural act to bring the
universe into being than to explain why a radioactive
nucleus decayed when it did.[31]

Now Davies, as a physicist, may not find it "such a surprise" to contemplate a universe appearing spontaneously,
without a definite cause, but I, as a Jewish heir to many centuries of philosophical and religious conditioning, find it one of
the most astonishing ideas imaginable! For many centuries,
Jewish philosophers debated whether God created the universe
from some pre-existent raw materials or from nothing. The latter possibility is rather awe-inspiring even when cast in the context of an omnipotent, eternal God who decides, at some point,
to create an entire universe out of literally nothing. But if we
take modern cosmology seriously, we may now have to think
about an even more startling possibility: that the universe may
have come into existence as a tiny quantum event, unbidden by
any cause *including a pre-existent omnipotent God!* This possibility raises some very challenging questions about the nature of
God, God's role in the creation of the universe, and God's role
in the lives of human beings.

3

CHAOS THEORY
When Random Things Happen to Regular People

ORDER OUT OF CHAOS

The thinkers of the ancient world often conceived of the creation of the world as the imposition of order on primordial chaos. Ancient Egyptians, Mesopotamians, Greeks, and others described the precreation state of things as an undifferentiated, and often watery, mixture of elements. The first real step in creation myths is often the initial separation of such elements into categories: heaven above and earth below, dry land and seas, and so on. This process bears a close resemblance to the best-known ancient Israelite cosmogonic story, recounted in the first chapter of Genesis. The creation there is preceded by a state called *tohu vavohu*, which most modern Bible translations render as "unformed and void"[1] or "a formless void"[2] (Gen. 1:2). The creation process that fills that void is one of separations: On the first day light is created and then separated from darkness, on the second the dome of the sky is created to separate water above the dome of the sky from water below, on the third

water is separated from dry land, and so on. The resulting
world is one of clear distinctions between categories, species,
and nations. It was God's creative power that had "subdued"
and ordered the disordered precreation state of things, and that
same power kept chaos at bay. God is portrayed traditionally as
the master of distinctions and separations. We can see this in
the *Havdalah* blessing recited at the end of the Sabbath on
Saturday evening. It acknowledges God as the one who "separates the holy from the ordinary, light from darkness, Israel
from the other nations, the seventh day from the six days of
work." Having originally created an ordered universe out of
primordial chaos is not enough, though. God must continue to
maintain order in the world, or else the forces of chaos would
reassert themselves and overwhelm the cosmos. There is a clear
sense in much of premodern Jewish thought that were it not for
God's continued watchfulness, primordial chaos would break
through and engulf the order of creation. God's providence
maintains the rhythms of the universe, from the smallest level
to the grandest. On the level of the very small, for example, we
have God's constant maintenance of the proper functioning of
our bodies. The liturgy of the daily morning service includes a
blessing that credits God with having created the human body
with a complex network of tubes and orifices:

> It is clearly known before Your glorious throne that if
> even one of them would be opened [when it should
> have stayed closed] or closed [when it should have
> stayed open] it would be impossible to survive before
> You. Blessed are You, Eternal One, who heals all flesh
> and does wonders.[3]

The fantastically complex, finely tuned order that is evident to even the most casual observer of the biological
processes of life is totally dependent, according to the blessing,

on God's power. On the level of the very large, we find the opening blessing of the daily evening service in which God is described as the one who "orders the stars in their courses in the sky, according to divine will." Again, any stargazer is awed by the precise order of the heavens, and the blessing attributes this order to God. It implies that without God the stars would simply wander the skies in a random and unpredictable—that is, disordered—fashion.

One final example will illustrate the depth of the ancient Jewish sense that chaos is held at bay from moment to moment only by the vigilant will of God. In the afternoon service of Yom Kippur, the Day of Atonement, there is a wrenching account of the brutal execution of ten great rabbinic sages by the Romans in the first half of the second century C.E. This deeply disturbing story reaches a shuddering climax when the executioner flays the skin off Rabbi Ishmael's face until he dies with a scream to God. Witnessing this horror, the heavenly angels cry out to God, "Is this the reward for Torah?" A voice from Heaven responds, "If I hear one more word, I will turn the universe back into water, and the earth back into *tohu vavohu*. This is a decree from before Me—accept it!"[4] This troubling response suggests that God too is pained by the torture being inflicted and cannot cope with the additional stress of challenges from the heavenly entourage. If they say one more word, God will simply allow the whole cosmos to revert to its original chaotic state. Apparently, the primordial chaos of *tohu vavohu* is held at bay from moment to moment by the conscious will of God.

CHAOS AS DIVINE PUNISHMENT

This sense of the divinely created and maintained order in the universe provides us human beings with a great deal of comfort. The notion that all the parts of the world are just exactly

where we expect them to be seems crucial to our ability to
maintain a sense of inner control and calm. No extra proof of
this assertion is needed by any parent of a two-year-old who
has ever tried to put the child to bed without following every
step of the accustomed bedtime ritual. The right steps must be
followed in precisely the right order—story, song, glass of
water, and so on—or disaster will result. This two-year-old's
rigid need for predictability and order does not seem to diminish significantly as we grow up. We may learn to control our
tantrums when familiar patterns are disrupted, but our sense
of dismay remains.

As important as cosmic order is for our psychological survival, however, it is even more critical for our physical survival.
Consider the example of the two blessings mentioned above.
Anyone who has encountered a victim of illness with uncontrollable diarrhea ("even one of them would be opened [when it
should have stayed closed]") or whose airway is obstructed and
thus cannot breathe ("or closed [when it should have stayed
open]") knows how quickly such bodily disorder can lead to
death. On the other hand, the travelers of the ancient world
depended for their very survival on "the stars in their courses in
the sky." Without heavenly order, they would never have been
able to navigate home. These and many other examples indicate
how our ancestors came to regard God's maintenance of order
and predictability in the world as an element of divine benefi-
cence and caring. Any deviation from the expected order of
things could be taken as a sign of divine displeasure. Our literature is replete with examples of God's anger being expressed in
this way, often in the form of the withholding of rain. (Note, by
the way, that drought is seen in any society as a deviation from
the expected order, but even more so in a climate like that of
Israel, where there is one clearly defined rainy season and
another clearly defined dry season. Any farmer in Israel knows
better than to expect rain through the summer, but knows

equally well that if the rains have not come by late October or November there will be serious—perhaps fatal—consequences.) In perhaps the best-known case, that of Noah and the flood, God's wrath is expressed by sending too much rain—a flood meant to destroy the world. That this punishment is seen by the biblical text as primarily a violation of the *order* of the world can be seen clearly by the very end of God's statement of regret and repentance after the flood:

> The Eternal said to Himself, "Never again will I curse the soil because of humans, since the devisings of the human heart are evil from youth, nor will I ever again destroy all life, as I have done. For all the days of the earth, seedtime and harvest, cold and heat, summer and winter, and day and night will never cease." (Gen. 9:21–22)

The last sentence of this passage demonstrates the degree to which the text sees the flood as a violation of order, a temporary return to chaos. God's promise never to bring another such flood is couched as a commitment never to allow the order and rhythm of the world to be disrupted.

FROM DIVINE MASTERY TO DETERMINISM

This ancient, religious perception of the relationship between God and natural order gradually changed over the centuries, eventually giving way to a philosophical doctrine known as determinism. As we have seen in chapter 2, the core of determinism asserts that the universe functions in a (theoretically) completely predictable manner. French mathematician Pierre Simon de Laplace put it this way:

An intellect which at any given moment knew all the forces that animate Nature and the mutual positions of the beings that comprise it, if this intellect were vast enough to submit its data to analysis, could condense into a single formula the movement of the greatest bodies of the universe and that of the lightest atom: for such an intellect nothing could be uncertain; and the future just like the past would be present before its eyes.[5]

Order in the universe is every bit as important in this modern philosophical framework as it was in the ancient religious one. But now, the order of nature is seen as a built-in and inviolable feature of existence, not one being maintained from moment to moment by the beneficent will of God. The religious implications of such a shift are staggering. First, it implies that universal, unchangeable, and theoretically knowable laws are at the heart of the universe, rather than the will of God, if by will of God we mean a (potentially capricious) force within God that is independent of any other constraint. In other words, whereas earlier religious views saw God as free to act in whatever way God chose, the clockwork view requires that God act in accordance with natural law. God cannot "choose," for example, to reverse the effects of gravity or to stop the movement of heavenly bodies. God cannot perform miracles, if by "miracles" we mean the suspension or violation of natural laws. Second, the universe and the divine forces traditionally thought to drive it are not at all mysterious. As we can know what happened at any point in the past, so too, in theory, we can predict absolutely and completely what will happen at any point in the future. It is easy to appreciate the religious crisis precipitated by such an approach. God's power is no longer absolute in a certain sense, and appeal to God, through prayer, for example, makes much less sense. After all, if we use the metaphor of a clockwork universe, it doesn't make much sense to pray that the clock speed up, slow down, reverse direction, or stop! The clock-maker's job was to create a reliable timepiece. If the clock maker has succeeded, it doesn't make much sense, now that the clock is sitting on my mantel, to plead with the clock-maker to slow it down, even if the irregularity would serve a very good cause. And such a plea is no more or less absurd if it comes from a saint or a sinner—the mechanism doesn't care, nor, by extension, does its builder. The belief in prayer and its efficacy, the idea of reward and punishment, and the belief that God intervenes in history in an ongoing way— these are just a few of the mainstays of classical religion in general and Judaism in particular that suffered the consequences of the "scientific revolution."

To a large extent, this crisis was the hallmark of the modern age. We were deeply convinced of the absolute control, predictability, and (theoretical) knowability of natural law. If there were elements of nature that eluded our understanding, even large elements, it was only a matter of time, hard work, and research funding before we conquered each new frontier of knowledge. This optimistic confidence, however, would not last.

The birth of quantum theory dealt a staggering blow to such comfortable certainty. We have already seen how its assertion of the importance of uncertainty on the smallest level of physical reality shook the foundations of our sense of how the world works. The effect, however, was—and continues to be for many—limited and negligible because of the very tiny level on which quantum effects occur. In fact, on a macro level, say, the level of billiard balls, rocket ships, and planets, we can predict position and momentum at any future time with such tremendous accuracy that any theoretical imprecision is in practice nonexistent. Although the Rabbis of the early talmudic era had to declare the start of the new lunar month only after receiving testimony from reliable witnesses that they had seen the first sliver of new moon, today I can look up astronomical tables that will tell me to within fractions of a second when the new lunar month will begin one hundred years from now! So quantum effects are an interesting curiosity on a quantum level, but for us classic (that is, nonquantum) creatures, they don't make much of a difference. In that pragmatic respect, quantum theory was a false alarm; our sense that the universe is ultimately predictable had been shaken but came through mostly unscathed. (These observations do not undermine the discussion in chapter 2. The effects of quantum uncertainty on a practical, observable level are negligible, but its existence still has profound philosophical implications for how the universe functions.)

FROM CLOCKS TO CHAOS

Enter chaos theory. In the couple of decades following the middle of the twentieth century, a slowly growing group of scientists from diverse disciplines—notably meteorology and mathematics—began to develop ideas that would first be presented to the nontechnical public in James Gleick's 1987 book *Chaos: Making a New Science*. The scientists who made up this group were drawn to investigate chaotic phenomena in nature, for example, turbulence in streams of fluid, apparently random fluctuations in animal populations, unpredictable changes in an economy, and many others. It is this work, and its effects on Jewish thought, belief, and life, that will occupy us for the rest of this chapter.

Intuition tells us, and many areas of science confirm, that understanding *most* of the factors of a system *nearly* perfectly will give us a nearly perfect understanding of the final outcome and that such a nearly perfect understanding is perfectly adequate for any normal human endeavor. In the words of biologist Arthur T. Winfree:

> The basic idea of Western science is that you don't have to take into account the falling of a leaf on some planet in another galaxy when you're trying to account for the motion of a billiard ball on a pool table on earth. Very small influences can be neglected.[6]

But this comfortable, intuitive sense turns out to be wrong in many dynamic systems, that is, systems that change and evolve continuously such that all changes up to any given point affect the course of development beyond that point. Often, in such systems, microscopically tiny changes or irregularities can and do lead to tremendous changes in the future state of the system. This phenomenon is known technically as "sensitive dependence on initial conditions." Edward Lorenz, the MIT meteorologist who first identified the phenomenon in 1963, dubbed it somewhat more colorfully the butterfly effect, based on the assertion that a butterfly flapping its wings in Asia today may have an effect on North American weather next month. Mathematician Ian Stewart explains this curious effect with reference to its original formulation:

> Lorenz ends his 1963 paper with some speculations about the possibility of weather forecasting. His argument is simple and original. Imagine recording a very accurate series of measurements of the state of the atmosphere, comparable to those that you wish to use for forecasting. Collect such data for a very long time.
>
> > The crucial point is then whether analogues must have occurred since the state of the

atmosphere was first observed. By analogues we mean two or more states of the atmosphere which resemble each other so closely that the differences may be ascribed to errors in observation.[7]

If two analogues *have* occurred, then you will make identical predictions of the future weather, starting from either of them. That is, your weather-predicting scheme must predict *periodic* variation of the weather. But this is nonsense; the whole difficulty with weather-prediction is that the weather is *not* periodic.[8]

The problem with predicting the weather, it turns out, is *not* that the forces driving the weather are "random" or "ruled by chance" or in any way theoretically unpredictable. In fact, the weather is governed by forces that are completely predictable and follow ironclad rules of physics: the physics of fluid flow, convection, evaporation, condensation, and so on. But because the system is characterized by sensitive dependence on initial conditions, that is, the butterfly effect, tiny changes or variations in conditions often lead quickly to tremendous changes in the overall system. So the problem is that making predictions based on the relatively simple laws of physics that govern the system would require completely accurate measurements of the current state. *Completely* accurate. Not "fairly accurate" or "almost completely accurate." But two problems prevent completely accurate measurement. The first problem is that any given measurement is necessarily limited in its accuracy by the design of the measuring device. So, for example, if one were to measure air temperature, clearly an important factor in weather prediction, one would need some sort of thermometer. How finely calibrated could it be? To tenths of a degree? Hundredths of a degree? Thousandths?

Ten-thousandths? It's easy to see that no matter how fine the calibration, any measurement of temperature (or wind speed, or humidity, or anything else) is still "rounded off." If our thermometer is accurate to .0001 degrees Celsius, it cannot distinguish between a temperature of 20.12321 degrees and a temperature of 20.12323 degrees. But surely such a tiny difference couldn't matter, could it? If the system is characterized by sensitive dependence on initial conditions—the butterfly effect—it could indeed. Two weather patterns that only differed by .00002 degrees Celsius would certainly stay pretty much the same for a while but might then diverge markedly. The second problem is that weather is such a vast system that getting a completely accurate measurement, even if our instruments were up to the task, would be impossible. Returning to the challenge of measuring air temperature, and assuming a magical thermometer that measured temperature with infinite accuracy, where would we measure the temperature? Would we impose an imaginary grid of squares one mile on a side over the whole earth and measure the temperature at each grid intersection, at the surface and at 1,000-foot increments of altitude up to 40,000 feet? But even this Herculean task would still leave lots and lots of space without thermometers, and the butterfly effect postulates that a very small "bubble" of air in between measuring points that was a degree warmer or colder could wreak havoc with our forecasting in no time! Given the immensity of this imaginary forecasting system, with the surface of the earth virtually covered by magical thermometers, and seeing that such a system would still not provide perfectly accurate measurement, it is not hard to understand the inaccuracy of the real-world system. We are told that the temperature at the airport is 56 degrees, and downtown it's 59, and there's a 40 percent chance of showers tomorrow—and we all take it with a large grain of salt and express surprise when the forecasters occasionally get it right!

WEATHER AND JEWISH BELIEF

Now comes the critical question: What does the butterfly effect, or the weather, have to do with Jewish thought, or Jewish belief, or the metaphors by which we think and believe?

Probably since human beings first evolved, and certainly since they began writing literature that has survived to our day, the weather has been an immensely powerful and uncontrollable force in human life. Sailors are acutely aware of weather's power to return them home safely, sink them in storms, or becalm them until they die of hunger or thirst. Farmers know that the weather is the single most important factor in determining whether they and their families and communities prosper or starve. Whole communities know that their very survival depends on how violent the weather will be—whether blizzards, hurricanes, tornadoes, or drought strike here or elsewhere. And even in our own day, when it seems that we have gained control over so many areas of life, the weather is on the short list of uncontrollables. Every winter still sees major metropolitan areas paralyzed by blizzards, and every summer residents of the Caribbean and Florida wait to see if this will be the year of the next monster hurricane. Given the tremendous power and completely uncontrollable nature of the weather, it is no surprise at all that religious folk have attributed its control to the gods, or to God. Let us consider just a few examples.

In chapter 11 of Deuteronomy, in a section included in the liturgy twice daily (as the second paragraph of *Shema Yisrael*), we find the following:

> If you carefully heed My commandments which I command you today, loving the Eternal your God and serving Him with all your heart and life, then I [God] will grant you the rain in your land at its proper time, both early rain and late rain, and you will gather in new grain,

wine and oil, and I will place grass in your fields for your cattle and you will eat and be satisfied. Be careful that your heart not be seduced so that you go astray and serve other gods and bow down to them. [If you do this] the Eternal's anger will blaze out against you. He will close up the skies and there will be no rain. The earth will not yield its produce and you will quickly perish from off of the good land which the Eternal is giving you. (Deut. 11:13–17)

This passage is grounded in a few basic assumptions. First, the relationship between the people of Israel and God is predicated on Israel's fulfillment of two requirements: The people must obey God's laws, including (but not limited to) loving and serving God, and they must remain faithful *only* to God, eschewing any relationships with or worship of other gods. Second, Israel's fulfillment of these requirements will be rewarded by God, while its failure to fulfill them will be punished. These two assertions form an important element of the core of biblical theology, especially the version of that theology expressed in the Book of Deuteronomy. The important observation for our current purposes, however, is that the divine reward and punishment for fulfillment or violation of the terms of this relationship will come in the form of beneficial or harmful weather, specifically, the granting or withholding by God of the rains necessary for agriculture. Given that having plentiful, good food fulfills a basic human need and starvation is one of humanity's greatest dreads, then God's promise to grant enough rain if the people are obedient, or to bring drought if they are disloyal, is indeed an effective reinforcement device. More important, this passage makes it clear that ancient Israel saw climate as a tool used by God to enforce divine will, by rewarding and punishing, respectively, with good and bad weather.

These assumptions applied not only to divine control of collective behavior, but occasionally to control of an individual's behavior as well. Consider the beginning and the end of the biblical account of the prophet Jonah. In chapter 1 of the book, God sends Jonah to prophesy to the people of Nineveh, and Jonah, for reasons of his own, does not accept the job. Instead he tries to flee from God by sailing in a ship bound from Jaffa to Tarsus. This attempt to avoid the prophetic mission angers God, so God causes a storm to assail the ship. At first the sailors try to row back to the harbor. When that fails, and the ship is in danger of sinking, Jonah finally admits that the storm is his fault and convinces the sailors to throw him overboard. After some argument,[9] the sailors agree, and sure enough, as soon as they toss Jonah into the sea, the storm abates. In chapter 4, Jonah, having done his duty, is upset that the people of Nineveh have repented completely in response to his prophetic admonitions and that God has consequently decided to forgive them and not punish them.[10] To teach Jonah a lesson,[11] God stations him on a hillside overlooking the city, causes a leafy shade plant to grow up to provide Jonah relief from the hot sun, then the next day provides a worm to attack and kill the plant, followed by a withering east wind and a scorching sun. When Jonah laments the heat and mourns the disappearance of the plant that had given him shade the previous day, God points out to him that his distress over the shade plant, for which he did not labor and which he enjoyed for only a day, is but a tiny fraction of God's distress over the fate of the people of Nineveh. So here again, God uses control of weather phenomena—first a storm at sea and then a heat wave and accompanying wind—to control behavior and to teach, though the student in this case is a single individual and not an entire people.

We could examine an extensive series of examples in the same vein. A large part of the talmudic tractate *Ta'anit* is devoted to the circumstances under which fasting is appropriate as a response to the lack of rain in the autumn rainy season in the land of Israel. And even in our own day, insurance policies still refer to "acts of God" by which they mean, among other things, floods, hurricanes, tornadoes, and so on. The point is simple: We have, throughout our history, seen the control of weather as one of the primary ways in which God expresses pleasure or displeasure and rewards and punishes.

What will happen to our religious thought and belief, and to the metaphor systems by which we express them, when we adjust our thinking about weather and its causes to be more in line with scientific thought? The first stage of such an adjustment, what we might call the "prechaos" stage, would involve the realization that weather phenomena are not doled out at will by a God who uses them to reward good behavior and punish disloyalty. Such views are seen as ancient, obsolete, and, frankly, somewhat pathetic. Yes, the modern scientific person argues, it is tragic when communities are ravaged by flood or storm or drought. But it's not mysterious. It's a simple (or not-so-simple, but at least understandable and predictable) matter of physics: convection, fluid flow, evaporation, and so on. The people of India are not deliberately "chosen" for affliction by killing drought, nor are those of Florida "targeted" to be the victims of Hurricane Andrew. These phenomena are part of a complex atmospheric system that we will eventually understand and ultimately be able to control. These are natural phenomena.

Rabbi Harold Kushner in his best-selling book *When Bad Things Happen to Good People* comments eloquently on the relationship between such phenomena and God:

> Laws of nature treat everyone alike. They do not make exceptions for nice people.... God does not reach down to interrupt the workings of laws of nature to pro-

tect the righteous from harm. ... God does not cause it
and cannot stop it....

I don't believe that an earthquake that kills thousands of innocent victims without reason is an act of
God. It is an act of nature.[12]

Prechaos scientific understandings often leave religious
individuals feeling a bit foolish. Traditional faith teaches one
model, while science presents another. The religious person feels
he or she is unable to maintain his adherence to his faith and
"believe in" science as well. By divorcing God from natural
phenomena, Kushner hopes to preserve the possibility of faith,
even in the face of natural catastrophes. The alternative to
removing God from the system is to trivialize God by portray-
ing God as a set of natural laws that can eventually be understood, computer-modeled, and predicted.

For either the naturalist approach or the approach advocated by Kushner, the proper behavioral response to concern
about the weather is neither prayer nor repentance, but rather,
preparation of irrigation systems, purchase of flood insurance,
the building of "hurricane-proof" houses, and so on. The
prechaos developments in scientific understanding create in us
a growing sense of human control. Technology, it seems, is
unlimited, at least in theory, in its (eventual) ability to understand and predict natural phenomena. And although there is little serious talk about such things, I would suggest that the leap
from the confidence in human ability to understand and predict
to the human ability to control natural phenomena is a small
one indeed. As I have observed elsewhere, we tend to harbor an
unspoken expectation that it is only a matter of time, research
funding, and continued ingenuity before we gain control over
the weather. And if I am exaggerating the substance of these
secret expectations, then certainly the spirit is there. So at the
same time that the prechaos modern understanding of weather

trivializes or negates the role of God, it elevates and glorifies the power of humankind.

In the specific context of Jewish religious culture, these developments seriously undermine our ability to find meaning in traditional language. For example, every single day of the year, Jewish tradition prescribes the recitation of a series of blessings known as the *Tefillah* (literally, "the prayer").[13] The second of these blessings focuses on God's power to resurrect the dead—a cornerstone of belief for the early Rabbis of the talmudic era. The blessing opens as follows:

> You are forever mighty, Eternal God, You are the Resurrector of the dead, causing great salvation. You sustain the living with kindness, and resurrect the dead in great mercy.

But from early winter until the beginning of Passover in the spring, we add after the words "causing great salvation" the phrase "causing the wind to blow and the rain to fall."[14] The traditional understanding of this blessing is that it acknowledges God's absolute power over life and death, as evidenced most dramatically by the unique divine power to resurrect the dead. The phrase appears to use God's power over wind and rain as an illustration of the general power over life and death, since proper rainfall or its absence, in an agricultural society, can spell the difference between life and death for the community. The illustration, however, can seem archaic, naïve, or just plain silly to a modern Jew who has learned even as much meteorology as one can pick up by watching the weather channel. And when the illustration no longer makes sense, the more general power that it was intended to illustrate can easily lose its meaning as well. Thus we see again, as we have seen in other cases, how foolish traditional practice and language can seem to the modern, well-educated Jew.

THE EFFECTS OF BUTTERFLIES ON JEWS

But what happens when we factor into our understanding some of the elements of chaos theory? The weather is clearly a dynamic system that exhibits sensitive dependence on initial conditions. Indeed, we might think of the weather as the paradigm for all dynamic systems that exhibit the butterfly effect; Edward Lorenz was, after all, creating computer models of weather patterns when he first identified the phenomenon. There is no randomness in the weather system. We are not dealing with chance events. Every single part of the system is absolutely determined by the previous history of the system and a relatively small number of physical principles. But because of the butterfly effect, we know that it is theoretically (not just practically) impossible for us to measure the prior state of the system with 100 percent accuracy, since no real-world measurement of any of the relevant variables can be 100 percent accurate. Furthermore, it is impossible to measure all parts of the system with *any* degree of accuracy, since to do so would require placing measuring devices over the entire surface of the earth and at every single altitude up to the farthest reaches of the atmosphere—there would be no more room for us. And thus we know that the weather forecast will become grossly inaccurate after a remarkably short period of time, perhaps as little as a few days or a week. Once we understand deeply that these limitations will not be overcome with time, effort, and ingenuity we are struck by two realizations: (1) The system, despite the fact that it is controlled by a relatively small number of fairly simple physical laws, is fundamentally beyond our abilities of understanding and mastery; (2) arbitrarily tiny acts and events that seem completely insignificant to us may well have a significance far out of proportion to their size and apparent importance, as the system develops.

The first of these realizations has the effect minimally of stripping away all hubris from our human sense of power and control. The system is not so large—after all, we can get outside it, circle it, and observe it from a distance in a space shuttle. It is governed by rules that are completely comprehensible to us. Yet we are still barred from understanding and predicting its future state! We may have some sense of the general contours of its development, but we absolutely cannot say with any certainty what will happen at a given future time.

This seems to me a highly useful metaphor for speaking about some aspects of God's interaction with the world and with us. According to traditional religious language and thought, God is "supposed to" behave in certain fairly predictable ways. For example, God is supposed to reward good behavior and punish bad behavior. This seems to be a straightforward and simple principle. Now let us suppose for a moment that these traditional assumptions about how God is "supposed to" respond are true. How are we to explain the apparent rewards of the wicked and sufferings by the saintly? This is the problem of *theodicy* that has plagued religious thinkers for many centuries. The Rabbis of the talmudic period, building on ideas conceived probably in the Greco-Roman world, posited the existence of a "world to come" (*olam haba* in Hebrew), a realm of life after death in which righteous and wicked would get their just rewards. The problem for many people is that the very existence of *olam haba* must be taken on faith—it cannot be proven. Thus many skeptics find the entire answer of just rewards coming not in this life but in the next just a bit too convenient.

Chaos theory, as a metaphor, gives us a different approach. The rules of the system all work, just as advertised. Hot air always rises, and God always rewards good behavior. But knowing the rules does *not* enable us to predict the outcomes on any but the shortest or narrowest of scales, because we cannot possibly know with precise accuracy the current state of the system. If the proverbial butterfly's flapping of wings in Asia can affect the weather in North America, is it not possible that the righteous person's thoughtlessly dismissive remark to a stranger on a bus years ago, or the murderer's kind smile to a child in a rare moment of good cheer in childhood, might have a grossly disproportionate and completely unanticipated effect on the future outcome of the world? In both cases—that of the weather and that of human behavior and interaction—the system is simply too vast and too complicated for us to be able to predict future outcomes with any certainty. Even after the fact, historians cannot agree on what caused the war or the economic recession, nor can meteorologists agree on why last weekend's predicted snowstorm never materialized.

Our inability to understand fully what has happened and to predict what will happen leads us in two directions. The first involves how we respond when human beings, especially innocent ones, are stricken, either by great natural tragedy or by great human evil. Because our overall sense of right and wrong leads us to believe that good people should be rewarded, we complain about the system when we see good folks suffer. We claim that the system does not work or that God is unjust. Such responses reflect confusion and frustration that the system, on a gross level, seems to have behaved in a random manner. The truth, however, is that human behavior and interaction may be as complex and dynamic as the weather and that conclusions about the injustice of the universe may make as little sense as proclaiming that the laws of physics—convection, condensation, thermodynamics—do not work, since this morning's forecast promised a sunny day but I got soaked in the rain. It is reasonable to conclude that there was something wrong with the forecast, and perhaps with the measurements and models on which it was based, *not* with the basic rules that govern the weather. But when it comes to evil and tragedy striking human beings, we assume that the rules governing the system were wrong! If we take the metaphor of the butterfly effect to heart, we may be more circumspect about, even if no less saddened by, the tragedies that periodically infect human life. Of course, this conclusion is based on a somewhat tenuous analogy. Weather phenomena are clearly and demonstrably regulated by well-understood and thoroughly reliable physical laws. The fate of human beings and its relationship to their behavior, on the other hand, are fairly mysterious, and even when the rules of human behavior are quite clear they are not like the laws of physics. All physicists, in all cultures and places, agree that a gas heated under a given set of conditions will behave in a particular way. On the other hand, people in diverse cultures, societies, religions, and eras do not agree universally about the rules that ought to govern human behavior. This flaw in the analogy, however, does not necessarily undermine its central conclusion, namely, that phenomena as complex as human behavior can certainly be affected in profound and unanticipated ways by extremely small factors. Such effects need not be seen as random but may, instead, be seen as the disproportionate impact of tiny variables that we have described in the phenomenon of "sensitive dependence on initial conditions," or the butterfly effect.

The second realization that comes from an understanding of the butterfly effect, namely, that tiny behaviors and events can have huge consequences down the line, may serve to caution us against judging our own behavior, or that of others, based solely on its "macro" features. A small kindness to a person who seems completely insignificant may have effects far in excess of its apparent importance, as may a small and seemingly insignificant cruelty. The butterfly effect may teach us that every act, every word, every interaction must be undertaken with the awareness that it could be the butterfly's wings. This insight is especially important in the realm of *tikkun olam*, or fixing the world. When we engage in activities designed to improve the human condition, relieve suffering, or solve problems, we are often overwhelmed by the vastness of the need and the tiny impact of our actions. We hear of thousands killed or left homeless by a massive earthquake in Turkey, and in response we contribute to relief organizations. It is the right thing to do. But the vast scale of the devastation makes us wonder if our check for $50 or $100 is really worth anything at all. When confronted with such frustrating situations, I often think back to a line I remember reading in high school in Upton Sinclair's *The Jungle* where a character was told that she was "standing upon the brink of the pit of hell, and throwing in snowballs to lower the temperature."[15] How futile it seems! But the butterfly effect reminds us that every once in a while, one particular snowball has an effect that eventually cools down the whole place. The fact that it is impossible to know which, if any, of the snowballs will have an effect simply leads us to regard each positive act, no matter how apparently insignificant, as if it might change the world. Conversely, each act of insensitivity, degradation, or disrespect, no matter how trivial, could be the butterfly that causes the next killer tornado in Kansas. In other words, we are cautioned against the idea that the effect of small actions is always insignificant when viewed in the big picture.

It is important to remember, though, that this system of metaphor, in sensitizing us to the potential impact of small deeds, does *not* permit us to ignore the big events or actions of life and concentrate only on the details. After all, a butterfly in Asia *may* have an effect on the weather in Florida next month, but a hurricane in the Caribbean will *definitely* affect it! Similarly, although a small passing kindness toward a despondent person may have unanticipated positive effects at a later time, proactive efforts to help the person cope with the problems he or she is facing will certainly have an impact.

These are clearly not new or revolutionary ideas. They are not meant to be. They can, however, provide a road back into a traditional language that, for many modern Jews, has become foreign and incomprehensible. By using the metaphor of the butterfly effect, we may be able to recognize, reclaim, and find meaning in some of the old language. Describing God as the one who "causes the wind to blow and the rain to fall" now seems quite a bit less silly if by using this image we suggest that God is, like the weather, vast without being mysterious, understandable without being predictable, and highly aware of and sensitive to the smallest actions, the most insignificant words, deeds, and people.

With regard to the importance of human action, the principle of the butterfly effect suggests a new understanding for an often-quoted piece of ancient Jewish text. In the description in the Mishnah's tractate *Sanhedrin* of how testimony was to be taken from witnesses in capital cases, we read the following:

> Humankind was originally created as a single individual [i.e., Adam], to teach that whoever destroys a single human life, Scripture accounts it to him as if he had destroyed an entire world, and whoever saves a single human life, Scripture accounts it to him as if he had saved an entire world. (*Mishnah Sanhedrin* 4:5)[16]

This wonderful text, which has often served as an inspiration for those who toil to improve the world, is usually understood to mean that the value of human life is so great that, in a sense, any single human being's life is already seen as having infinite value. Since infinity cannot be "enlarged" by adding another infinity, or two more infinities, or a billion more, the destruction or preservation of even one life is posited as having value equal to the destruction or saving of all lives. The tremendous dignity and value conferred upon human beings by this view is unquestionably moving. Yet some might claim that the emphasis thus placed on the value of any one life might blunt our sensitivity to the need to protect, defend, and upgrade many lives, in fact, all lives. In response to this critique, the metaphor of the butterfly effect can add another dimension to the text. The Mishnah may be understood as saying that the destruction (or preservation) of even one human life—a small thing on a planet with over six billion human inhabitants!—might in some unpredictable, but completely deterministic, way lead to the destruction (or preservation) of many lives, or all lives. Once again, remember that this metaphor is in no way intended to de-emphasize the importance or value of protecting large groups of people or whole societies. I am not suggesting that one be counted as having discharged his or her obligation by saving one life, if many lives remain imperiled. My purpose, rather, is to sensitize us to the possible impact of our actions toward a single individual.

SACRED NUMBERS, SACRED WORDS, AND THE GAP BETWEEN REALITY AND PERFECTION

In colloquial usage, the word *chaos* can also mean "irregularity," that is, the opposite of smoothness or regularity. As applied to the world of physical shapes, these ideas of chaos and regularity raise an interesting issue. In high school, we all learned geometry, that branch of mathematics that deals with the physical shape of the world. But the geometry that we learned did *not* really address the shape of the world. Rather, it addressed a world of idealized, perfect shapes: circles, squares, parallelograms, and so on. This perfect, idealized world came with perfect, idealized rules. So, for example, the interior angles of a triangle add up to 180 degrees, the circumference of a circle is pi times its diameter, and so on. Perhaps one of the most memorable of the rules is the Pythagorean theorem that states that in any triangle in which one of the three angles is a right

(90-degree) angle, the squared length of the side opposite that right angle (the hypotenuse) equals the sum of the squared lengths of the other two sides. This famous rule is named for the ancient Greek mathematician and religious leader Pythagoras (ca. 560–500 B.C.E.). At the core of Pythagoras's teaching was an absolute reverence for the purity and perfection of numbers (which he considered divine) and numerical relationships. According to Margaret Wertheim's analysis of Pythagoras's impact on later mathematical thinking, he worshipped numbers because

> to him they seemed timeless, immutable, and incorruptible. In this numbers stood in sharp contrast to the all-too-obvious fact that everything in the material, or natural, world is subject to corruption, decay, and death. Four flowers might wither, four melons might rot, four men might die, four streams might dry up, four mountains might crumble, but the number 4 itself seemed eternal and indestructible—like the gods. Pythagoras equated divinity with timeless stasis and immutability, qualities which cannot be found anywhere in nature. Indeed the whole point of the number-gods was that they were beyond nature, with its inherent transience and mortality.[17]

It is not clear exactly what the relationship was between the Pythagoreans and the Jews, but it is certainly reasonable to assume that Jews of the time were familiar with, and perhaps even influenced by, some of these mathematical-religious notions. When the Persians invaded Egypt in 525 B.C.E., Pythagoras, who had been living and studying there, was taken captive to Babylon. It was in Babylon that he continued his mathematical studies. Wertheim comments that

[t]he Babylonians were … great astronomers and mathematicians. Lindberg notes their mathematics was "an
order of magnitude superior to that of the Egyptians."
From them Pythagoras may well have learned the theorem for which he is still famous today.… Although we
are taught in school that this is the Pythagorean
Theorem, historians of mathematics believe it was
almost certainly known to the Babylonians before
him.[18]

Students of Jewish history will immediately realize that
this mathematically enriched environment, sixth-century
Babylonian society, was precisely where the intellectual elite of
the Jewish people were living, having been deported from Judea
after the destruction of the First Temple by the Babylonians in
586 B.C.E. So although there is no historical evidence for a
direct and explicit connection between Pythagoras himself or
his followers and the leading Jewish (or more correctly, Judean)
thinkers of the day, there is no doubt that they functioned in
the same environment. The likelihood of cultural/intellectual
cross-pollination is quite high, given what we know of how
quickly the Judean captives grew to feel comfortable in their
Babylonian surroundings. Despite their initial grief at the
Temple's destruction and their own displacement, fewer than
half of the deportees (or their descendants) chose to return
home to Judea, when, less than a century after the initial depor-
tation, the Persian conquerors of Babylon allowed them the
opportunity to do so.

This cultural influence is certainly apparent in the later
appearance in rabbinic literature of *gematria* (from the same
Greek word that gives us the English *geometry*), the system of
finding meaning in words of Torah based on their numerical
value as derived from the numerical value of each of the letters
in the Hebrew alphabet. The Rabbis of the talmudic era really

believed that the hidden meaning of the words could sometimes be discovered by understanding and manipulating their numerical value. They also really believed that the words were God's own words, and therefore that *gematria* was one of the ways human beings could discover what God intended. This being the case, we could easily take the statement quoted above, in which Wertheim describes Pythagoras's view of numbers and the "number-gods" and apply it directly to the rabbinic view of words in the Torah: "eternal and indestructible ... timeless stasis and immutability, qualities which cannot be found anywhere in nature ... beyond nature, with its inherent transience and mortality." These descriptive terms are completely consistent with rabbinic teachings that the first Torah, God's Torah, was written before the creation of the world, that it was written in letters of black fire on a background of white fire, and that God used it as a blueprint for the creation of the world. The words are eternal, indestructible. These qualities are described vividly in the famous story, read on Yom Kippur as part of the synagogue service, of the martyrdom of Rabbi Hananiah ben Teradyon by the Romans. According to the Talmud, the renowned sage was wrapped in a Torah scroll and burned alive. As the flames consumed him, his students asked him, "What do you see?" He answered, "The parchment is burning, but the letters are flying away" (*Avodah Zarah* 18a). Unlike the material, natural world, the words of God are eternal, perfect, indestructible. In this respect, they are just like Pythagoras's numbers.

In both these systems, that is, the system of God and God's words and the system of perfect numbers and numerical relationships, there is a certain disconnect between the realm of things immaterial, pure, and eternal and the realm in which we live. On a religious level, this disconnect is expressed as *transcendence*, the idea that God is absolutely and completely apart from the world and that we cannot bridge the gap that separates God from us. This complex topic has been addressed by countless theologians and philosophers. For now, I only want to address one element of the issue, namely, the degree to which God's transcendence is an important cause of classic religious frustration, by which I mean the sense that one wishes to be close to God, the creative power and life force of the universe, but cannot cross the barrier. In a sense, a great deal of religious life is devoted to finding ways to cross the chasm that separates us from God. So, for example, the practitioners of classical Kabbalah (Jewish mysticism) in thirteenth-century Spain identified God's essence as *En Sof,* meaning "endless" or "boundless." This core of God's self was seen as absolutely and completely mysterious and inaccessible to humankind or, for that matter, to the created world in any way. To cope with this unbridgeable gap, the kabbalists developed a system of ten *sefirot,* or emanations—manifestations of God's essence in forms less hidden from the real world. We will examine this system in some detail in chapter 4.

On a mathematical level, the disconnect between mathematical theory and the reality of life in the world (which is the mathematical equivalent of the idea of transcendence) may be expressed in the realization that, in the words of mathematician Benoit Mandelbrot, "Clouds are not spheres, mountains are not cones, coastlines are not circles, and bark is not smooth, nor does lightning travel in a straight line."[19] In other words, while the "world" of traditional mathematics in general and geometry in particular is populated by perfect, regular shapes, the real world in which we live has few, if any, of these idealized shapes. Instead, life is filled with irregular shapes, shapes with wiggles and bumps and "imperfections" in them, shapes that are, in comparison to the smooth and regular shapes of our high school geometry textbooks, chaotic. For Euclid and his followers, this disconnect was simply an eloquent proof of the fact that the "real" world was an imperfect approximation, a flawed image of the "ideal world." For me, however, this classical geometric notion is as unsatisfying as the Kabbalah would have been without the *sefirot*. If geometry is not about the real world, but only about an idealized version of that real world, then the same frustration felt by religious folk at their inability to access God is felt by all of us at the lack of correspondence between the perfect, regular order of geometrical shapes and the irregular shape of the real world in which we live.

IDEAL AND REAL GEOMETRY: FRACTALS

The gap between geometric idealism and the shape of reality can be bridged through the concept of *fractals*. In 1975, Benoit Mandelbrot, a European-born mathematician at IBM, coined the term *fractal* to describe a particular kind of real-world shape. The simplest definition I have found for *fractal* (curiously, a fractal is easier to understand by observing it than by reading a verbal definition) is offered by mathematician John Casti.

> Fractals are curves that are irregular all over. Moreover, they have exactly the same degree of irregularity at all scales of measurement. So it doesn't matter whether you look at a fractal from far away or up close with a microscope—in either case you'll see exactly the same picture.[20]

In other words, a fractal is an object that is not smooth or regular, but in which the pattern of irregularity remains the same regardless of how small or large a piece of the fractal you examine. Literally, if you hold a large fractal object in your hand and break off a tiny piece and look at it under magnification, it will be exactly like the original object. You can keep breaking off smaller and smaller pieces until there is nothing visible left, and each piece will still be exactly like the original.

This characteristic, called *self-similarity,* and is one of the most important features of fractals and is the outcome of *recursion,* a relatively simple mathematical operation that is performed, and then performed again on the result, and then again, and so on. A very simple example of recursion is the Sierpinski carpet. It is constructed as follows: Start with a black square. Divide it into ninths like a tic-tac-toe board. Remove the center square. Then take each of the remaining eight squares and perform the same operation, that is, divide each into ninths and remove its center. Keep going forever, as illustrated in figure 3.1.

A second example of this process is hardly necessary, but I want to present it simply because of the Jewish iconic echoes of

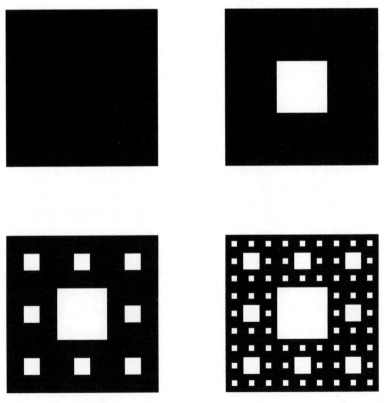

Figure 3.1: The Sierpinski carpet, created by the endless repetition of a simple process.

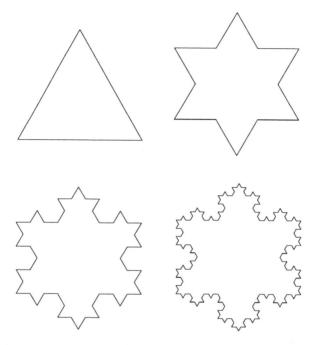

Figure 3.2: The Koch snowflake, like the Sierpinski carpet, reflects the continued repetition of a simple process.

the second step in the process of its creation. Called the Koch snowflake, or Koch curve, it is produced by starting with a triangle with sides of equal length. The middle third of each side is then used as the base for another triangle, thereby producing a Magen David, or Star of David. The process of building another triangle on the middle third of each exposed side of each triangle is repeated, as illustrated in figure 3.2.

The Sierpinski carpet, the Koch snowflake, and other fractals created by mathematicians are idealized shapes. They don't "look like" any objects in the real world, though they do share mathematical features with real-world objects. And since Mandelbrot himself lamented that although the word *geometry* was etymologically rooted in "measurements of the world" but, in reality, had little to do with things in the real world (hence his comment, cited above, that "clouds are not spheres"), it seems crucial that we examine not only idealized fractals created in the heads of mathematicians but real-world fractals. Mandelbrot and other writers include the following among the many examples of fractal structures or objects in nature:

lightning

the branching of river systems (tiny streams feeding larger streams feeding rivers)

the branching structure of the bronchi in the lungs

trees (trunk to limbs to branches to ever smaller twigs)

the contours of clouds

the coastlines of islands and continents

the distribution of stars, star systems, and galaxies in space

the distribution of noise in an electronic signal

the distribution of (raw) diamonds throughout the earth

the surfaces of proteins, like hemoglobin

the surface of the polio virus

All these phenomena, and many others, exhibit the remarkable fractal characteristic of self-similarity. This is truly a fantastic list! It spans a wide range of natural phenomena on many scales and suggests that there is something essentially "fractal" about the shape of the universe in a literal, as well as a metaphorical, sense.

Another intriguing feature of some classes of fractals is that their circumference is virtually infinite, even though they can be circumscribed in a finite space. To understand this apparently paradoxical claim, consider the strange question asked by Mandelbrot in one of his early papers: How long is the coastline of Britain?[21] At first glance the question is simple. One should be able to find its answer in any good atlas. But on further reflection, it turns out that the answer is critically dependent on the *scale* of the unit of measure! That is, if one were to build a huge set of dividers spanning one kilometer and "walk them" all around the coast, the result would be one number. But if one then measured again, closing the dividers to, say, one-half kilometer, the answer would be different, and clearly greater, since coastline features—bays, inlets, outcroppings, and other irregularities—between one-half kilometer and one kilometer in size would not have registered in the first measuring, but would show up in the second. Decrease the span of the dividers even more and measure again, and again and again and again. Each time the result will be larger! Eventually, you would close the dividers down to a fraction of a millimeter, or less, and the result would still continue to grow as the now tiny dividers had to be walked around every tiny pebble, every grain of sand. So we see that the measurement of the coastline, a wonderful example of a fractal, has no practical limit! Yet we all know that Britain is not infinitely large. Thus we have the strange realization that, for some types of fractals, the boundary of a shape is infinite, or nearly so, while the whole shape can occupy a finite area!

THE FRACTAL SHAPE OF GOD

Given these few remarkable features of fractals, I now want to propose a radical idea: As we develop a new vocabulary of religious metaphors, might it be useful to think of God's shape as fractal? Of course, many centuries of Jewish intellectual conditioning make us recoil at applying such concrete, physical terms to God, but I suggest we resist the impulse to draw back in shock. In fact, as was noted earlier, it is only since the Middle Ages that Jews, originally under the guidance of Moses

Maimonides and other, similar rational philosophers, have embraced with devotion the idea that God is incorporeal, non-physical, invisible.[22] In earlier eras, however, Jewish literature is replete with physical-sounding language about God—God's eye, God's arm, God's finger, God's mouth, and so on. In fact, Maimonides spends a great deal of time in his main philosophical work, *Moreh Nevukhim (The Guide for the Perplexed)*, carefully explaining why each of these expressions, as they appear in the Bible, is not to be taken literally. They are metaphors, figures of speech, which must not mislead us into the serious error of thinking that there might be a physical or corporeal aspect to God.

I am certainly comfortable with this approach. I have discussed such figures of speech at great length as the metaphors by which we get our mental hands around an idea that, without concrete metaphors, is just too vast to contemplate. The theme of this book from the outset has been the need to develop a new set of metaphors to augment and, in some cases, to replace old metaphors that have lost their usefulness. This being the case, let us consider carefully the metaphor of the shape of God being fractal.

The metaphor appeals to me for several reasons. First, the fractal notions of scaling and self-similarity seem thoroughly appropriate for thinking about God. The structure of a fractal looks pretty much the same regardless of how much or how little of it you examine, how close you are or how far away. We see structural similarities in natural phenomena spanning a vast range: from galactic clusters, to the mighty trees growing in a forest, to the bronchial structure of the mice scurrying beneath those trees. When I pay attention to such structural similarities, they fill me with wonder. If we assume that there are basic structural similarities between the universe and the creative process(es) that designed it, then it makes sense to think of the fractal nature of the universe, visible at scales from the submicroscopic to the supergalactic, as reflective of the "shape" of God. What does that mean? Simply that when I contemplate the structure of a tree, the series of branchings-off that lead from the trunk to the tiniest twigs, what I am contemplating is in some sense reflective of God. And the fact that the structure is self-similar means that I can contemplate the "whole picture" of God, the entire divine structure and nature, as it were, in a single flash of lightning or the veins on a single leaf. According to one traditional explanation of the statement in Genesis that God made humans in God's own image, when I interact with a human being, I can "see through" that individual to the God in whose image he or she is created. As that understanding changes my relationship to other people, leading me to value their uniqueness and their inherent and infinite worth, so regarding any of the many fractal-shaped phenomena of nature as geometric images of God can change not only my ability to sense God's presence, but my view of the world in which I live. This thought process may be extended, in traditional Jewish terms, from the realm of nature to that of Torah. It is a widespread belief that the Torah is holy, and that its holiness can be seen no matter how much or how little of the book you look at. The holiness is equally palpable in the whole book, in a single story or section of laws, in a single verse, in a single word, or even in a single letter. The premodern proponents of this view did not know of the language of fractals, but that is what they were describing, nevertheless.

The concept of an infinitely long yet completely circumscribed coastline provides the second reason I am attracted to the notion of a fractal-shaped God. It is quite common to speak about God with the language of infinity. We teach Sunday school students that God is infinitely everything—infinitely wise, powerful, enduring—but then are unable to answer their simple questions about what any of these assertions could possibly mean. And similarly, although on a far deeper level of sophistication, the classical kabbalists spoke of God's essential self as *En Sof,* literally "without end," that is, infinite, but stipulated right away that there was nothing that could be known about this essential, infinite divine nature. Only the *sefirot,* the emanations of God, could be known. After all, how could anyone, especially any finite being, ever claim to understand infinity? I believe that the metaphor of the coastline gives us a way to understand, or at least to think about, divine infinity. What does it mean to claim that the coastline of Britain is infinitely long? A pilot in a helicopter could fly along the entire coast in a finite amount of time. Indeed, a well-equipped and persistent walker could walk it in a finite number of weeks. In fact, Mandelbrot's claim does not deny these obvious indications of finitude. He simply observes that the finer the lens—that is, the smaller the unit of measurement—that one uses to examine the coast, the longer it becomes. In a similar sense, if we look at the universe on an astronomical scale we are awed and humbled by the "wisdom"—that is, the beauty, the vastness, and the structure—of the cosmos. We are moved to say, as does the psalm quoted in each morning's service, "How great are your works, O God, you made them all with wisdom!" (Ps. 104:24). The universe seems to reflect an awesome power. But this power, and the "wisdom" whose existence we infer from it, are no less apparent if we look at smaller and smaller scales of reality. The awe inspired by a starry night is no different from that inspired by a stormy sea, or a single whale leaping from the waves, or, for that matter, by a sleeping child or the tightly fisted hand of a newborn infant. Indeed, the structure of a DNA strand and that of a galaxy both seem to indicate the presence of a sophisticated, structuring force, an agency of order in the universe. So just as the coastline of Britain "grows" infinitely large as we measure it in smaller and smaller increments, I am awed by the way the "measurements" of God grow without limit as we examine them on ever-smaller scales.

It is curious that the early thinkers and writers on chaos theory were drawn to the strange conclusion that the more one studied seemingly chaotic, or irregular, or unpredictable phenomena, the more order one sensed in them. It seems ironic that in the discussion of chaos we sense, through notions of scaling and self-similarity, God as the force that imposes the same order on the universe regardless of the scale on which we examine it.

TURBULENCE AND PHASE TRANSITIONS

In many respects, fluids seem to be far more important to the life of the universe than solids. Fluids are dynamic—they move and flow and change—while solids, more or less, just sit there. On a poetic level, fluids seem alive—if life be marked by movement and change—while solids seem far less so. The Hebrew phrase *mayim chayyim*, "living water," that is, natural water (from a spring or stream or river as opposed to water drawn from a well), which first occurs in the Bible and is used throughout later stages of Jewish literature, seems to capture this notion. It is not surprising that scientists often muse about the close relationship between the amount of life on our planet and the amount of liquid water, which would not exist if we were just a bit farther from the sun—in which case it would all freeze—or just a bit closer—in which case it would boil off and drift away into space. The movement of water around the earth, whether in rivers and oceans or in the atmosphere as rain and snow, is absolutely critical for the maintenance of life. Similarly, the flow of blood in an organism is critical for life. Both the planetary and the bodily circulatory systems *are* the life force.

But this fluidic life force can flow in either of two ways. It can flow smoothly, or it can become turbulent. Turbulence is a form of chaos. Like other forms of chaos it is nonregular and unpredictable, but also deterministic: Its behavior is governed absolutely by a set of physical laws. It exhibits sensitive dependence on initial conditions (the butterfly effect) in that two particles in adjacent regions of the fluid at one point are likely to take paths that will diverge wildly and carry them very far apart in a very short time. According to the latest understanding of turbulent phenomena, turbulence can be generated by a very simple set of dynamic forces; it is not the result of highly (or infinitely) complex causes. Its structure is also somewhat fractal, in that the large whorls and eddies in a turbulent flow contain within them smaller whorls and eddies so that the overall structure is self-similar. In these respects, turbulence is quite similar to other chaotic phenomena.

What is noteworthy in regard to turbulence, however, is the great mystery surrounding its onset. Other examples of chaos in nature seem to be chaotic by their very nature. The weather, for example, is *always* chaotic, even though some weather patterns may seem a bit more or a bit less so for a short time. (The extent to which we *expect* meteorological phenomena to be chaotic is reflected in the expressions of surprise on television and radio forecasts after seven or eight days of calm, sunny, moderate weather!) The branching structure of trees or river systems or the irregular shape of clouds or coastlines are by their very nature fractal. As we have seen, such shapes demonstrate their "bumpiness" on every scale. We would be shocked if we were to see a perfectly smooth or absolutely straight section of coastline or cloud. We cannot imagine these phenomena ever existing in a nonchaotic state. But fluid flow is different. We *can* imagine smooth, regular fluid flow—such flow is called *laminar flow*—and we have seen it. A smoothly flowing river or the water coming out of a tap can be calm and regular. But such flows can very easily become chaotic or turbulent. Some transitions from laminar to turbulent fluid flow are relatively easy to understand on an intuitive if not a mathematical level. A slow-moving river, flowing smoothly, can become turbulent as it flows around a fallen tree or some other object that disrupts its path. But in other cases, the onset of turbulence seems more mysterious. In a poetically simple passage, Ian Stewart describes how fluid flow goes by stages from smooth to turbulent as a tap is slowly and gradually opened. As the rate of flow is slowly increased, steady, rhythmically dripping drops suddenly lose their even rhythm and become irregular. As the rate of flow continues to increase, the dripping gives way to a smooth laminar flow, but as the increase continues still further the laminar flow breaks up, develops eddies, and splits into multiple flows.[23] This familiar phenomenon is a wonderful demonstration of how turbulence starts. Nothing has apparently obstructed the flow of the water. *All* that has changed is the amount of water flowing through the tap, and even that has not been changed in a sudden manner, but rather slowly and steadily. So what accounts for the turbulence? It seems that the mere addition of energy to the system, even if that increase is slow and steady, eventually pushes the system through what are called *phase transitions* where the nature of the system changes rather suddenly. Common examples of phase transitions are what happens when water, being heated steadily, reaches the boiling point and becomes a gas, or, conversely, when its temperature is slowly and steadily reduced until it freezes and becomes crystalline ice. Such phase transitions, and many less dramatic ones, are prime candidates for points in a system where turbulence will develop.

The idea of phase transitions and their propensity for exhibiting turbulence suggests an old and extremely well-known metaphor in human life in general and in Jewish life in particular. We have always been highly sensitive to and concerned about the "phase transitions" that we experience in life. Two rather ordinary examples are sunrise and sunset. These completely normal phenomena, which result from a steady, gradual, uninterrupted turning of the planet, result in rather dramatic changes in the nature of the environment in which we live. The transition from daylight to the darkness of night and back again radically changes our experience of life. During the day, we can see what is around us. The world is familiar and fairly easy to control. Evening arrives, and the world becomes mysterious and shadowy. We cannot see very well, and our ability to distinguish and identify colors is impaired. We are put at a tremendous disadvantage relative to creatures, especially potentially dangerous ones, who see well at night. The normal human condition entails a degree of nervous discomfort in the dark. Then morning comes, the darkness evaporates, and once again we feel safe. Evolution has added to the depth of the experience of these daily phase transitions by providing us with a "body clock," an internal rhythm that adjusts our moods and makes us feel alert or drowsy based on the amount of light around us. Even we moderns, whose mastery of our environment is tremendous, are stymied on night-shift jobs or transoceanic flights by our inability to defeat the power of our internal clocks.

Given the importance of the differences between our experiences of day and night, it is no great surprise that the phase transitions, the periods when day becomes night and when night then becomes day, are times when metaphorical "turbulence" is common in human life. Thus we find that dusk and dawn are times well suited for anxiety, wonder, concern, and the need for some stabilizing force. Jewish tradition, together with many other religious traditions, responds to this need by prescribing prayer. The morning service (*shacharit*) and the evening service (*ma'ariv* or *arvit*) may be recited, respectively, well into the morning and the night. But the tradition prefers that they be recited at or near the cusp, during the phase transition. Each service consists of two basic elements: the recitation of *Shema Yisrael* in which we remind ourselves of God's oneness, and the *Tefillah* or *Amidah*, in which we address prayers, including petitions, directly to God. Both these elements seem precisely tuned to respond to phase-transition anxiety. In a time when we are experiencing the shift from one mode of being to another, rather different mode of being (being human by night and being human by day), the assertion of God's unity can be tremendously comforting. And in the transition from light to dark or dark to light, the opportunity to address our needs to God can alleviate some of the anxiety of the moment. In addition, if we invoke the earlier use of the metaphor of the fractal as the shape of God, a fractal-shaped God is perhaps most appropriately addressed in a phase-transition time (since, apparently, many phase-transition phenomena exhibit fractal characteristics—eddies within eddies within eddies, which create structures of scaling and self-similarity).

Aside from being fraught with anxiety, these phase-transition periods between light and darkness also end up being important creative times in the Jewish imagination. There is a fascinating textual tradition found, among other places, in *Pirkei Avot*, that tells of ten crucial things being created by God just at twilight at the end of the sixth and final day of creation. The text is as follows:

> Ten things were created on Sabbath eve at twilight. They are: (1) the mouth of the earth, (2) the mouth of the well, (3) the mouth of the she-ass, (4) the rainbow, (5) the manna, (6) the staff, (7) the *shamir*, (8) the writing, (9) the writing implement, (10) and the tablets. Some say also: the evil spirits, the grave of Moses and the ram of Abraham our ancestor. Others say: the tongs made with tongs. (*Pirkei Avot* 5:9)[24]

Some of the items on this remarkable list are less readily identifiable than others, so a brief description of all is in order.

The "mouth of the earth" refers to a rebellion against the authority of Moses and Aaron by 250 rebels under the leadership of a Levite named Korach. The uprising was resolved by God when "the earth opened up its mouth and swallowed them" (Num. 16:32).

The "mouth of the well" refers to a legendary well that is said to have followed the Israelites throughout the desert, supplying them water, as long as Moses's sister Miriam was alive.[25]

The "mouth of the she-ass" refers to the story of Balaam, a magician hired by the Moabite king Balak to curse the Israelites. As Balaam traveled to do Balak's bidding, an angel of God, invisible to Balaam but visible to his she-ass, blocked his path. When he struck the animal, she opened her mouth and spoke to him of the blessed nature of the Israelites, whereupon Balaam decided to bless the Israelites instead of cursing them (see Num. 22 and 23).

The "rainbow" is the sign of the covenant placed in the clouds after the flood, as a reminder to God never to destroy the world with a flood again (see Gen. 9:13).

The "manna" was the miraculous food that God provided to the Israelites during their forty years of desert wandering (Ex. 16:15).

The "staff" is the staff carried by Moses, with which he performed wonders, both while in Egypt and during the desert wandering.

The "*shamir*" was a tiny mythical worm that could cut through rock. The Torah (Ex. 20:22) prohibited the use of iron tools for cutting altar stones (and, by extension, for cutting stones used in building the Temple), probably because iron was typically used to fashion weapons and its use on altar stones would defile them. Thus, according to rabbinic legend, the *shamir* was used to cut the stones for the Temple, and when the Temple was destroyed, the worm disappeared.[26]

There is some disagreement among commentaries about the meaning of the next two items on the list. Some say that the "writing" refers to the shape of the letters carved into the two tablets of the law that God gave to Moses and that the "writing implement" refers to the physical process by which the letters were formed. Others (notably Maimonides) see the "writing" as the content of the words on the tablets and the "writing implement" as the physical shapes of the letters. In either case, the underlying focus is a rabbinic tradition regarding the miraculous nature of the writing on the tablets. The Torah tells us that the tablets were written on "both their sides" (Ex. 32:15), which the Rabbis understood to mean that the letters were carved through all the way from one face of the stone to the other, yet miraculously they could be read regardless of which side one looked at. Furthermore, two of the Hebrew letters needed to write the Ten Commandments, namely *samech* ס and final *mem* ם, are completely closed loops. If one were to carve them entirely through a physical tablet, the inside would fall out! Yet, miraculously, according to rabbinic tradition, God wrote these letters such that the insides did not fall out.

The last item on the list is the tablets themselves, which, according to Exodus 32:16, were "the work of God." Finally, the Mishnah adds four other items that some include on the list, without clarifying whether they are meant to replace items already enumerated or to be added, thereby creating a longer list. The additions are: the "evil spirits," a general category of demons; the "grave of Moses," the location of which, according to Deuteronomy 34:10, is "known to no person, to this very day"; the "ram of Abraham," that is, the ram that Abraham sacrificed on Mount Moriah instead of sacrificing his son Isaac; and the "tongs made with tongs." This last item is confusing, since the real meaning is "the tongs made *without* tongs," and in fact, there are some editions of *Pirkei Avot* in English that translate interpretively, "the original tongs, for tongs can [in human experience] be made only by means of tongs."[27] The reference is to a philosophical/logical curiosity relating to the fact that one normally forges a new pair of tongs by holding the metal in the flame with a pair of tongs! So where did the very first pair of tongs come from? The tradition says that they were created in this powerful phase-transition time at sunset just before the first Shabbat. This issue of the tongs is simply a convenient hook on which to hang the larger philosophical question of cause and effect. In a universe in which everything was caused by something prior, where did the first things, which had no prior causal agents, come from?

Every item on this list is somehow miraculous. More specifically, each either comes into existence as the result of a miraculous process (the closed-loop letters on the tablets or the tongs) or was created to provide a miraculous intervention in later history (the mouth of the well, the manna, the *shamir*). Because they all exist somehow outside the normal "rules of the game," it seems appropriate that they are all traced back to a moment of creation at twilight before Shabbat, at the end of the creation week. Note that their moment of creation is a *double* phase transition: It is both a transition from light to darkness and also a transition from weekday to primordial Sabbath. No wonder that such a double phase transition would be thought of as having unusually high potential for creative turbulence. If we imagine the normal course of the universe as being fairly smooth or, in fluid dynamics terms, a "laminar flow," it makes sense to think of miracles, that is, suspensions or violations of the typical course of things, as a manifestation of turbulence.

It is important to point out that these observations are neither new nor original. Many anthropologists of religion have noted the propitiousness of dusk and dawn as prayer times. And on a grander scale, Professor Jacob Neusner has suggested that many of the concerns of the Mishnah (the first compilation of oral-legal traditions compiled in Israel about 200 C.E. and forming the basis of the Talmud) surround transitional areas of life: the eve of Sabbath and holidays, the transition times of marriage and divorce, and many others. The reason I dwell upon these well-worn observations is that I believe we can see them in a new way when we view them through the metaphor lens of turbulence, which occurs at phase transitions throughout the natural world. It renders our tradition's responses to transitions more understandable, less "primitive and superstitious" (and I use these terms deliberately in their harshest and most negative senses). It brings our human, cultural construction of reality into harmony with the fabric of the universe, as understood by science. It does not prove anything, but it may give us another way of understanding our tradition, and the more paths to understanding that can be created, the more people may understand.

CHALLAH DOUGH

Why *do* butterflies affect the weather? That is to say, why are chaotic systems chaotic? Why do they exhibit sensitive dependence on initial conditions? Most specifically, why do two points in such a system, which are arbitrarily close to one another as the system gets going, end up unpredictably far apart in a relatively short time, or unpredictably very close together a short time later? The mechanism responsible for this characteristic behavior of chaos is called *stretching and folding*. The idea is described succinctly by Stephen Kellert:

> The action of a chaotic system will take nearby points and stretch them apart in a certain direction, thus creating the local divergence responsible for unpredictability. But the system also acts to "fold" together points that are at some distance, causing a convergence of trajectories in a different direction.[28]

Figure 3.3: The process of kneading challah dough, stretching and folding.

This may sound somewhat confusing and may be hard to understand on an abstract level. But this is a case where abstraction is not the tool of choice in seeking understanding. Forget about abstract concepts. Imagine that you are kneading a lump of challah dough. To describe kneading dough is far more difficult than to watch it being done, but I shall try. With the dough on a waist-high table in front of you, mash it flat with the heels of your two hands, but allow one hand to slide farther ahead of the other, thus stretching the dough. As you stretch it, you rotate it—and simultaneously fold the now stretched-out dough back over on itself. Repeat this process in a rhythmic way again and again (see figure 3.3). Now imagine two points that are right next to each other in the prekneaded lump of dough, perhaps two raisins, and visualize how they travel throughout the dough relative to one another as you knead it. It's easy to see how the two points quickly become independent of one another, moving unpredictably around the batch of dough, at one moment quite near each other and, at the next, quite far apart.[29] Thus the essence of the unpredictability and the sensitive dependence on initial conditions that are so prominent in chaos theory can be understood practically, if not technically, by kneading challah.

This observation seems extraordinarily important on a symbolic level. Bread plays a key role in traditional Jewish ritual life. It defines a meal. That is to say, an eating event is only a meal if it includes bread. You can eat a multicourse feast, but if there is no bread included, you are not required by traditional Jewish law to recite *Birkat Hamazon*, the blessing after the meal. And whereas every different category of food must have a particular blessing recited over it before it is eaten, if one precedes the entire eating event by reciting *Hamotzi* (the blessing over bread) and eating a piece of bread, that one blessing suffices for all subsequent categories of food. In recognition of the meal-defining nature of bread, the Rabbis of the talmudic period, when they searched for ways to replace the functions of the sacrificial cult after the destruction of the Temple, suggested that every table be considered an altar, every home a Temple, every Jew a *kohen* (that is, a priest, one of the male descendants of Aaron who alone were authorized to officiate in the Temple), and every meal a sacrifice. This "make-believe" Temple cult led to the institution of two traditional practices: ritual hand washing with a blessing (*n'tilat yadayim*) before eating bread and the salting of the first bite of bread. There are numerous explanations for the origins of both these practices. In this context, however, the relevant suggestion for the origin of pre-*Hamotzi* hand washing is that it is an imitation of the ritual hand washing prescribed for the priests before performing the sacrificial rites in the Temple. Likewise regarding the use of salt, there is a requirement in the Torah (Lev. 2:13) that every sacrifice must be salted. Thus it is the bread with which we mark the beginning of the meal that symbolizes the sacrifices offered to God. If we bear in mind that, in the time of the Temple, the sacrifices brought by our ancestors were the primary means by which they communicated with God, we could say that bread was thought of by the Rabbis as one of the symbolic mechanisms by which our post-Temple relationship with God is maintained.

A final observation about bread. People often think that Kiddush (or "making Kiddush") refers to a blessing over wine. This is not quite the case. The Kiddush is a set of two blessings recited on the eve of Shabbat and festivals. The first of the two is typically the one-line blessing over wine. It is the second blessing that is technically Kiddush (the word means "sanctification"). This blessing (in its Shabbat version) talks about God's sanctification of Shabbat and of the people of Israel and invokes two ancient core memories: the creation of the world and the Exodus from Egypt. In many respects, these function as the two most basic pillars on which our relationship with God stands. Interestingly, the Kiddush blessing may be recited over wine or, if no wine is available, over bread. But it *may not* be recited over grapes or wheat. Many have commented that this limitation teaches us that Kiddush, that is, sanctification, results from a partnership between God's natural world and the human technological "improvement" of that world. Wheat and grapes are simple products of nature. Bread and wine are quintessential examples of what human ingenuity can create out of the simple ingredients provided by nature. The sanctification (*kiddush*) of Shabbat is not just about God. It is about the partnership between God and human beings.

We now live in an age of immense affluence. Rarely do we think of bread as a staple. I would suggest, however, that the ancient importance of this food could be recovered in some measure by seeing it as symbolic, in the stretching and folding necessary to prepare it, of the dynamics that govern the flow of every chaotic system. Furthermore, lest we slip into the old habit of thinking of chaos as a destructive force, something inimical to the creative powers of life, let us remember what the most amateur bread baker learns early on, namely, how crucial proper kneading of dough is for the baking of good bread. If bread is the symbol of life, the representation of human creativity and genius at its peak, and the symbol of our communication with God, then the fact that it simply *cannot* be made without the chaotic stretching and folding that is called kneading tells us quite a bit about the place of chaos in the universe.

4

ALBERT EINSTEIN AND SPECIAL RELATIVITY

The Cosmic Speed Limit

THREE OBSERVATIONS ABOUT EINSTEIN

Observation 1: I began thinking about writing this book in early 1997. At the time, I was considering *New Jewish Metaphors for Einstein's Descendants* as a possible working title. I intended the word *descendants* in the title in a strictly figurative manner, for I had an intuitive sense that anyone who muses about modern physics is, in a sense, a descendant, follower, or student of Albert Einstein.

Observation 2: In the summer of 1999, as millennial fever gripped us all, I began to get e-mail messages about a small controversy that was raging over a poll being conducted by *Time* magazine to help the editors select their "person of the century." The controversy concerned the numerous votes cast for Adolf Hitler. Many said that his nomination was an abhorrence, while others countered that the magazine was not looking for the *best* person of the century, but rather for the person who had had the greatest influence. When the poll was finally completed and results tabulated, the winner, judged the most influential person of the century, was not the German dictator who murdered six million Jews but the German Jewish physicist Albert Einstein.

Observation 3: I conducted an experiment in which I taped unlabeled photographs of three great twentieth-century physicists—I. I. Rabi, Niels Bohr, and Albert Einstein—to a sheet of paper and asked everyone I could find in my office to identify them. Ten people agreed to participate. Nine identified Einstein with the briefest glance. Only one was able to identify Bohr and Rabi. Clearly, Einstein is a well-known figure, an icon of the twentieth century. I asked a few respondents what they could tell me about Einstein. One said, "E = mc^2" but couldn't explain what it meant. Another said, "the theory of relativity" but, again, couldn't explain what that meant.

Einstein has become a nearly universally recognized icon in our society. Yet what fascinates me is that, despite the familiarity of those sad eyes, that bushy mustache, and that wild fringe of hair, very few people can understand, much less explain, Einstein's contributions to human knowledge. This cannot be blamed on the general level of ignorance in our society, since I would think that many ordinary folks (that is, nonscientists) who *could* tell you that "Newton discovered gravity when an apple fell on his head," or that Darwin figured out "the survival of the fittest," could *not* explain, in even a rudimentary way, what the theory of relativity is about. I myself have found relativity harder to understand than any other single idea in physics. Apparently, Einstein's work resulted in some of the subtlest, most elusive, and toughest ideas that human minds have ever developed.

But so what? Why do I dwell on the fact that one *does* have to be a rocket scientist to understand Einstein? Remember that our goal all along has been to ponder how the revolutionary advancements in twentieth-century physics would influence the metaphor-language with which we think about, and discuss,

Jewish lives, beliefs, texts, and so on. For such an influence to occur, however, the principles hammered out by the physicists must trickle down, in at least some vague form, to the consciousness of common people who do not have degrees in science and who do not spend much time thinking deeply about science. Consider the case of gravity. One need not understand Newton's laws of gravity, nor be able to calculate gravitational forces using those laws, nor *certainly* understand Einstein's theory of gravity as laid out in his theory of general relativity to understand the basic ideas quite well: If you drop something, it falls down. Big rocks are harder to lift than little rocks. And astronauts in space float around because there's no gravity (well, almost none, but that's an unnecessary level of detail for most practical purposes). In other words, despite a complete lack of technical expertise, all of us have a general sense of gravity. It seems, however, that most people do *not* have a sense of relativity. This being so, I must at least entertain the possibility that, despite Einstein's larger-than-life stature in the minds and imaginations of us all, his theories may not trickle down very much to most of us. Without trickle-down, there can be little if any effect on the way ordinary people think and speak. What an irony it would be if the unquestionable father of modern physics, the one who fired the first mental shot in the revolution that altered the way human beings see and interact with the world, were himself to have had limited influence on the general perceptions of common folks!

This being said, I shall nevertheless try to extract at least a few basic principles from Einstein's work and speculate on their application in the world of Jewish metaphor.

SPECIAL RELATIVITY: BASIC PRINCIPLES

There are actually two theories of relativity, not one. The first, published by Einstein in 1905, is the *special* theory of relativity, and the second, published a bit more than a decade later, is the *general* theory of relativity. (We will explore general relativity in detail in the next chapter.) The special theory starts out with a thoroughly counterintuitive and mystifying assertion, namely that the speed of light (in a vacuum) is absolutely constant, regardless of the motion of the observer or light source. What does this mean? It is best explained by any one of a handful of simple analogies. Let us assume that you usually walk at 4 miles per hour (mph). If you walk down the aisle of an airliner cruising at 400 mph, your fellow passengers will perceive your speed as 4 mph. But if the airliner were made of a transparent material, an observer on the ground would perceive your walking speed differently. If you were walking in the direction of the plane's flight, from the tail back to your seat near the front, the ground-based observer would measure your speed as 404 mph, that is, the 4 mph of your pace plus the 400 mph of the flight. Conversely, if you were to return to the rear of the plane, thus walking opposite the direction of flight, the observer on the ground would measure your speed to be 396 mph, though moving *backward*. For although you are walking forward at 4 miles per hour, the plane is still carrying you in the other direction at 400 mph. This is not a deep insight, nor is it surprising. It works just as well if you shout from one end of the plane to the other and compare the speed of the sound waves as measured by a fellow passenger and the speed as measured by the observer on the ground. In fact, the principle is commonplace in air travel, where the pilot may announce that, while our airspeed is 400 mph, we are bucking a 75 mph headwind, so our *ground speed* is only 325 mph, which is why we will arrive in, say, Chicago behind schedule!

All this intuition collapses like a house of cards when light is used in the example. We know that the speed of light is about 670,000,000 mph.[1] If you sit in your seat in the first row of coach and aim a flashlight beam back toward the rear of the plane, your fellow passengers will measure the speed of the light beam as 670,000,000 mph. *But so will the observer on the ground!* For some mysterious reason, the ground-based observer will *not* measure the beam as traveling at 669,999,600 (that is, 670,000,000 – 400) mph. Similarly, if you shine your flashlight beam in the direction of the plane's flight, the ground-based observer will not measure it as 670,000,400 mph. No matter how fast, or in what direction, the flashlight is moving relative to the observer, the light it generates will *always* be seen as moving at the same, constant 670,000,000 mph! *The first major insight of special relativity, then, is that light travels at a constant, fixed speed, regardless of the speed or direction of the light source or the observer.*[2]

One clarification must be made here: The word *light* is actually just a convenient label for all electromagnetic energy, which comes in many forms that differ from one another only in their wavelength and their frequency. (See figure 1.1 on page 6 and the accompanying explanation.) Electromagnetic energy at different wavelengths and frequencies has different names. So, what we know as FM radio transmission waves, microwaves, x-rays, gamma rays, and others are all included in the broad category of "light" (along with visible light of all colors, of course) when we refer to the fixed, constant speed of light.

The second important insight of special relativity is as counterintuitive as the first. In everyday experience, we think of speed as having practical but not theoretical limits. For example, a typical, pretty good, new car will easily achieve speeds of 70 mph. In an emergency, or an attempt to seek dangerous thrills, it can probably achieve speeds of 90 mph, perhaps even 100 mph. Let us assume that the absolute best speed of a new car is 110 mph. It just won't go any faster. We have the sense, however, that this is *not* a theoretical limit. We know this because we've seen racecars on television that can go much faster. In fact, we can't imagine a rational claim by a racecar company to have built "the fastest possible car." It may be the fastest this year, or at this race, but eventually someone will build a faster one by developing lighter materials, better fuel, sleeker design, and so on. The same intuitive sense would apply to aircraft, or Olympic marathon runners. Apparently, the speed of a thing can always be a little faster. This intuitive assumption is crushed out of existence by the special theory of relativity, which says that *no object in the universe except light can travel at the speed of light and* nothing *can go faster than the speed of light, under any circumstances.* I have read a bunch of different explanations of why this is so and have become convinced that this is one of those cases where "you just can't really understand it without the math." But in the interest of *sort of* understanding it, let me try to convey the most useful and sensible explanation I have encountered. This involves Einstein's famous equation $E = mc^2$. What this means is that there is a relationship in the universe between the energy of an object and its mass (mass being the amount of "stuff" in a thing). In the equation, the term c stands for the speed of light, which, as we have seen, is constant. If you square a constant, that is, multiply it by itself, it is still constant. So the equation states that you can calculate the energy in an object by multiplying its mass times the speed of light squared. Of course, this also means that you can find the mass of the object by dividing its energy by c^2. Now the faster a thing goes, the more energy it has. Which means that as a thing goes faster, its mass *increases*. This makes no sense intuitively, partly because the effect is so tiny as to be unimportant (and undetectable) at the speeds we are accustomed to, even the speeds of very fast jets or space shuttles. But apparently, as a thing approaches the speed of light, its mass increases dramatically, that is, it very quickly gets much heavier. As the object gets closer and closer to light speed, its mass increases at a faster rate and it takes a greater amount of energy to boost its speed any higher. As the object's speed approaches closer to light speed, its mass increases without limit, and thus, according to physicist Brian Greene,

> it would require a push with an *infinite* amount of energy to reach or to cross the light barrier. This, of course, is impossible and hence absolutely nothing can travel faster than the speed of light.[3]

SPECIAL RELATIVITY AND JEWISH THOUGHT

These two facts about light, namely that its speed is absolutely constant to all observers regardless of the observers' motion and that nothing can go as fast as light, are the beginnings of special relativity. In a little while, we will explore the role of time in the theory, but before doing so, let's pause and see how these first insights about light might be useful in creating new Jewish metaphors. We have seen that light does *not* move instantaneously from place to place; in other words, that its speed is *not* infinite. But it does move *faster* than anything else in the universe possibly can. It is a noninfinite absolute. Its motion represents a limit that physical objects can approach (in theory), but can never, never reach or surpass.

Now the concept of infinity is one of the hardest things for a human mind to grasp. We may use the word easily, but we have no real way of comprehending a quantity that is unending. On one level, understanding an idea requires that we define it, and defining it requires that we set some boundaries around it. An infinite thing, by definition, is boundless, and that makes it very hard, if not impossible, to define and understand.

The medieval Jewish mystics clearly understood this difficulty. They spoke of God in two distinct and rather different ways. The first was *En Sof*, literally "without end."[4]

Theologian Karen Armstrong captures the sense of *En Sof* as follows:

> [T]he Kabbalists made use of the ... distinction between the essence of God and the God whom we glimpse in revelation and creation. God himself is essentially unknowable, inconceivable and impersonal. They called the hidden God *En Sof* (literally, "without end"). We know nothing whatever about *En Sof:* he is not even mentioned in the Bible or the Talmud.... Unlike YHWH, *En Sof* had no documented name; "he" is not a person. Indeed it is more accurate to refer to the Godhead as "It."[5]

The two most important features of *En Sof* are that it represents the true essence of God and that it is absolutely, completely hidden and unknowable. The infinite essence of God is beyond any and all human perception or understanding. This conclusion is desperately frustrating to anyone who seeks, wonders about, or longs for some glimpse of the divine nature of reality. To assert from the beginning that this particular goal of the religious life is fundamentally impossible to achieve is to undermine fundamentally the religious imagination. The mystics avoided this grim conclusion by describing a second form or aspect of God, distinct from, but not unrelated to, the unknowable *En Sof*. This is the system of ten *sefirot* (literally "numberings," but variously translated as "spheres," "aspects," or "emanations"), a series of "unfoldings" of God that become manifest as God creates the world and reveals the divine self to human beings. Each of these sefirot has a name (indeed, most are known, in the complexity of kabbalistic tradition, by any of several names), and each has qualities and characteristics. They are often depicted graphically in what has come to be known as the "map" of the *sefirot* (see figure 4.1).

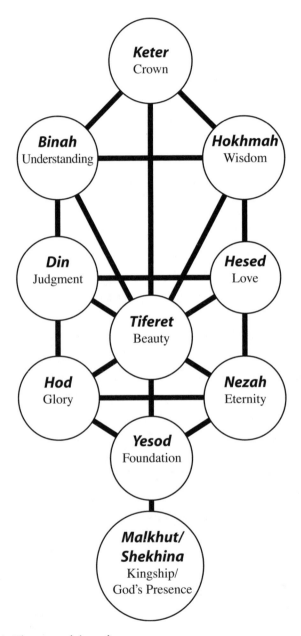

Figure 4.1: The map of the *sefirot*.

The *sefirot* are the aspect of God to which we can relate, the aspect spoken of in sacred literature, encountered in revelation, addressed in prayer, and so on. Of these, perhaps the most familiar to contemporary Jews is *Shekhinah*, the feminine presence of God who dwells in and among the people of Israel.[6]

This system of *sefirot*, often dismissed by modern folks who pride themselves on being hard-boiled rationalists, is remarkable in several ways. First of all, like the electromagnetic spectrum, it is *not* infinite, though it does describe a power that is absolute and that cannot be matched or surpassed by anything else in the universe. Each of the *sefirot* has its own identity, its own name and characteristics, although the kabbalists understand that each *sefirah* is simply a different form, or aspect, of God. Similarly, each form of electromagnetic radiation—visible light, microwaves, infrared radiation, x-rays—has its own name and its own properties, but we understand that they are all merely different forms (different wavelengths and frequencies) of one another. And, crucially, the *sefirot* are, for the kabbalist, the aspects of God the Unknowable that are *by their nature* knowable. In a way, light, in its various forms, defines communication, and therefore knowledge. If you gain knowledge about a thing by seeing it, that knowledge has come to you by means of reflected light, or radiation. The various forms of electromagnetic radiation are not the essence of the universe, but they are the only means available to us by which we can know the universe. Thus there seem to be several structural and metaphorical similarities between what the kabbalists called the *sefirot* and what we think of as the electromagnetic spectrum.

I am *not* suggesting that light and the various other forms of radiation are God! But then again, the kabbalists never really suggested that the *sefirot* "are" God. God, they claimed, is essentially *En Sof*, without boundary or definition, unknowable. The *sefirot* are the aspect of God that we can know, relate to, and deal with. In like fashion, I suggest that whereas the essence of God may be beyond any perception or knowledge, we might find in the phenomenon of light—whether visible or not—a metaphor for those aspects of God that are accessible to us.

GOD AS LIGHT IN ANCIENT TEXTS

As we consider this metaphor of light as representative of some aspects of God, we should remember that this is by no means a new idea. Rather, it is found throughout Jewish literary history—and very likely throughout the literary history of many other religions as well.[7] Let us take a look at three typical examples. The first is Psalm 27:

> [A psalm] of David:
>   The Eternal is my light and my help; whom shall I fear?
>   The Eternal is my life's refuge; of whom shall I be afraid?
>   (Ps. 27:1)

The next example comes from *Sifrei BeMidbar*, an early talmudic-era *midrash* on the Book of Numbers. This passage expounds upon the priestly blessing set out in Numbers 6:22–27:

> "May the Eternal cause His face to shine upon you ..." (Num. 6:25)—that is, may He give you the light of His face. Rabbi Nathan says: This is the light of the Shekhinah, as it is written, "Arise! Shine! For your light has come.... Behold! Darkness shall cover the earth, and dense fog [shall cover] the nations, [but upon you the Eternal will shine]"[8] (Is. 60:1–2), and it is also written,

"God will be gracious to us and bless us, may He cause His face to shine with us, Selah!" (Ps. 67:2), and it is also written, "The Eternal is God, and He will shine for us!" (Ps. 118:27).[9]

And lastly, an example from another *midrash* called *Pesikta DeRav Kahana*:

Rabbi Samuel bar Nachman said: Whereas in this world one walks by the light of the sun during the day, and by the light of the moon at night, in the world to come, we will not walk by the light of the sun by day or by the light of the moon by night. What is the reason? "No more will you have the sun for light during the day, or the shining of the moon for illumination ..." (Is. 60:19). But by what light will we walk? By the light of the Holy Blessed One, for it is written, "... for the Eternal shall be a light to you forever, and the days of your mourning shall be complete." (Is. 60:20)[10]

All three examples constitute minor variations on a single theme. The first example, from Psalm 27, is relatively easy to understand. The ancient Hebrew poetry found throughout the Bible did not rely upon rhyme or what we would recognize as meter to achieve its poetic form, but depended instead on a device called *parallelism*. In this structure, a line is divided into two half-lines, each of which contains the same thought expressed in more or less the same number of elements. That is, each element in the first half of the line is roughly parallel or equivalent to an element in the second half. Thus to understand the meaning of a term, we simply look at its parallel term in the other half-line. Here, the term "my light and my help" in the first half-line is parallel to the term "my life's refuge" in the second. Both phrases evoke protection and safety, especially since both half-lines end with an expression of the author's sense of security. So this use of the light metaphor is rooted in the primal sense of fear and danger associated with darkness and the corresponding sense of comfort and safety associated with light.

The passage from *Sifrei BeMidbar* appears to start from exactly the same association. In trying to explain the passage from Numbers, it uses two other biblical texts. The first, from near the end of the Book of Isaiah, foresees a future time of redemption for the nation of Israel when "Darkness shall cover the earth, and dense fog [shall cover] the nations," but when, by contrast, "upon you [Israel] the Eternal will shine." This is a fairly common prophetic notion of future salvation for Israel, where Israel's safety and prosperity are contrasted to the downfall of the nations that have formerly oppressed it. And lest there be any doubt as to the meaning of the metaphors of darkness, fog, and light, the *midrash* continues with a second biblical text (from Ps. 67) in which the poetic term "cause God's face to shine with us" in the second half-line is parallel to the term "will be gracious to us and bless us" in the first half-line. Here again, light is a symbol of God's grace and blessing, as opposed to darkness, which symbolizes the absence of these highly positive things.

The passage from *Pesikta DeRav Kahana* is perhaps the clearest of all, since it explicitly distinguishes between conditions in "this world" and those in the future, redeemed, messianic "world to come." The difference, according to the *midrash,* is that in the world to come, God's light will play the illumination role that is played by the sun and moon in this world. And again, lest we be unsure of the meaning of the metaphor, a second biblical text is employed (by coincidence, from the same chapter of Isaiah cited in the previous example) to make it clear: God's status as "a light to you forever" is associated with the promise that "the days of your mourning shall be complete." In other words, while there is mourning in this world, there will be none in the world to come. In all three examples, the metaphor of God as light, or God as the source of light, is used to convey a sense of God as a source of protection, comfort, safety, and happiness.

A NEW TWIST ON GOD AS LIGHT

Given the widespread appearance of this God-as-light metaphor throughout Jewish literature, and other religious literature as well, how is the metaphor I am suggesting any different from its tried-and-true ancient counterpart? How can God as light be a *new* Jewish metaphor in the century after Einstein? First of all, the ancient sense of the metaphor is rooted in a dualistic sense of the universe in which there are two possible states, light and darkness. When there is light, we can see, and we feel safe, or if not safe then at least in control. By contrast, when it is dark, we cannot see, and the lack of sight makes us feel uncomfortable and threatened. Light is good; darkness is bad. "God said, 'Let there be light!' and there was light. God saw that the light was *good*" (Gen. 1:3–4). When I think about the meaning of this ancient use of the metaphor, it sounds primitive and unsophisticated. My children, when they were very little, needed to have a night-light left on in their bedrooms as they slept. Being in a dark environment made them anxious and afraid. It is little wonder that religious metaphors based on the sense of light being good and darkness being bad leave us feeling that the whole ancient enterprise of religious thought and language is rather childish!

By contrast, a new metaphor of light as representative of God leads us to several somewhat more sophisticated insights. First of all, we now use the word *light* to indicate all forms of electromagnetic radiation. And though not all can be seen by the human eye, all are "signals" that can transmit information—and therefore understanding—about the world. Thus the metaphor continues to be about "seeing," although it moves that idea from the narrow confines of "visual perception" to a much broader sense of "knowing." Furthermore, whereas the ancients' association of light with God might have led them to imagine a dark place, or a dark era, as being abandoned by God, we have been taught by modern cosmology that the cosmic background radiation, that is, the very faint microwave "echo" of the Big Bang, is everywhere in the "darkness" of space and that it is fairly uniformly distributed throughout the universe. We moderns cannot conceive of a place with *no* energy, a place where the temperature reaches absolute zero. Even in the laboratory, physicists have not succeeded in creating temperatures that cold. According to our modern incarnation of the metaphor, since heat is yet another form of light, the fact that it permeates the entire universe in at least some minimal fashion leads us back to a traditional conclusion that we have seen before: There is no space that is utterly devoid of God's presence. "The whole earth is filled with God's glory" (Is. 6:3).[11]

But let us refocus on the specific insights regarding light that are generated by special relativity. The first insight was that *light travels at a constant, fixed speed, regardless of the speed or direction of the light source or the observer.* What can this insight teach us, as a modern metaphor, about contemporary Jewish life and meaning? The answer may lie in the issue of human hierarchy. All of ancient society in general, and ancient religious society in particular, was highly hierarchical. From the very beginning of the creation story, in which human beings are placed over the rest of the created world, with only God's authority above them, through every single element of biblical society, the world is arranged in a clearly hierarchical manner. With regard to power in society, men are superior to women. With regard to covenantal responsibility, the people of Israel are superior to those of the other nations. With regard to the service of God, the *kohanim*, that is, the priests, are pre-eminent, the Levites have a somewhat less prominent status, and both of those groups "outrank" the common Israelites. The land of Israel in general and Jerusalem in particular are the places that God has "chosen to make His name dwell there" and are therefore holier than other locations. Such hierarchies are simply the most basic fact of ancient human life. Such hierarchical inequities have continued into the modern era as well, creating a society of racism, ageism, and many other forms of inequality among human beings. By contrast, however, the special theory of relativity allows no person, no group, no place any privileged position with regard to the speed of light. According to its ironclad rule, the fastest of the fast are no closer to the speed of light than the slowest of the slow! It is as if the theory of relativity were saying to the human inhabitants of earth, "Look, folks, in all sorts of ways you have carved up power, resources, and countless markers of status in vastly unequal proportions among yourselves, but in this one respect you are all equal. With regard to light speed, no one has, or ever can have, an advantage!"

This is a deeply revolutionary, almost messianic idea. That there would be a standard in the universe with regard to which *all* humans beings are truly equal, not just in theory but in fact, is astonishingly idealistic. The question is: Does Judaism have *anything* to say about such an idea? There is, in fact, at least one such instance. My colleague and friend, Rabbi Irving "Yitz" Greenberg, has for years taught about the fundamental equality that pertains among all human beings as a result of our shared status as images of God.[12] Working primarily with Genesis 1:26 ("God said, 'Let us make the human in our image, after our likeness'") and other similar verses, Greenberg roots his entire philosophy in the belief that every human being is an image of God and, therefore, equal in value and status to every other human being. Of course, the problem for Greenberg, and to some extent for all of us, arises when we look for the expression of this absolute and universal equality in real life. In the reality of human life in general and Jewish life in particular, there are countless *in*equalities that are woven deeply into the fabric of culture and law. So, for example, the traditional prohibition of work on Shabbat can be interpreted in part as an ideal statement of human equality. On Shabbat, we behave as if there are no masters and slaves, no employers and employees, no executives and underlings. In reality, however, the traditional Jewish world assigns women the tasks, even on Shabbat, of child-care and food preparation (and let us admit openly that despite the numerous legal restrictions placed on cooking and preparing food on Shabbat, nevertheless the serving and the cleaning up of festive Shabbat meals creates a huge amount of real work). Another example is found in a general principle in the Talmud that groups women, slaves, and minors together in a category exempt from large areas of religious obligations and barred from others. Clearly there is no true equality in Jewish religious life as it developed over the centuries. Perhaps the most troubling element of the traditional social structure is the very presence of slaves and slavery. This institution, the ultimate testimony to the lack of equality in a society, is written into the Torah in some detail (see, for example, Ex. 21:2–11 and Lev. 25:44–45). How do we explain it? Greenberg teaches that the Torah and the society it creates are reality-based, not ideal. The Torah's laws regarding slavery, he claims, represent a significant improvement over the state of slavery in non-Israelite cultures. The fact, for example, that the Shabbat prohibition on work extended to slaves as well (see Ex. 20:10), or that Hebrew slaves (i.e., indentured servants) may only be kept for six years (Ex.21:1–6), are incremental steps toward the eventual abolition of slavery. In a messianic world, of course, there will be no slavery, but for the time being we can only try to move the world toward such a perfected state a step at a time. Whether or not one is convinced by this argument, special relativity as a religious metaphor posits an ideal state in which all humans are absolutely equal in relation to God. In a world in which people continue to slaughter one another over religious differences, this stands as a shining goal for which we ought to strive.

LIGHT SPEED, AND GOD, ARE FINITE

The second main insight of special relativity was the curiously counterintuitive statement that no object in the universe except light can travel at the speed of light, and *nothing* can go faster than the speed of light, under any circumstances. I have already commented on the noninfinite but nevertheless very great speed of light as suggestive of the *sefirot,* those observable aspects of God that are not *En Sof* (without end, infinite) but still reflective of some of God's immense power. I now want to make one more observation about this basic truth regarding light and the rest of the universe. We have mused about situations where we could not possibly imagine anything *beyond* the limit of a particular physical quantity. So, for example, it can be argued that it makes no sense to ask about what happened before the Big Bang. According to the understanding of the Big Bang that sees time itself as one of the results of the event, the idea of "before" is absurd when applied to the Big Bang. With light speed, however, this is not the case. Light speed, at 670,000,000 mph, is not the fastest speed we can imagine. We can *imagine* 671,000,000 mph, though physicists tell us nothing could travel that fast. Fans of the *Star Trek* television shows and movies can easily imagine faster speeds, since warp one was light speed and was, for the Starship *Enterprise,* like being out for a leisurely Sunday drive. The point of all this is merely to point out clearly what was surely already obvious: The speed of light is *not* infinite. Though the laws of physics assure us that nothing in our universe can equal or surpass that speed, nevertheless we can *imagine* speeds greater than that of light. In terms of translation to religious metaphor, this idea intrigues me for one very important reason. God is often spoken of as "infinitely powerful" or, more commonly, as "omnipotent." Such terms and the ideas they reflect lead to some amusing mind games. For example, I remember being fascinated as a teenager by the question: "Can God create a rock too heavy for God to lift?" Answer whichever way you like, yes or no, and you come face to face with a contradiction to the idea that God can do anything, that is, that God is omnipotent! Beyond the level of adolescent mind games, however, we encounter a much more serious realm of questioning stemming from the claim of God's omnipotence. It is the realm of moral questioning regarding the apparent contradiction between God's power and God's goodness. This dilemma is summed up neatly by Archibald MacLeish in his play *J.B.*: "If God is God He is not good, / If God is good He is not God."[13] In other words, if God is truly omnipotent (this is the intention behind "If God is God"), then God must not be all good, for there is clearly evil and undeserved misfortune in the world, which an omnipotent God could eliminate. This idea has brought on in many people serious crises of faith and has caused them much anger and bitterness. Innocent children die agonizing deaths, while unspeakably cruel and evil dictators live long, comfortable lives. On the other hand, if God is good and therefore (we assume) is as appalled as we are at the senseless pain and cruelty that often fill human life, then the fact that God allows such things to go on must mean that God is, after all, limited and not omnipotent. In the face of Sunday school lessons about an omnipotent *and* loving God, such data make no sense.

We looked briefly at the problem of theodicy in chapter 3, where I suggested that the butterfly effect might give us one way of approaching the issue. We turn now to another approach, articulated by Mordecai M. Kaplan. Kaplan revolutionized Jewish philosophy by daring to define God. His very clear definition was: *God is the Power that makes for salvation.* In two typical passages he writes:

> From the adoption of the frame of human values which derive their significance from man's striving for salvation, perfection or self-transcendence, it is but one logical step to the belief in God as the Power that impels man to pursue that course and that enables him at least to come within sight of its destination.[14]
>
> The purpose of speaking of God as "the Power that makes for salvation" is to identify the particular human experiences which enable us to feel the impact of the process in the environment and in ourselves which impels us to grow and improve physically, mentally, morally and spiritually.[15]

Kaplan is saying that God is the label we give to the power that makes us do good things in the world. The bad things aren't God, nor are they God's doing. This clearly resolves the problem of theodicy, but the price paid for the resolution is God's omnipotence. Thus freed from the burden of being in control of, and responsible for, everything, God can now be seen only in the good parts of life.

Kaplan's position strikes a satisfying chord in many people. By regarding God as a *good* and *powerful* force, but one that is not *infinite*, we are able to maintain some belief in God, or at least to feel comfortable with the language of that belief, while not having to worry about the serious problems that confront the world regularly. Returning to the metaphor of light, we can appreciate the illuminating power of the energy and marvel at its immense (but not infinite) speed, while still being aware that the universe is full of dark places, shadows, and regions where the light either cannot reach or has not reached yet. The fact that there are dark places in the universe does not lead most people to be disappointed in, or angry at, light, nor does it cause them to lose faith in light. We would do well to allow some of our tolerance for darkness in the universe to carry over into our religious lives, where so many of us *are* disappointed in, or angry at, God for the fact that there are so many places not yet illuminated by "divine light." I have often met people who say they cannot believe in a God who would allow cruelty or pain to persist in the lives of innocent people. This is a clear case where a new metaphor derived from physics would help us out. The truth learned from the metaphor was poignantly anticipated and understood by a victim of the Holocaust whose graffiti on a wall in Cologne, Germany, proposed a clear analogy: "I believe in the sun, even when it is not shining ... I believe in God, even when He is silent."

THE ROLE OF TIME IN SPECIAL RELATIVITY

The last element of special relativity that we will raise is, for me, the most puzzling. It concerns the nature of time, and the fact that, as a logical result of the constant speed of light, time flows at different rates for people (or objects) that are in motion relative to one another. I have found this idea by far the most difficult to grasp, despite having read a dozen or more clever attempts to describe it without mathematics. I shall try to explain it, and then explore its meaning in the realm of religious thought.

Of all the explanations of this strange relationship between time and motion that I have read, that of Columbia University physicist Brian Greene has appealed to me most.[16] He starts with a functional definition of time as that which is measured by the regular ticking of clocks. He then proposes a device called a *light clock* (see figure 4.2A) consisting of two parallel mirrors held in a bracket so that they face each other, with one photon of light bouncing back and forth between them. (Photons are the smallest, simplest particles of light that can exist.) Since the speed of light is constant, the time for the photon to make one roundtrip from mirror A to mirror B and back again is also constant, and thus the device can indeed be used to measure time. Now he proposes a setup in which one light clock is stationary and another, identical light clock slides by from left to right. (See figure 4.2B.) The photon in the stationary clock seems to us, the stationary observers, to move straight up and straight down again. But from our perspective, the photon in the moving light clock travels up at an angle, for

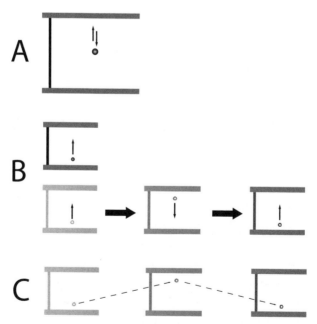

Figure 4.2: A: A light clock. Each "trip" of the single photon from the top mirror to the bottom mirror and back to the top mirror is one "tick" of the clock. B: Two identical light clocks, one sitting still, the other moving from left to right. C: The dotted line traces out the path of the photon in the moving light clock from B.

if it were to travel straight up from its starting point, it would miss the upper mirror since the device would have moved to the right in the time it took the photon to travel from bottom to top. Again, the downward path of the photon in the moving clock will have to be diagonal, for the same reason its upward path was diagonal. Thus the roundtrip of the photon in the moving clock is in the shape of an inverted V, while the path of the photon in the stationary clock is in the shape of a simple I. Even without the benefit of high school geometry, it is easy to see that the photon in the moving clock has a longer path to traverse than that in the stationary one. (See figure 4.2C.) And since the speed of the two photons is identical and constant, it will take the photon in the moving clock longer to make its longer trip; that is, the moving clock will tick *more slowly* than the stationary clock. In other words, time, which is defined as that which is measured by the regular ticking of clocks, flows more slowly for the moving clock *from our perspective*! These last three words are crucial, for if we were tiny creatures living on the moving light clock, the path of its photon would seem to us to be straight up and straight down, while the path of the photon on the other clock (the one we have been calling "stationary") would seem diagonal. Thus, from the perspective of creatures living on the moving clock, time flows more slowly for the stationary clock.

This last point can be put another way: The creatures on the moving clock can arbitrarily decide that *they* are stationary and the "stationary" clock is actually moving from right to left. According to the understanding of special relativity, neither group's claim to be "stationary" can be privileged over the other group's similar claim. In fact, special relativity teaches that it is *impossible* to detect constant, uniform motion—in other words, motion that is straight, without turning or swerving and without acceleration or deceleration. This part of the theory is easy to understand if you've ever been in a train that has stopped at a station while another train is parked on the adjacent track, so all you can see out of the windows on that side is the other train. If the other train starts to move in one direction, it is impossible to tell, for a moment or two, whether it is moving one way or your train is moving the other way. The only way to be certain is to look out the other window and see if the station is still there. According to special relativity, all constant, uniform motion is like that, except that there is no "window on the other side" to check.

To return to the time being measured by the two light clocks, it is important to point out that, at normal speeds traveled by human beings and their contraptions, the effect on time is so tiny as to be virtually impossible to detect, while at speeds that are some significant fraction of the speed of light, they become much more pronounced. That having been said, however, Greene reports a 1971 experiment in which cesium-beam atomic clocks were flown on commercial airliners for forty hours and were then compared to identical, earthbound clocks. The clocks that had been airborne *had indeed* ticked more slowly![17] So we may summarize this bizarre notion by saying that if an object X is in motion relative to another object Y, then *from Y's perspective, time will pass more slowly for X than for Y, and the closer X's speed comes to the speed of light, the slower time will flow for X.*

This notion is one of the most challenging for us to assimilate, not only because we have no everyday experience with it and thus cannot visualize it, but also because a key part of the human condition is our clear, sometimes agonizing sense of the flow of time. We are keenly aware that time moves on, that we cannot stop it or slow it down or speed it up, that we are, in essence, its prisoners. Unlike the realm of space, which (it seems to us) we have mastered, time is utterly beyond our control. This being so, the notion that time could be slowed is indeed tantalizing. But, alas, scientists tell us—and special relativity confirms—that we humans are incapable of traveling at speeds great enough to make the control of time a realistic possibility. And so the idea of being freed from the shackles of time evaporates as quickly as it appears.

THE RELATIVITY OF TIME: MORTAL CREATURES AND THEIR IMMORTAL GOD

But what would control of time really mean? If it *weren't* impossible in practical terms, what difference would it make? Our enslavement to the inexorable flow of time is, in a sense, the core of our mortality. It is closely bound up with our birth, maturation, aging, and death. This overwhelming notion is at the heart of human religion. The fact that we are mortal, *and that we are aware of our mortality*, drives us to seek meaning, to seek salvation, and to imagine a God who is eternal. In fact, the possibility of being in relationship with an eternal, immortal God is, I think, tremendously important to the religious life. Such a relationship takes the sting out of our own sense of mortality. If we cannot live forever, at least we can have contact with God who does live forever. But what does God's immortality mean? More specifically, what does it mean in the context of the notion of the relativity of time, suggested by Einstein's theory of special relativity?

By way of an answer, I offer two observations: one from the language of ancient Jewish literature, the other from a contemporary interpretation of special relativity. The first is a verse from the biblical Book of Psalms: "For a thousand years in Your eyes are as yesterday when it has passed, and a watch[18] in the night" (Ps. 90:4). This verse is, in its context, quite straightforward and clear in its meaning. The entire psalm describes God by comparing human insignificance and frailty to the majesty, power, and eternity of God. One rather traditional commentary explains that

The Psalmist proclaims that time has no meaning with God. In the estimation of man a thousand years is a vast stretch of time; in God's estimation it is like a day—not as the hours drag slowly by—which is gone and in retrospect appears so very short. Nay, it is less even than that, the Psalmist continues, it is like a night-watch ..., of which the sleeper takes no reckoning and which has vanished on his waking.[19]

This particular verse conveys the eternity and power of God as compared to the fleeting insignificance of humankind. The intended relationship could be compared to the case of a wise elder who says to a child, "For you, ten years is a lifetime, but for me it seems like nothing at all." Such a statement is not meant to suggest that the two *really* experience time differently, but merely that their perspectives differ because of the amount of time each has lived. The child will understand the elder's perspective when the former achieves the age of the latter (although by then the latter will be long dead). The comparison only collapses when we realize that we (the "children") will *never* achieve the age of the elder (that is, God), since, as the psalmist has told us in verse 2 of the same psalm, "You are God from eternity to eternity."

But we are now in a position to reinterpret the meaning of the verse in the light of special relativity. If, as suggested earlier, we use light as a metaphor for God, then indeed time moves at a different *and much slower rate* for God than for human beings. When we ask how much slower time moves for God, we encounter a startling answer. In Brian Greene's brilliant elucidation of special relativity, he explains that, according to Einstein (who himself adopted the idea from the work of mathematician Hermann Minkowski), time is to be thought of as a dimension, similar to the three spatial dimensions of length, width, and height. Now let us imagine two objects moving in parallel paths, going north to south at precisely the same speed. Obviously, the two will arrive at any given line drawn east-west along their path at the same instant. But if one object alters its course so that it is moving diagonally, say to the southwest, it will arrive at the arbitrary east-west line *after* the object that travels directly north to south. Even though the two objects move at the exact same speed, the diagonally moving object is using some of its speed to move east to west, thus its north-to-south speed will be decreased. If, instead of moving diagonally, this object moved directly east to west, that is, at right angles to the path of the north-to-south-moving object, the east-to-west-moving object would *never* arrive at the "finish line." Now comes what Greene correctly labels as a "leap":

> Einstein proclaimed that all objects in the universe are *always* traveling through spacetime at one fixed speed—that of light.... We are presently talking about an object's speed through *all four* dimensions—three space and one time—and it is the object's speed in this generalized sense that is equal to that of light. To understand this more fully and to reveal its importance, we note that ... this one fixed speed can be shared between the different dimensions—different space *and* time dimensions, that is. If an object is sitting still (relative to us) and consequently does not move through space at all, then ... all of the object's motion is used to travel through one dimension—in this case, the time dimension.... If an object does move through space, however, this means that some of the previous motion through time must be diverted.... [T]his sharing of motion implies that the object will travel more slowly through time than its stationary counterparts, since some of its motion is now being used to move through space.... We now see that time slows down when an

object moves relative to us because this diverts some of its motion through time into motion through space ...

We also see that this framework immediately incorporates the fact that there is a limit to an object's spatial velocity: the maximum speed through space occurs if *all* of an object's motion through time is diverted to motion through space. This occurs when all of its previous light-speed motion through time is diverted to light-speed motion through space.... [S]omething traveling at light-speed through space will have no speed left for motion through time. Thus light does not get old; a photon that emerged from the big bang is the same age today as it was then. There is no passage of time at light speed.[20]

The insight of the end of this passage hit me like a revelation when I first read it. The question of God and time is a difficult one. Many people complain that they were taught as children about an image of God as "an old man with a long white beard," and although I am not personally aware of any Sunday school curriculum or picture book that *actually* ever portrayed God in this fashion, the complaint is sufficiently common to suggest that somewhere along the line (probably courtesy of the Book of Daniel, as we shall see) this image became a part of our collective imagination. It clearly appears in kabbalistic tradition. The term *Attika Kadisha*, or the Holy Ancient One, appears as a name of God in the Zohar (the foundational thirteenth-century Spanish mystical text),[21] the works of Lurianic Kabbalah (from the mystical circle of Rabbi Isaac Luria, Safed, sixteenth century),[22] the works of Shabbetai Zvi (a seventeenth-century false messiah from Turkey),[23] and elsewhere.[24] A related phrase, "Ancient of Days," first appears in the biblical story of Daniel (chapter 7, verses 9, 13, and 22). In this strange and unique passage, Daniel describes a dream he has had, in which he has seen four fearsome beasts. As Daniel watched,

> Thrones were set in place, and the Ancient of Days took His seat. His garment was like white snow, and the hair of His head was like lamb's wool. His throne was tongues of flame, its wheels were blazing fire. A river of fire streamed forth before Him. Thousands upon thousands served Him, myriads upon myriads attended Him. The court sat and the books were opened. (Dan. 7:9–10)[25]

This bizarre vision, which may well owe much to the Hellenistic environment (ca. 170s–160s B.C.E. in Judea) in which Daniel lived, clearly portrays God in anthropomorphic terms (God has garments, a head, hair, and sits on a throne). Two questions need to be asked in this regard. First, why are many modern folks so uncomfortable with this anthropomorphic portrayal? And second, why did the author of Daniel (or that of the Zohar, or the Lurianic texts, or Shabbetai Zvi) use this sort of language? The answer to the first question, I think, lies in the fact that we have come to have a much larger view of the universe and the power(s) that must have brought it into being than did our ancestors. In a world in which the earth and its human inhabitants were seen as the crown of creation and the central focus of the universe and its creator, it makes some sense to imagine the creator as looking like us, only more so. After all, the first chapter of Genesis tells us that God made humans in God's own image, so in a certain sense it is completely reasonable to look at ourselves and imagine God as a much bigger, stronger, flashier version of the same basic design. The problem is that today we have a much humbler sense of our place in the universe. Our galaxy, our sun, and our planet are rather ordinary objects hidden among billions of galaxies, stars, and planets of similar types. And, according to many (who argue, in large part, based on the logical improbability of any evolutionary phenomenon in a universe so vast being "unique"), our own lives, imaginations, creative abilities, and intelligence are quite likely fairly ordinary as well, although, unlike the many galaxies, stars, and planets, we haven't yet found other intelligent life. All this being the case, we feel a bit foolish imagining God, the creator of the whole system, as a being more or less like ourselves, even a bigger, stronger, faster version.[26] Thus it makes sense that people complain about that portrayal of God as the "old man in heaven with the long white beard," even though we now have a better idea where the image may have originated!

The answer to the question of why the ancient authors would have used such highly anthropomorphic language seems to lie in the central assumption I have stated throughout this book, namely, that human beings can only speak of (and therefore think of) the powers that create and control all of existence in metaphorical terms. The use of metaphor allows us to have some understanding of, and control over, forces so vast that they overwhelm and silence us when we try to contemplate them directly. When an ancient text speaks of the Ancient of Days, describing him as an old man with hair like lamb's wool, wearing white, with rivers of fire flowing forth from him, what it says is that this power is so much older and wiser and more powerful than we are, or even than our planet is, that we feel like small, frightened children in its presence. These feelings are legitimate and real, and I suggest that they have *not* changed, despite our broader view of the universe. We *still* feel overwhelmed by the vastness of the universe and its power. We are *still*, with all our knowledge, our understanding, and our technology, like very small children. If the old metaphors that expressed those feelings no longer ring true, for the various reasons discussed above, we need new metaphors. One such metaphor is that of light, which always travels at the fastest speed possible, much faster than we can *ever* hope to go, and which *never* ages! We who are lifelong inmates in the prison of time, unable to break free of its grip, condemned to age and die, and, as humans, perhaps uniquely aware of this fate would do well to stand in awe before a power that is not subject at all to the inexorable passage of time. "[A] photon that emerged from the big bang is the same age today as it was then."[27] It would be not a leap, but a very small step indeed, to restate Greene's observation in what sounds like less scientific and more spiritual language: The light that burst forth at the very first moment of the universe's birth, when God said, *"Yehi or* (Let there be light!)" is the same age today as it was then. "Time has no meaning with God."[28]

5

GENERAL RELATIVITY
Jewish Meaning in Curved Space

As Einstein contemplated his special theory of relativity, he recognized a fundamental problem arising from one of its essential elements. He wrestled with that problem for more than ten years before finally solving it. The problem was this: Special relativity tells us that no object or force can travel instantaneously from one place to another; all objects and forces in the universe are absolutely limited to traveling at or below light speed. This basic truth seemed in conflict with Newton's theory of gravitation. That theory posited that all bodies in the universe attract all other bodies in the universe with a force (gravity) that is determined by the mass of the bodies and by the distance between them. The greater the mass, the stronger its gravitational pull on other objects will be; the farther away one object is from another, the weaker the gravitational force between them will be. It is the effect of distance on gravitation that presents a problem when viewed through the lens of special relativity. For if we assume that two objects are, say, ninety-three million miles apart (as the earth and the sun are) and then we imagine one of them suddenly exploding, such that its mass is suddenly reduced by a great deal, then according to Newton's theory of gravitation, the other object would *immediately* feel the decrease in the gravitational pull resulting from the decrease in mass of the object that had exploded. This immediate decrease in gravitational attraction could only happen if the force called gravity traveled instantaneously between the two objects. Special relativity dictates that nothing can travel faster than light, which makes the trip between the sun and the earth in about eight minutes. To resolve this conflict, Einstein had to rethink completely what gravity is and how it works.

Bear in mind that Newton's theory of gravitation had been around for more than two centuries and had been tested experimentally, that is, proven, many times. It accurately predicted all sorts of observable, measurable phenomena in the universe. It was generally agreed to be true! The special theory of relativity, on the other hand, was "just" a theory, still very new, and hardly the much-tested "truth" that Newton's laws had become. Yet Einstein was so deeply certain that special relativity was true that he assumed that the proven laws of Newton were flawed based on that belief. I point this out only because the thought process involved seems strangely reminiscent of a thought process commonly encountered in the realm of religious belief. It is not unusual to find people clinging to a religious belief even though it disagrees with what everyone knows to be true. Sometimes the belief even flies in the face of what the empirical evidence demonstrates. We often think that religious belief is driven by faith (often called "blind" faith), while scientific knowledge or thinking is driven by an impartial and detached observation and analysis of data. It turns out, however, that both these human quests are sometimes driven by a deep faith in the truth of a proposition that is apparently unsupported by observed data. I am not claiming that religious belief is arrived at by the same kind of logical reasoning that leads theoreticians to new insights in science, but it is interesting to me how similar the strength of faith in the two processes seems.

Einstein's faith in the universal "speed limit" set by special relativity and the resulting suspicion that all was not right with Newton's sense of instantaneous gravitational effects were not the only goads driving him to rethink gravity. He was also bothered by the fact that Newton's law of gravitation, although it predicted the behaviors of planets, cannonballs, and falling apples with nearly perfect precision, did not explain what specific mechanism causes gravity. In fact, Newton made specific note of the utterly mysterious nature of the force whose action he had so thoroughly come to understand when he wrote: "Gravity must be caused by an agent acting constantly according to certain laws; but whether this agent be material or immaterial, I have left to the consideration of my readers."[1]

In 1907, Einstein developed an idea that started him on the road to an understanding of Newton's mysterious force. The idea began with the realization that the force of gravity is, in many ways, similar to the force of accelerated motion. That is, if you are in a vehicle that is accelerating, you are pressed backward in the direction opposite the direction of the vehicle's motion. This feeling is indistinguishable, said Einstein, from the feelings induced by gravity. In fact, we now take this insight for granted; we have all learned from books or movies about space flight how the G forces (G is for gravity) build up during take off, squashing the astronauts back in their seats. The similarity between the action of gravity and that of acceleration, dubbed the *equivalence principle*, was an important step toward unlocking Newton's mystery, simply because it suggested that gravity is somehow caused by a mechanism similar to the very common and well-understood phenomenon of accelerated motion.

Although the details of the journey from Einstein's 1907 realization of the equivalence between gravitation and inertia

(inertia is closely related to accelerated motion) are said to be devilishly difficult, the most general outline seems to be as follows:[2] The most commonly experienced indication of the equivalence principle is the feeling of riding in an elevator. As the elevator accelerates upward, the passengers inside feel pressed down onto its floor. This feeling is typically attributed to inertia, that is, the force in nature that tends to keep stationary objects stationary and moving objects moving, unless either is acted on by some other force. The equivalence principle says that we are equally justified in attributing the effect on the passengers to a gravitational field that is created by the elevator's upward acceleration. Apparently, one way of understanding the essence of general relativity is to say that it is impossible to say in any absolute way whether the elevator is moving upward through a fixed space or whether the space around the elevator is moving downward while the elevator itself remains stationary. It is not just that one cannot tell the difference without visual points of reference (as in the case of the two trains in the station). Rather, general relativity says that, in the case of the elevator, *there is no difference*! Thus, while special relativity taught that it is impossible to determine absolute motion in the case of uniform motion, that is, motion in a straight line with no changes in speed or direction (this being the case of the two trains), general relativity made it impossible to determine absolute motion even where acceleration is involved.

Now this does not explain all of general relativity by any means. The next step will involve the work of a mathematician named Minkowski that revolutionized the way we think about space. But before venturing into that heady territory, I want to consider for a moment the impact of general relativity's undoing of the notion of absolute motion. In his explanation, Martin Gardner writes the following:

> The ancient argument over whether the earth rotates
> or the heavens revolve around it (as Aristotle taught) is
> seen to be no more than an argument over the simplest
> choice of a frame of reference. Obviously the most con-
> venient choice is the universe. Relative to the universe
> we say that the earth rotates and inertia makes its equa-
> tor bulge. Nothing except inconvenience prevents us
> from choosing the earth as a fixed frame of reference. In
> the latter case we say that the cosmos rotates around
> the earth, generating a gravitational field that acts
> upon the equator.... Do the heavens revolve or does
> the earth rotate? The question is meaningless. A wait-
> ress might just as sensibly ask a customer if he wanted
> ice cream on top of his pie or the pie placed under his
> ice cream.[3]

In this era of space shuttles, an international space station,
and the Hubble space telescope, Gardner's statement is rather
astonishing! As the latter half of the twentieth century passed,
and we humans became increasingly familiar with, if not quite
yet comfortable in, outer space, we seem to have drawn an ironclad conclusion that our own place in the universe is a rather
unassuming one, without any special privilege. Our location is
often defined as a medium-sized planet circling around an average star, which is one of millions on the outer edge of one of the
arms of a typical spiral galaxy, which is one of billions. This
modesty is more graphically described in a somewhat tongue-
in-cheek poster, which shows a vast galaxy-scape filled with
stars, with an arrow pointing to a particular spot off to one
side, and a label on the arrow like those seen on zoo maps proclaiming "You are here!" But Gardner's statement about pie
and ice cream says that, in an absolute sense, the question of

whether the earth spins through space or space dances around a stationary earth is a meaningless one! What is going on here?

GENERAL RELATIVITY
AND RELIGIOUS PERSPECTIVE

I think perhaps the issue is not one of science at all, but one of belief, self-image, and philosophy. It is quite clear that in ancient times, we believed that the earth, and our own existence upon it, were the most privileged of positions. The entire creation tale of Genesis tells us, in its very first line, that it will be the story of God's creation of "the heavens and the earth." It becomes clear, as we read, that "heavens" is to the ancient text what "outer space" or "the cosmos" is to us. The second and third days of the six-day creation process, as well as the last two, deal exclusively with processes on the earth. Only the first day (on which light is created and then separated from darkness) and the fourth day (on which sun, moon, and stars are created) deal with anything beyond the earth itself. And even when the other celestial bodies are created, the text portrays them clearly as being in service to the earth:

> God said: Let there be lights in the dome of the sky to separate between the day and the night. They shall be for signs and for seasons and for days and for years. And they shall serve as lights in the dome of the heavens to shine upon the earth. And it was so. (Gen. 1:14–15)

The sun, moon, and stars are created *for the purpose* of giving light to the earth and of distinguishing days, seasons, and years on the earth. According to this ancient account, the earth and its inhabitants are clearly the central focus of the universe and of God. So thoroughly accepted and deeply believed was this conclusion that when Nicolaus Copernicus (1473–1543) rejected it in favor of his[4] heliocentric system, teaching that the sun, not the earth, was the center of the universe, he was seen as a great religious heretic.

Today, of course, were anyone to claim that the earth is the center of the universe, he would be denounced and dismissed as a religious reactionary, a throwback, in league with creationists and the Flat Earth Society. Yet Gardner tells us that according to general relativity there is no difference. What is at stake here is not so much the brightly lit, equation-endorsed truth of science, but rather how we human beings see ourselves in the context of the larger reality in which we live. The ancients saw us as the pinnacle of creation, the "apple of God's eye," while we moderns tend to see ourselves as a bit of lint on the shoulder of the universe. As Gardner's pie-serving waitress points out, however, neither position is "right" if by that we mean that the other must be "wrong." Rather, it is a matter of choice regarding how we wish to see ourselves. It is similar to the well-known "figure-ground" illusion, which can be seen as a drawing of either two faces looking at each other or a goblet. Neither perception is wrong, for both are right; we can easily switch from one image to the other and back. So it is with the relationship between the earth and the cosmos. More important than the question of which view is right is the question of which gives life greater meaning. This, of course, is the quintessential religious question. And in answer to it I would cite an old Hasidic teaching about a great teacher who kept in his pockets two pieces of paper. Written on one were the words, "I am but dust and ashes." On the other was written, "The whole world was created for my sake alone."[5] It is important to live in the tension between these two convictions, seeing ourselves at times as being the most important beings in the entire universe, the hub around which all else revolves, and at other times as completely insignificant. For there are times in which our human condition desperately requires the balm of believing that we matter, that

the cosmos cares about us. These are times of despair and loneliness, when we feel abandoned and uncared for. At such times,
we are best served by the ability to believe that "the world was
created for my sake alone." On the other hand, there are times
when we risk destroying ourselves and large chunks of the
world around us because of our limitless human pride in our
powers and abilities. These are the times when a healthy dose
of abject humility—"I am but dust and ashes"—can save us
from ourselves.

SPACE-TIME IS CURVED

There is one more important idea in the theory of relativity,
namely, the curvature, or warping, of space-time. The idea
required Einstein to rely heavily on the work of the Lithuanian-
born German mathematician Hermann Minkowski.[6] He pioneered the notion that time is a dimension very similar to (but
not identical to) the three space dimensions about which we are
accustomed to thinking, namely, length, width, and height. His
notion resulted in the now fairly common term *space-time*,
which denotes the four-dimensional matrix in which all things
exist. If an object is at rest in space (although the very idea of
being "at rest" begins to lose its meaning as we think more and
more about relativity), it is still "in motion" along the dimension of time, that is, its existence continues from moment to
moment. If it were possible to draw a four-dimensional graph,
the "world line" (the term itself is apparently Minkowski's) of
such a stationary object would be parallel to the time axis of the
graph. (Since drawing, or even imagining, a four-dimensional
graph is impossible, most authors ask us to imagine only two
spatial dimensions, then use the third axis of the 3-D graph to
represent time.) Minkowski's description of the unity of space
and time, given in a lecture he delivered in Cologne, Germany,
in 1908, is considered canonical and often quoted in writings

on relativity: "Henceforth space by itself and time by itself, are doomed to fade away into mere shadows, and only a kind of union of the two will preserve an independent reality."[7] Although the deep mathematical understanding of Minkowski's space-time is quite mystifying, the basic idea as Einstein made use of it is fairly straightforward. When we think of a three-dimensional coordinate grid that is used to specify the positions of objects in space, we generally think of the lines that make up that grid as being straight. Lines on the grid that denote the same dimension (for example, all the lines on the grid that lie east-west) are parallel to one another. Being parallel to one another, according to what we all learned in high school geometry, they never meet. Those lines intersect other lines that define other dimensions on the grid (that is, the north-south or up-down lines) at right angles. The shortest distance between any two points in the grid, again according to high school geometry, is a straight line. The space described by such a rigid grid of parallel and perpendicular lines is called a "flat space." Einstein's theory of general relativity says that *the presence of mass or energy in the universe warps or curves the space-time around it* (remember that the grid we are now thinking about is not composed of merely three dimensions but four, the fourth being time). Physicists often use the analogy of a flat rubber sheet (representing space-time) to describe the theory nonmathematically. If the sheet is completely flat, and we place a ping-pong ball on it and give it a push, the ball will roll straight across the rubber in the direction of the push. Now we place a heavy bowling ball (representing any large chunk of mass or energy) on the sheet. The ball will deform, or warp, the flatness of the sheet. If we place the ping-pong ball on the sheet again and give it a push, its course will not be straight (unless we happen to have pushed it toward the exact point where the bowling ball is sitting), but will bend toward the center of the depression, or warping, caused by the heavy weight.

Although the analogy is not perfect, it allows us to visualize a bit of what general relativity teaches about how gravity works. A somewhat more accurate image comes from one of the theory's first experimental proofs. In 1919, an expedition led by the astronomer Sir Arthur Eddington took photographs during a solar eclipse that proved that the mass of the sun causes the light from distant stars to bend toward it as that light passes nearby. This effect, called gravitational lensing (because a lens bends light rays, and in this case the light rays are being bent not by going through a curved glass surface but by passing near a massive object), shows how the sun's mass warps the space-time around it, causing all things in the neighborhood to curve from their previous "straight" course. Note that the sun does not "pull" on the light rays, any more than the bowling ball on the rubber sheet pulls on the ping-pong ball. Rather, the space-time through which the light rays are traveling is warped by the sun's presence, and so the light rays, still traveling, as always, the "straightest" possible path, travel a path through the curved space-time, which seems to bend.

WARPED TIME TICKS MORE SLOWLY

Note that both these models, the rubber sheet and the sun, have allowed us to visualize what the warping of *space* is all about, but neither has allowed us to visualize the warping of *time*. Yet it is critical for Einstein's theory, based in Minkowski's ideas, that the entity called *space-time*, warped by the presence of mass or energy, is a *four*-dimensional grid. Apparently, the warping of time causes time to slow down in the presence of a gravitational field. This has been verified experimentally by synchronizing extremely accurate clocks, then taking one to the top of a tall tower and leaving the other at ground level. The one at the top of the tower, being farther from the center of the gravitational field, or from the earth's center, will tick a tiny bit faster than the one on the ground. I am assured by all the books that discuss this phenomenon that the effect is not caused simply by the slowing or speeding up of the physical clock mechanism, but by the slowing or speeding up of time itself. Incidentally, because of the equivalence principle that asserts that gravity and acceleration are basically the same thing, time will also run more slowly in an accelerating situation, say, a spacecraft accelerating to escape velocity.

Under normal circumstances, such as those in an accelerating airliner or those encountered when we place synchronized clocks in the basement and on the one hundredth floor of a tall building, the effect on time is very, very tiny and measurable only by the most sophisticated laboratory equipment. Even in circumstances that we might think of as gravitationally extreme, the effect is small. For example, on the surface of the sun, a clock would run slower than it does on earth by only about sixty-four seconds per year.[8] But there is a circumstance in the universe where the effect would be clearly noticeable, although by the time we noticed it, it would, ironically, be too late! I refer to the phenomenon called a *black hole*.

The existence of black holes, though they were then called "dark stars," was first predicted in 1783 by an English scientist named John Michell.[9] In his day, light was thought to be made up of tiny particles called corpuscles, which would be affected by gravity as would any other particle. Given the constant speed of light, already known to the scientists of the time, Michell hypothesized (using Newton's laws of gravitation) a star with a given mass and a small enough circumference that its gravity would be so strong as to require an escape velocity higher than that of light. In such a case, light rays emitted from the surface of the star would shoot outward but, unable to reach escape velocity, would fall back to the star like a pebble tossed high into the sky. Such a star would be invisible from the earth, since it could emit no light. Thus it was called a dark star. In the early nineteenth century, however, scientists began to think of light more as a wave than as a particle and became uncertain about how a wave of energy, with no mass, would be affected by gravity. The dark star idea was abandoned until 1915, when it was revived by Karl Schwarzschild, a German physicist who began to consider the implications of general relativity almost immediately after Einstein first published it. Schwarzschild's version of Michell's dark star, which came to be known as a Schwarzschild singularity, was based on Einstein's understanding of gravity as space-time curvature. Before describing the mechanism he imagined, however, it is important to point out why Michell's dark star mechanism conflicts with Einstein's theory. Michell's notion is based on the idea that the gravity of a star would pull on the particles of light emitted by the star, slowing them more and more as they shoot outward from the stellar surface until they finally slow to zero speed, then "fall" back into the star. According to this description, inhabitants of a planet very near the star *would* see its light, because they would be within the area where the light was still moving outward, that is, before it had slowed so much that it would fall back to the star. This is like the situation of a missile launched from a planet's surface at less than escape velocity. If a target is sufficiently close to the surface, it can be hit by the missile, but targets much farther away are safe, since the missile will be slowed, stopped, and pulled back to the planet by its gravity. The problem with this approach when it comes to light, however, is that Einstein's special theory of relativity assures us that the speed of light, unlike the speed of a missile or any other massive object, is constant. It *cannot* be slowed down.

Schwarzschild's approach was different. He focused on the fact that, according to the general theory of relativity, space-time is warped in the presence of mass—this is what we know as gravity. *Time* flows more slowly in a gravitational field; the stronger the gravity, the slower the flow of time, as we have seen. Remember now that light travels as energy waves that can be described by two numbers: the frequency (the number of waves that pass a given point in space each second) and the wavelength (the distance between the crest of one wave and the crest of the next). Since the overall speed of light is constant, the lower the frequency is, the longer the wavelength must be. It is clear that frequency is determined in part by the flow of time at the point where the light wave is emitted, since frequency is a measure of waves *per second*. Now a star has a given amount of gravity, that is, it has a particular amount of power to warp space-time. But, in the prime of its life, it also has a given size. The huge amount of burning, exploding gas in the star's interior exerts enough pressure to keep the star "inflated," counteracting the star's tendency to collapse under its own gravity. But as a star ages, it uses up more and more of its nuclear fuel. The more it uses up, the less pressure the thermonuclear reaction exerts inside, and the more the star's gravity wins the battle to collapse the mass of the star into a smaller and denser package. Since the strength of gravity is determined by the mass of an object and by how close you are to the object, as the star's mass collapses into a smaller and smaller region, the star's surface is closer and closer to its core, and thus the gravity at the surface increases more and more. As the gravitational field at the surface of the star grows stronger, and the flow of time grows more sluggish, the frequency of the light waves diminishes and their wavelength increases more and more. We have seen elsewhere that as the wavelength of light increases, the light is red-shifted, that is, its color appears redder, since red light has a longer wavelength than light of other colors. In cases where the star's mass is sufficiently large and its diameter is sufficiently small, its gravitational field becomes so strong that it creates an *event horizon*. This is a region where any matter that enters will be

drawn by gravity into the star and *never can escape it again.*
Additionally, and more importantly, no energy of any kind can
get out,[10] since the huge gravitational effect inside the event
horizon effectively freezes time and thus infinitely stretches the
wavelength of any energy emitted. This infinite stretching of
wavelength essentially drains all the energy out of the wave. In
somewhat more technical parlance, the black hole red-shifts
the energy right out of existence.

This is as far as my explanation of general relativity can
go. A story (perhaps apocryphal) is told about a comment made
to the great British astronomer Sir Arthur Eddington (whose
1919 expedition demonstrated gravitational lensing) to the
effect that only three people in the world really understood general relativity. Eddington is said to have not replied for a
moment, and, when questioned, to have said, "I am trying to
think who the third person is!"[11] The details of the theory are
probably among the most difficult ideas human beings have
ever developed. But these few general ideas—the curvature of
space-time, which accounts for both gravitational "attraction"
and the slowing of time in a gravitational field, and the strange
characteristics of black holes—seem a sufficient base for our
nontechnical understanding of the theory. I want to make a few
brief comments now on the implications of general relativity for
Jewish metaphor.

JEWISH METAPHORS FROM GENERAL RELATIVITY

In the discussion of special relativity and the use of light as a
metaphor for God, I suggested that God-as-Light does not age,
or even experience time, since, according to Brian Greene, photons do not age. We can now return to this idea from a somewhat different direction. Remember that according to general
relativity, the presence of mass or energy warps the space-time

of the universe, and that one effect of the warping is the slowing of time in the area. The greater the mass or energy, the stronger the gravity, and the more severe the warping. If we imagine God to be pure energy, then once again we see that time, for God, would proceed at a far slower pace than it would for the rest of the universe. In fact, if we imagine God's power being sufficiently strong, we can imagine the gravitational warping of space-time around God being so pronounced that it would create an event horizon, like that which surrounds a black hole, around God. Remember that one of the primary features of a black hole is that (virtually) no signals can escape it. It is hidden from the rest of the universe, cloaked in its event horizon. Astronomers can detect its presence by observing its gravitational effect on other objects in the universe, but it cannot be observed directly.

The idea that God is hidden, cloaked, and unknowable is an ancient one, and its evolution in Jewish thought has an interesting history. It has no place in the earliest collective memories of the Jewish people, those memories being of a God who chooses to reveal the divine self to the Jews and to enter into a covenant relationship (in Hebrew, a *brit*) with them. So, for example, with both Abraham and Moses, it is God who initiates the contact. In Abraham's case, God suddenly speaks to Abraham and, without even an introduction, tells him to leave his ancestral homeland and go to the land that God will show him, there to become a great nation (see Gen. 12:1–3). Similarly, in Moses's case, God accosts Moses from inside a burning bush and instructs him—this time after a proper introduction—to lead the Israelites out of Egyptian slavery (see Ex. 3). Neither of these figures sought God; rather, in both cases God took the initiative to interact with them. Given these earliest experiences that seem so clearly to demonstrate God's desire to be in contact with us, it is somewhat surprising to find God threatening the Israelites toward the end of Deuteronomy:

The Eternal said to Moses: When you are lying with your
fathers, this people will rise up and go whoring after the
foreign gods of the land into which they are coming.
They will leave Me and break My covenant which I have
made with them. On that day, My anger will burn
against them. I shall leave them *and I shall hide My face
from them.* They shall be consumed, and many evils and
troubles will find them. And they will say, on that day, "Is
it not because our God is not in our midst that these
evils have found us?" *Yet I will keep my face hidden* on
that day, because of the evil they have done in turning
after other gods. (Deut. 31:16–18)

This clear expression of God's anger at the people is the
first of many such expressions in the Bible. The hiding of God's
face (or, to avoid the discomfort at such anthropomorphic language, God's presence) becomes a standard biblical response to
Israelite disloyalty or infidelity to the relationship with God.[12]
Apparently, according to this earliest phase of the Jewish people's imagining, God initially wished to enter into a relationship
with them, but insisted that the relationship be an exclusive
one. When they violated the exclusiveness of the bond, God
responded angrily and punitively by hiding from them, that is,
turning away, not paying attention, and, consequently, with-
drawing the loving protection that they had been shown before
their infidelity. God's hiddenness is a response to their sinful-
ness and, we assume, can be reversed by their repentance.

This image of divine hiddenness, however, does not seem
to me to be connected with the metaphor of the hiddenness of
a black hole. The biblical image is one of a God who *chooses*
to be concealed from the people and who can just as easily
choose to emerge from hiding and reconnect with the people,
when they resolve to be faithful to the covenant. Hiddenness is
not in God's nature; it is merely a form of punishment that

God can elect to employ, at will. This model of hiddenness has been invoked by various thinkers in their attempts to grapple with human evil in general and the Holocaust in particular. The great twentieth-century philosopher Martin Buber suggested that the Holocaust represented divine hiddenness, which he called an "eclipse of God."[13] The term is an interesting one to me, because it invokes an astronomical metaphor, but the metaphor is problematic. As Buber himself points out, "An eclipse of the sun is something that occurs between the sun and our eyes, not in the sun itself."[14] In other words, the language of "eclipse" suggests that nothing has changed in the sun (or in God) but that some other object (or force) has interposed itself between the sun and us, blocking the light temporarily. The hiddenness of God as imagined biblically, on the other hand, results from a decision made by God to "not shine" for some period of time. Leaving aside the problems with the metaphor of eclipse, however, there are still numerous theological questions left starkly unanswered by the use of divine hiddenness in explaining the Holocaust. They are summed up in a blistering litany in a recent book entitled *God and Evil*, by David Birnbaum. A small excerpt will suffice to communicate the tone of his challenge:

> If the *Hester* [i.e., hiddenness] was punishment, for what sin(s)? Were six million people, including a million children, so guilty? Was a warning given, and, if not, why not? Even if the forebears were the sinners, was the denouement commensurate? Under what possible moral schema should innocents born during the Holocaust period be forced to pay so horribly for others' sins?[15]

These questions and others like them are the classic building blocks of the problem of resolving God's presence/power/

goodness with the existence of evil. As I have pointed out before, the questions are virtually unchanged since the days of Job. The central problem is that all these queries rest on an assumption that God makes decisions, to punish or reward, to be revealed or hidden, and so on. It is in this incomprehensible divine decision making that most of us get so tangled, frustrated, and angry. The next stage in the historical development of the idea of a hidden God may relieve some of these feelings of frustration and anger. It also resonates more clearly, I think, with the metaphor of the black hole. This is the stage of the Kabbalah, or Jewish mystical tradition, in which the essence of God is seen as being completely transcendent, that is, completely unavailable to human perception or knowledge. In contrast to the position of the biblical and rabbinic sources, which see divine hiddenness as a choice made by God at certain times in response to human behavior, the medieval mystics saw hiddenness as a defining element of God's very nature. God does not *choose* to be hidden, any more than humans *choose* to be mortal. In his initial description of this essential divine concealment, Gershom Scholem writes:

> [W]hile the living God, the God of religion of whom these writings [i.e., Bible and Talmud] bear witness, has innumerable names ... the *deus absconditus* [literally, "hidden God"], the God who is hidden in His own self, can only be named in a metaphorical sense and with the help of words which, mystically speaking, are not real names at all. The favorite formulae of the early Spanish kabbalists ... [include] "Root of all Roots," "Great Reality," "Indifferent Unity," and, above all, *En Sof*. The latter designation reveals the impersonal character of this aspect of the hidden God from the standpoint of man.[16]

Earlier, in my exploration of special relativity, I suggested that the ancient metaphor of God as Light might be reunderstood by reference to a modern understanding of the electromagnetic spectrum. The various wavelengths of energy that comprise that spectrum could be likened to the kabbalistic notion of the *sefirot,* the accessible, knowable emanations of divinity. Each has its own characteristics, but they all share two characteristics: First, they are all forms of the *non*infinite and, therefore, knowable aspect of God; and second, they are distinct and separate from the infinite and, therefore, fundamentally unknowable essence of God, or *En Sof.* Now, with reference to the metaphor of a black hole, which so severely warps space-time in its immediate area as to conceal it utterly from the rest of the universe, we return to this mystical twofold notion of divinity. On the one hand is a visible, accessible aspect of God, with which religious human beings can interact and which we can describe and discuss. This is the creative power in the universe, that which brings the world and us into being and sustains us. It is closely analogous to the spectrum of electromagnetic radiation, including visible light and all the other forms of nonvisible energy. The spectrum of energy is indeed responsible, directly or indirectly, for the creation and sustenance of the life of the universe. Its power is absolute and absolutely beyond us, but it is by no means infinite. We can understand it in greater and greater detail, although we can never match it or exceed it. This power is related to God, attached to God, but it is not the essence of God. On the other hand is the essential nature of God, the unknowable, hidden God, *En Sof. En Sof* is completely self-contained, without reference to the rest of the universe, although the universe may be aware of its existence. This is analogous to the black hole, the ultimate mystery.

One may justifiably ask what the purpose of such astrophysical metaphors might be. What is gained by comparing

God to light or to a black hole? I suggest that what is gained is
a potential reduction in our anger at God. There is a good deal
of talk about how angry people are at God for God's silence
and inaction in the face of tragedy and cruelty. The two
metaphors we have explored here seem to me to cut the legs out
from under such anger, at least to some extent. If we liken God
to light (in all its visible and nonvisible forms) it becomes less
meaningful to hold God responsible, or to rage at God, for
tragedies, whether they be natural or of human design. If someone locks me in a closet, or blindfolds me, I do not hold the
light responsible for not penetrating the darkness that surrounds me. Nor does the fact that shadows exist, or that people sometimes construct and use windowless dungeons, in any
way diminish the beauty or the life-giving properties of light.
And if we liken God to a black hole, we see how little sense it
would make to curse the black hole for not revealing its secrets!
If the nature of the phenomenon is to be concealed and
absolutely shrouded in mystery, then we may wonder about it,
think and dream about it, and be amazed by it, but we are kidding ourselves if we assume that the phenomenon will ever, "in
its great love and mercy," reveal itself.

Of course, the disadvantage of thinking about God in
these ways is that many of the metaphorical assumptions with
which we have lived for centuries have to be questioned, modified, or given up altogether. But that is the heart of the process
that I have been exploring all along: the shift in metaphors. If
God is a king, and the king refuses to talk to me, then there is
some chance that I can convince him to change his mind and
decide to talk. Given what I know of human nature, I assume
that a human king (and thus, by analogy, a divine king) can
choose to talk or be silent, to remain secluded in the palace or
go out among his subjects, to protect his people or abandon
them. These assumptions, obviously, make far less sense if I use
a different metaphor, for example, light, instead of king, when

I imagine God. Such a shift from highly personal, anthropo-morphic metaphors to more natural ones will raise its own questions, most notably the question of whether one can have a relationship with an impersonal force of nature. Since this vast question relates not only to relativity, but to virtually every topic addressed in these pages, it is best left for consideration later on.

6

STRING THEORY
Tying It All Together

A CONFLICT AT THE HEART OF PHYSICS

From the very outset, my goal has been to mine the treasures of modern physics for new Jewish metaphors. This goal made it impossible to avoid relativity, which changed the way we think about the "stage" on which we play out our lives, the backdrops called time and space. By the same token, it was impossible not to address the mystery and weirdness of quantum theory, which describes the behavior of the smallest players on the stage. Both these fundamental theories about how reality is put together leave the contemporary nonscientist thinker reeling as he or she tries to get comfortable with a number of bizarre assertions about existence that not only lie outside our everyday experience but fly in the face of our gut sense of how the "stuff" of the universe is put together. What we will now discover is that, as startling as the insights of relativity and quantum theory are, their mutual incompatibility and the challenges it raises are even more so. The incompatibility will be addressed by a fairly new, unproven, and incomplete theory called string theory, which is, perhaps not surprisingly, every bit as strange as the two earlier theories it seeks to reconcile. In this chapter I describe string theory and, as always, consider what implications it has for Jewish life, thought, and belief.[1]

First of all, we must reveal the conflict, or incompatibility, between the worldviews of relativity and quantum theory. General relativity, in its portrait of gravity, assumes that the space-time stage on which the universe plays is, in the absence of matter and energy, flat and calm. This flatness is warped, or deformed, by the presence of matter or energy (which are merely different forms of the same stuff), and this warping or curvature of space-time is gravity. General relativity describes massive bodies, such as planets, stars, and galaxies, and their interactions to an astonishing degree of accuracy. Quantum theory, on the other hand, is interested in describing only the tiniest particles of the universe—subatomic particles, atoms, and perhaps the odd grain of dust, but nothing larger. On these levels, its predictions are also breathtakingly accurate. As we have seen, the picture it presents of reality is one of a seething, roiling turmoil of activity. This frenzy, according to the uncertainty principle, characterizes even "empty" space. When examined on a sufficiently tiny size scale, and a sufficiently brief time scale, such "emptiness" is filled with particle-antiparticle pairs that constantly pop into existence and annihilate each other. The smaller the area considered, and the shorter the time span, the more turbulent this "quantum foam"[2] is. We experience space-time as flat and calm because, on average, the energy associated with the spontaneous appearance of particles and antiparticles cancels out as the members of each particle-antiparticle pair annihilate one another, so *on average*, and on large enough space scales and time scales, "nothing" is happening.

A problem arises between these two theories when an object both has a large mass and is tiny. This unusual pairing of traits occurs in at least two places: the singularity at the very center of a black hole and the very first moment of the Big Bang. In such situations, and in any other cases of great mass but tiny size, both general relativity and quantum theory must be applied, the former because it is the only way to account for the effects of gravity, and the latter because it is the only way to account for the behavior of very tiny objects. But when the two theories are applied together, they yield results that are mathematically absurd and impossible. Mathematical issues notwithstanding, it is easy to imagine the problem based on the two descriptions of space-time laid out earlier. General relativity can only be useful in describing the gravitational effects and behaviors of a large object if it assumes a flat, calm space-time, which will then be deformed by the presence of mass or energy (remember the flat rubber sheet and the bowling ball). But when a tiny object also has great mass, quantum theory comes along with its picture of a frenzied, foaming space-time. Suddenly, the tiny area of the rubber sheet, onto which we are about to place our fantastically tiny but hugely heavy bowling ball, is not flat but constantly undulating, bucking, twisting, and shivering. It seems impossible to predict what effect the presence of the mini–bowling ball will have!

At first glance, it is not clear why this incompatibility between quantum theory and general relativity should be such a problem. Why can't physics be content with one theory that works brilliantly when it comes to predicting the behavior of big things, like celestial bodies, and another that works equally well when it comes to predicting the behavior of very small things? After all, there are few instances in which both systems actually come into play, since generally things that are large have great mass, and things that are tiny have very little mass. And it seems rather safe and even reasonable to disregard the two examples mentioned—the Big Bang and the singularities at the centers of black holes—because neither of them can really be examined. The Big Bang, as a unique, onetime event very far in the past, need not concern us too much, nor should we worry a lot about the singularity at the center of each black hole, since, by definition, we can never know anything about such a singularity as it is completely concealed by its event horizon cloak. Nevertheless, physicists have yearned for decades for a theory that will unite gravity and quantum theory. This yearning, in and of itself, is an intriguing phenomenon.

IN SEARCH OF ONENESS

Most of the physicists whose works I have read appear to *need* to find a unity among the forces of nature and the different theories that describe and explain them. This word *need* ought not be taken lightly. This deep need is rooted in a fervent *belief*—likewise a word to be taken seriously—that the whole universe operates with a single set of principles, rather than with multiple sets. Consider the following passage in astronomer John Barrow's book *Theories of Everything*:

> As complexity has grown, so has physics fragmented into specializations, which in turn have found themselves partitioned into manageable pieces. Each has enjoyed its own successes in building up mathematical theories of the different fundamental forces of Nature. … The most striking aspect of these theories … is that until only recently they have been distinct in form and content, each compartmentalized from the others.... This goes against the grain of our belief in the unity of Nature.[3]

The last sentence is a powerful statement of faith. It seems to be based not in any empirical observation that everything in nature functions according to a single set of rules, for in fact, casual observation suggests just the opposite. Rather, it is based in a fundamental conviction that there *must* be a single set of rules, perhaps even a single rule, at the root of everything. This conviction is, to say the least, rather surprising. A faith that does not flow from observational data, but that flows instead from an intuitive belief that the world is ultimately grounded in oneness rather than twoness, sounds far more similar to religion than to science. Science normally proceeds from observation of the world to a deep understanding of what lies behind that which we observe. Religion, on the other hand, often holds firmly to a belief that seems to fly in the face of what is observed. For example, when people die, observation suggests that their lives are over. We know that they stop responding and behaving in ways that we characterize as signifying "aliveness," and we know that, without special chemical treatment, their bodies decompose and disappear in a matter of months. Nevertheless, religions of many sorts have clung fiercely to some version of a belief that there is another stage of life after death.

Such a belief, and many others like it, are often characterized as "irrational," convictions that stand outside the standard scientific practice of observing the world and drawing conclusions that fit the observations. Religion in general is often criticized, and sometimes even mocked, because it is so irrational. Yet Barrow, a serious scientist, expresses a deep faith that the universe, at its core, has a single set of rules, not a double set. Observation suggests that the opposite is the case. And experimentation suggests that each set of rules (those of general relativity and those of quantum mechanics) is "correct" and "true" for the realm in which it is applied. And still Barrow—and many others—persist in a belief in the unity of nature.

In fairness to the workings of science, it must be said that this belief is not based (at least not solely based) on some irrational gut feeling, but on an abiding belief in the truth of mathematics. Apparently, when one tries to apply both quantum mechanics and general relativity to a single set of data, one gets quantum probabilities (remember, these are the probabilities that a particular particle will be at a particular spot at a given moment) that are infinite. And since any probabilistic phenomenon can never have a probability greater than one (since a probability of one means that there is a 100 percent chance that a particular outcome will occur, and you simply can't have a greater chance than that), such results point to a flaw in the theory, if one believes deeply in the truth of mathematics. But it must also be noted that the language of physicists often implies that their faith is not based entirely on a belief in the rational truth of mathematical theory. After admitting that some physicists do not worry too much about the incompatibility of quantum mechanics and general relativity, Brian Greene writes:

> There are other physicists, however, who are deeply unsettled by the fact that the two foundational pillars of physics as we know it are at their core fundamentally incompatible.... The incompatibility, they argue, points to an essential flaw in our understanding of the physical universe. This opinion rests on an unprovable but profoundly felt view that the universe, if understood at its deepest and most elementary level, can be described by a logically sound theory whose parts are harmoniously united.[4]

From the standpoint of traditional Jewish thought and belief, one can hardly criticize this "unprovable" faith that there must be a single principle at work in the universe, since it has been shared by most Jewish thinkers throughout history. The prophet Isaiah quotes God as describing himself as the one and only God "who fashions light and creates darkness, makes peace and creates evil; I am Adonai who does all these" (Is. 45:7). Such a statement has generally been understood as a polemic against those who would hold the opposite view, based much more firmly in observations of the world, that light and darkness, or peace and evil, represent two fundamental realms that oppose each other by their very nature. The same polemic can be detected in the very ancient Jewish claim that Satan (the word itself is Hebrew—see the first chapter of Job) is not an enemy or opponent of God but rather a servant of God, on the payroll of the divine court, as it were. The image is developed more fully in Jewish folklore: A soul is judged, after death, in the divine court, where there are two angels running the proceedings, a prosecutor and a defender. The job of the former is to "convict" the soul, while that of the latter is to secure an acquittal. But, as is the case in our own courts, both sides work for the court, and, ultimately, the judge (that is, God) is in charge of both the prosecution and the defense.[5] And the rejection of all dualism that is so clear in the Bible and the folk accounts of the proceedings of God's court is certainly at the heart of much of Jewish philosophy. Moses Maimonides, for example, is unequivocal in his conviction that, at its very core, the creative power that gave rise to the world and keeps it functioning is absolutely one.

The deep belief that the universe, at its core, must function according to only *one* set of rules has led physicists to search tirelessly for a single theory that will overcome the apparent dualism of a world in which both quantum mechanics and general relativity are at work (even though, for all practical purposes, they do not both function in any given situation). There are at least two terms for such a unifying theory, namely, a TOE (theory of everything) and a GUT (grand unified theory). According to some physicists, string theory is a good candidate.

WHAT IS STUFF MADE OF?

For as long as human beings have been wondering about the world, we have been fascinated by the question, "What are things made of?" A bit of careful observation and critical thought reveals that the "stuff" that fills our world is probably not "elementary"; it can be broken down into simpler stuff. That stuff, in turn, can be reduced to simpler stuff, and so on and on. Is there a limit? Is there a point at which we are dealing with *the* simplest stuff of the universe?

From the time of ancient Greece, when many thought that the entire universe was made up of different combinations of the four elements (earth, air, fire, and water), not much progress was made in answering this question until the early twentieth century. During the last hundred years, however, tremendous progress has been made.[6] Without going into too much detail, the progression was something like this: The century started with a sense that everything was made of atoms (ironically, the word *atom* comes from the Greek meaning "indivisible"), but that soon gave way to a picture of the atom's internal structure of a nucleus with electrons going around it. That was followed by the discovery that the nucleus was made up of two different kinds of particles: positively charged ones called *protons* and others with no electrical charge called *neutrons*. In the 1960s, as particle physics began to blossom, it was finally determined that protons and neutrons were not elementary but were made up of simpler particles called *quarks* (a name chosen from the writings of James Joyce by Murray Gell-Mann, who won the Nobel Prize in 1969 for his work on quarks). Quarks come in six "flavors," and each of those comes in three "colors." (Note that these terms are simply imaginative and cute ways to distinguish elementary particles; they have nothing really to do with color or flavor as we experience them. It is interesting to see in this regard how playful—and filled with metaphor—the language of physics is.) Meanwhile, two other particles were discovered, the *neutrino* (also called the *electron-neutrino*, to distinguish it from other neutrino varieties) and the *muon*, both of which bear some resemblance to the electron. Finally, we must add the tau particle, the tau-neutrino, and the muon-neutrino. Each of these particles has its own characteristic mass. The least massive (the electron-neutrino) has a mass less than 10^{-8} (.00000001) times the mass of a proton, while the most massive is 189 times the mass of a proton. It is important to realize that many of these elementary particles are not normally found in ordinary matter, but only appear in the extremely high-energy collisions of particles in particle accelerators in physics labs—and presumably in the similarly high-energy state of the very early universe (shortly after the Big Bang).

This gaggle of elementary particles does not, however, tell the whole story of nature on its most elementary level. The particles that are the fundamental building blocks of the stuff of the universe interact through four basic forces of nature, namely, gravity, the electromagnetic force (which we experience as the basis of electricity and of magnetism), the strong nuclear force (which holds together the quarks that comprise a proton or neutron), and the weak nuclear force (which is responsible for the radioactive decay of radioactive elements like uranium and plutonium). Each of these forces is also associated with a particle that "carries" or transmits that force. The electromagnetic force is carried by a particle called the photon (which we have seen elsewhere described as the smallest possible package of light), the strong nuclear force by the gluon (so called because it glues the quarks together), the weak nuclear force by the weak gauge boson, and gravity by the graviton (which, unlike the other three, is theorized to exist but has not yet been observed experimentally). Three of these force-messenger particles have no mass, while the weak gauge boson has a mass of

86 or 97 times (there are two types) that of a proton. This entire set of matter particles and force particles is known as the *standard model.*

It is not hard to see why this theory of the elementary or fundamental stuff of the universe is so unsatisfying. The sheer number of particles that are claimed to be fundamental is troubling. Physicists for at least the last quarter of a century have searched for ways to simplify the picture. Intuitively, they believe that there must be a more basic way of understanding things that will involve fewer basic ingredients. Ideally, there ought to be a way of understanding the system as the product of just *one* basic ingredient that somehow appears in different guises, or assumes different forms, depending on the circumstances. In addition to the unsettling nature of the number of different particles, the wide range of their masses is also a source of consternation. Why should the universe, on its "simplest" level, be composed of so many different kinds of things?

As I ponder the discomfort and dissatisfaction that physicists express when asking this critical question, I imagine they must mirror the feelings of the early monotheists many centuries ago. All around them were people whose best analysis of the world was that it was controlled, on its most basic level, by a panoply of gods. One controlled the sea, another the sun, another the mountains, and so on and on. Each had its own characteristics, its own abode, and its own strengths and weaknesses. Each interacted with the others in complex ways. But among the societies in which such views prevailed, there must have been some who intuitively felt that the world must be simpler. Eventually this intuition developed into a belief that there was just one god controlling the entire system. This intuition, it should be noted, is not based on observation. Indeed, observation suggests a polytheistic model. There seems to be little to unite the forces of sunshine and the forces of thunderstorms. They seem, in fact, to be in constant tension. Sometimes one "wins," while at other times, the other "wins." A monumental leap of faith was required to imagine that a single deity controlled both.

FROM PARTICLES TO STRINGS

String theory, which was first investigated in 1974 and first proposed as a grand unified theory in 1984, replaces all the many particles of the standard model with a single fundamental thing: a string. These strings are one-dimensional, vibrating filament loops, on average about Planck length, that is, about 10^{-33} centimeters in length. Because of their extremely small size, they behave like point particles, or particles with no size, and have typically been treated that way (in the standard model, for example). But in fact, they are not points, but strings. The strings are not made of any substance; that is to say, they are not composed of anything we could identify—they *are* the fundamental substance of the universe. Curiously, it is not clear to me, as a nonscientist, if it could even be said with certainty that the strings are made of energy or of matter. A string vibrating in one way is labeled a "photon," by definition a packet of energy, while a string vibrating in another way gets the label "top quark" and is clearly a chunk (albeit a very tiny one) of matter. Yet the two strings are the same "stuff." This lack of clarity about the string's composition is important, for it may indicate the extent to which, on a fundamental level, the distinction between the two categories, matter and energy, blurs. We have learned this insight from Einstein's famous equation $E = mc^2$, which gives us a way to see that matter can be converted into energy and vice versa. But with strings the truth of the interchangeability of matter and energy goes farther, such that it is hard to say whether the strings are made of one or the other! In this way, string theory vastly simplifies the universe, getting rid of the multiplicity of fundamental particles and replacing them with a single element that appears as different particles depending on how it vibrates.

How does string theory resolve the conflict between general relativity and quantum mechanics? It does so, in a way, by cheating. The incompatibility between these two theories only becomes serious when there are significant quantum fluctuations that destroy the smoothly curving picture of space-time required by general relativity. This sort of quantum frenzy only becomes significant, however, on a distance or size scale shorter than Planck length. Since strings are, on average, about Planck length, quantum fluctuation presents no real problem. Brian Greene describes the resolution this way:

> *If the elementary constituent of the universe cannot probe sub-Planck-scale distances, then neither it nor anything made from it can be affected by the supposedly disastrous short-distance quantum undulations....* [O]ne can even say that the supposed tempestuous sub-Planckian quantum undulations *do not exist.*[7]

EXTRA DIMENSIONS

One of the most intriguing features of string theory is the picture it provides of the geometry of reality. Our experience of the world, as we have seen elsewhere, is that everything happens in three dimensions of space and one of time. The three spatial dimensions give us our sense of how the world is put together and how the things in the world relate to one another spatially: "The bird fluttered *down from* the power line and stood *on* the large boulder *next to* the tree." As we read these words, we can easily form a mental picture of the scene's geometry. All the elements of the scene can be visualized in the three-dimensional coordinate system of our everyday experience. But in the 1980s, string theorists searching for a way around some particularly difficult problems in their theory[8] revived a notion of additional spatial dimensions that was first proposed by a Polish mathematician named Theodor Kaluza in 1919.

Kaluza had proposed the existence of a fourth spatial dimension, in addition to the three with which we are familiar. String theory, however, requires that the universe have *nine* spatial dimensions and one time dimension,[9] instead of the three spatial dimensions and one time dimension to which we are accustomed in everyday life. Of the nine spatial dimensions, three are large—those are the three with which we are familiar—and six are curled up very tightly and can only be detected on the tiniest distance scales. These extra curled-up dimensions are mathematical requirements for string theory to work. They have not been experimentally observed, nor can they be (at least with today's technology), since they are detectable on a scale vastly smaller than that which we are able to probe. In fact, it is hard to imagine what they would look like if they were observed, since we cannot think of things in more than three spatial dimensions. According to the string theory view of the birth of the universe, the Big Bang started with a Planck-length-size nugget of "stuff" in which all nine spatial dimensions were equally tiny and equally curled up. Note that even this starting point is unorthodox, since the usual assumption of Big Bang cosmology, as we have discussed, is that the process started with zero size. But string theory does not permit anything to exist with zero size. It claims that the smallest possible thing, a string, is of nonzero size, roughly Planck length. In any event, at about the Planck time, that is, about 10^{-43} seconds after the Big Bang, three of the spatial dimensions began to expand at a tremendous rate, and kept on expanding thereafter, while the other six dimensions remained curled up.[10] All this leaves us with a picture of our world in which we function, on a macroscopic level, in our ordinary three (spatial) dimensions, but in which, on the tiniest subatomic level, the structure of reality also includes six more curled-up dimensions. This picture is important because the string theory view of the universe includes strings that wind around these tiny, curled-up dimensions. These wound strings have different properties from the unwound variety.

When Einstein formulated general relativity, the theory was based on the geometry of space-time. In string theory we find, once again, that geometry plays a central role. Apparently, the six tiny, curled-up dimensions cannot curl up in just any old way. Rather, their theoretical properties require that they curl up into a class of shapes called Calabi-Yau shapes, or Calabi-Yau spaces. These strange and beautiful six-dimensional mathematical creatures are named for two mathematicians, Eugenio Calabi and Shing-Tung Yau, whose pioneering research into the mathematical characteristics of these shapes has been quite important. The shapes apparently cannot be readily understood without a firm grounding in a great deal of advanced mathematics. Brian Greene's comment on the nontechnical grasp of them leaves us only one option: "Although the mathematics describing Calabi-Yau spaces is intricate and subtle, we can get an idea of what they look like with a picture."[11] And so, I invite you to spend a few moments contemplating figure 6.1 (see p. 194). To me, this image suggests complexity, multilayeredness, a sense of things twisted in on and curled around themselves and one another, with elements wound around elements wound around elements. It feels labyrinthine and tremendously deep, a space that, if we could enter into it, we could explore—or get lost in—for a long, long time without exhausting its possibilities or discovering all its hidden features. This is the shape of reality.

ANCIENT JEWISH STRINGS

When I first heard of string theory and briefly considered its place in the world of Jewish metaphor, I immediately thought of *tzitzit*, the stringlike ritual fringes, or tassels, worn on the corners of a garment by some Jews and on the corners of a *tallit*, or prayer shawl. I dismissed the thought as a silly joke, cute but not worth serious consideration. But then a strange thing happened. As I read about string theory, I kept returning to my initial reaction, and each time it seemed a bit less silly and a bit more interesting, so much so that I decided finally to explore the connection seriously. And so, we turn now to *tzitzit*.

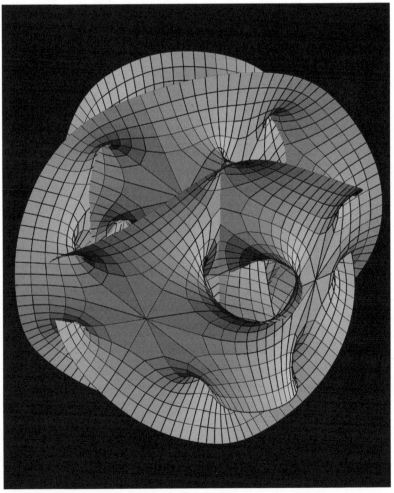

Figure 6.1: One example of a Calabi-Yau space.

The Hebrew word *tzitzit* (the plural form is *tzitziyot*, but it is more common to see the singular form, *tzitzit*, used in a colloquial way as both singular and plural) means simply "fringe." We first hear about fringes in the Bible, in the Book of Numbers, as follows:

> The Eternal said to Moses, "Speak to the Israelites and tell them to make themselves *tzitzit* on the corners of their garments for all their generations, and to put a string of blue [Hebrew: *tekhelet*] on the corner-*tzitzit*. This will be your *tzitzit*: you shall see it and remember all the commandments of the Eternal, and observe them, and not stray after your heart and after your eyes, after which you whore. Thus you shall remember and do all My commandments, and be holy to your God. I am the Eternal, your God, who brought you out of the land of Egypt to be your God. I, the Eternal, am your God. (Num. 15:37–41)

It is impossible to know exactly how this bit of biblical legislation was observed in biblical times, but eventually its observance developed into a very specific set of practices. Although early on the *tzitzit* may have been attached to all garments, or perhaps to all garments with corners, the prevailing custom eventually established that they were attached to just two garments, the *tallit* and the *tallit katan* (often mistranslated as a "small" *tallit*, but in reality, a *tallit* for a young person).[12] The *tallit* is a prayer shawl traditionally worn by men during the morning prayer service, wrapped around the shoulders and occasionally drawn like a hood over the head. The *tallit katan* is a poncholike affair, a rectangular garment with a hole for the head, often worn underneath the shirt, but occasionally, especially among some Hasidic groups, worn over the shirt so that it is visible under the coat. Both the *tallit* and the *tallit katan* have small holes at each corner with *tzitzit* attached through the holes. Generally speaking, neither is worn in the evening or at night because, according to the explanation in the Talmud, the biblical commandment specifically requires that one *see* the *tzitzit*, and this leads to the understanding that they need only be worn during daylight hours, when things are easily seen. It is customary, when reading the above-quoted passage from Numbers 15 (which appears in the prayer book following *Shema Yisrael*) to gather the four *tzitzit* together, wind them around the right index finger, and kiss them at each mention in the passage of the word *tzitzit*. In addition, the *tzitzit* are usually gathered together during the blessing preceding *Shema Yisrael* in the morning service when the words "Bring us in peace from the four corners of the earth" are read.

In ancient times, in accordance with the original biblical law, the *tzitzit* included one strand dyed a specific shade of purplish-blue called *tekhelet*. Most biblical historians identify this dye as having been made from a gland of a particular snail, *Murex trunculus*, found in the shallow waters off the coast of northern Israel and Lebanon. The dye was very expensive, because twelve thousand snails were required to manufacture just 1.4 grams of the stuff; thus it was generally used only by royalty. (Perhaps, in fact, *tekhelet* should be translated in the passage from Numbers 15 as "royal blue.") Thus the *tzitzit* required to be worn by all Jews were a sign, as it were, of their "royal" origins. Rabbinic literature, especially in conjunction with Rosh Hashanah (the New Year) and Yom Kippur (the Day of Atonement), often describes the Jewish people as children of a king, that is, God. During the Roman period, the Jewish population was so impoverished that few could afford even the tiny amount of *tekhelet* required to include one strand in each of the *tzitzit*. That fact, plus the decline of the *tekhelet*-manufacturing industry and the resulting scarcity of the dye, led to a suspension by the talmudic Rabbis of the requirement for *tekhelet* in the *tzitzit*. From that time on, they have been made with only white string.[13]

Although technically there is no difference whatsoever between the religious or symbolic meaning of the *tzitzit* of the *tallit gadol* and those of the *tallit katan*, in fact the two are commonly perceived as being quite different from one another. The reason for this perception is that a very wide variety of Jews occasionally wear a *tallit* during synagogue worship services. The most marginally observant, least frequent synagogue attendee will not think twice about putting on a *tallit* on Yom Kippur or at the Bar or Bat Mitzvah of a son or daughter. In the last few decades, women have also begun wearing a *tallit* in some congregations. The *tallit katan*, on the other hand, is typically worn by only a very narrow sector of the community—men and boys who self-identify as among the most observant and traditional of the Orthodox.

So what does the *tzitzit* have to do with string theory? According to the original biblical passage, the function of the *tzitzit* is to be a memory aid.

> "[Y]ou shall see it and remember all the commandments of the Eternal...." Thus you shall remember and do all My commandments, and be holy to your God. I am the Eternal, your God, who brought you out of the land of Egypt to be your God. (Num. 15:39–41)

How does the *tzitzit* perform its role as memory aid? There are two traditional explanations. The commonsense explanation is that there is nothing specific in the *tzitzit* that makes it useful in this regard, but rather that the arbitrary designation of this particular ritual object as a memory aid makes it so. This makes it the equivalent of the common folk custom of tying a string around one's finger as a reminder of something one wishes to remember. There is nothing inherent in a string tied round a finger that helps us remember, but the mere fact of having tied it there reminds us. The other explanation, more specifically rooted in Jewish tradition, sees the *tzitzit* as specifically and inherently designed as a memory aid. The tradition starts with the fact that every letter in the Hebrew alphabet has a number assigned to it. The first ten letters of the alphabet are the numbers 1 through 10, the next eight go up by increments of 10 (20, 30, 40) to 90, and the last four represent 100, 200, 300, and 400. In this way, any number can be represented by a series of letters, and any combination of letters, or word, has a numerical equivalent. The Hebrew word *tzitzit*, using this system, has the numerical equivalent of 600. Now each *tzitzit* is composed of eight strands of thread, or string (actually, there are four strands, but the way they are doubled over makes them appear to be eight). Furthermore, each *tzitzit* has five knots tied in it. A traditional explanation takes the numerical equivalence of the word *tzitzit*, 600, adds to it the eight strings and the five knots, and comes up with the sum of 613. This is a highly significant number in Jewish tradition; it is the number of commandments in the Torah. Thus the *tzitzit* specifically reminds the wearer of all the commandments, since its name, plus the number of its strings and its knots, add up to the number of commandments.

Neither of these explanations does much for the average contemporary Jew. The first explanation is likely to evoke the response that if the *tzitzit* is simply an arbitrary mnemonic, then it is no more (or less) effective than any other mnemonic, and in that case the strangeness, antiquity, and "superorthodox" feel of the thing are good reasons to reject it in favor of some more modern, less obtrusive mnemonic. The traditional explanation, although usually greeted as "cute" by those who have never heard it, seems more like a mathematical parlor trick, worthy of cocktail parties but not sufficiently important to take seriously. Besides, most Jews have no desire to be reminded constantly of all 613 commandments,[14] since many of those commandments are seen by most contemporary Jews as largely irrelevant (and occasionally abhorrent) in modern life.

I think string theory may suggest a third understanding of the mnemonic value of *tzitzit*, which is both more modern and more profound than the other two. To arrive at this understanding, we must first have some sense of how *tzitzit* are made and how they are used. To make *tzitzit*, start with 4 strings, 3 of the same length and 1 longer. Put them through the hole in the corner of the garment to which they are being tied with one end of all 4 strings held together, so that at the other end you have 3 strings that are the same length and the additional length of the fourth string hanging loose. Taking each bundle of 4 strings in one hand, you then tie a simple double knot. This results in a bundle of 8 strings, of which 7 are the same length and 1 is longer. Then wrap the longer string in tight, neat coils around the bundle of the other 7 strings, seven times. Split the whole bundle into two bundles of 4 strings each, and again tie a double knot. Repeat the process, this time wrapping the long string around the bundle of the other 7 strings eight times. The next repetition has eleven coils, and the final repetition has thirteen coils.[15] The whole thing is finished off with a final double knot. (See figure 6.2.) Thus the *tzitzit* is made of twisted cords (which if examined under a magnifying glass, are seen to be made in turn of twisted fibers) that are twisted and knotted around each other in a very complex pattern, most of which we do not see with a casual inspection. Then, during the part of the morning service in which we read the original biblical passage pertaining to the *tzitzit*, we gather all four *tzitzit* (from the four corners of the *tallit*) together and wrap them around the right index finger (see figure 6.3). It is this bundled, twisted, coiled, wrapped, and knotted thing that we look at when the text says, "you shall see *it* and remember all the commandments of the Eternal."

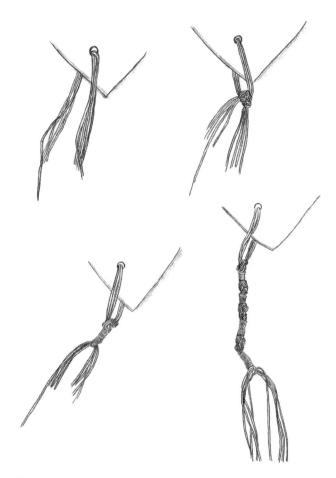

Figure 6.2: Tying *tzitzit*.

TZITZIT AS METAPHOR

What, exactly, do I see when I look at the bundled *tzitzit* coiled around my finger, and what does it mean to me? Before reading on, go back and compare figure 6.3 to figure 6.1. As I have read about string theory and its requirement for six curled-up, tiny spatial dimensions, the *tzitzit* have become a symbol of the multidimensionality and hiddenness that characterize all things. As I examine the knotted, twisted, curled bundle, I am acutely aware of its intricacy. I can clearly see some of the grosser levels of its coils, but as I examine it, I understand that there are many, many finer layers of twists, turns, and coils that I cannot see. Some of these are simply obscured because they lie underneath the parts I can see. I know they are there, and I could reveal them if I were to dissect the *tzitzit* with a sharp knife, or simply unwind them from my finger and untie and uncoil their strings. But others would still be hidden from my view, even if I were to untie my *tzitzit* so completely that only a pile of tangled string remained. Those levels of twists and coils are hidden because they exist on a scale beyond my ability to detect! If I look *very* closely, I can see that each

Figure 6.3: *Tzitzit* coiled around a worshipper's finger during the recitation of *Shema Yisrael*. This photograph should be compared to the Calabi-Yau space illustrated in figure 6.1. On an impressionistic level, the similarities between the two are remarkable.

strand of the *tzitzit* is manufactured by twisting together finer strands, but I know that, on a microscopic level, the twisting continues on increasingly fine levels of structure. If the strands are wool, which is most often the case, they are made of very complex organic molecules. The structure of these molecules is described as follows:

> Wool is composed of more than 20 amino acids which form long chains, or polymers, of protein. Two different types of cells, the para-cortex and the ortho-cortex, develop into a three-dimensional corkscrew pattern, or helical crimp, of great elasticity.[16]

Personally, I find this description rather technical and uninspiring. This is not the case, however, when I contemplate the accompanying drawing, figure 6.4.

When I first came across this image, I was awed by its complexity, by its layers upon layers of twists, coils, and unseen windings. It is remarkable to me that all this complex structure is hidden from the eye. The finest woolen thread that I might be able to see, or hold in my hand, or wind around my finger, contains within it all these layers of nested structural detail. Bundles of cells containing bundles of cells containing bundles of cells. Right-handed coils inside left-handed coils. All these features, invisible to the naked eye, give the wool its characteristics—elasticity, moisture absorption, insulation, and so on.

Yet even this microscopic detail is gross and huge in comparison to the submicroscopic structure deep inside it. The scale of it all is humbling: The finest level, at the top of figure 6.4, is .001 microns, or 10^{-7} centimeters. But the Planck length, the scale on which fundamental strings make up the universe of tiny, curled-up dimensions and Calabi-Yau spaces, is 10^{-33} centimeters, or twenty-six orders of magnitude smaller than the tiniest microscopic detail of the wool fiber! On that level again,

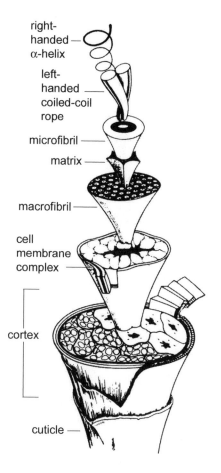

right-handed α-helix

left-handed coiled-coil rope

microfibril

matrix

macrofibril

cell membrane complex

cortex

cuticle

Figure 6.4: The microscopic structure of a wool fiber.

it is the specific structure, in this case the vibrational resonance patterns of the strings, that gives the "stuff" its characteristics, including whether it is what we know as matter or what we know as energy. All this in a simple length of woolen string.

What does it mean when the biblical/liturgical text says, "you shall see *it* and remember all the commandments of the Eternal" when the "it" that we see has so many microscopic and submicroscopic layers of hidden twists and coils? Or, to put the question a different way, what is the relationship between the *tzitzit*, as we now understand it, and the *mitzvot*, or commandments, that, according to much of Jewish tradition, lie at the heart of our relationship with God? How are the ritual fringes a useful mnemonic on a metaphorical level? Part of the answer is that the *mitzvot* are by no means straightforward or clear. In other words, our sense of *tzitzit* as a powerful symbol of a multidimensional, multilayered reality clearly undercuts any claim that our obligations in relationship with God are simple. A complex object cannot symbolize a simple reality. In fact, usually we construct symbols that are *simpler* than the realities to which they point. A flag, for example, is vastly simpler than the nation for which it stands, with all its history, political jockeying, and subtle ideological compromises. So initially, I assume at least that the system of *mitzvot* is as complex as, or more complex than, the *tzitzit*. We are not talking about a simple set of rules, be they 613 in number, or 10, or any other number, promulgated by a divine authority for us to hear and obey. The reality *must* be subtler and more complex. The *tzitzit* as symbol, and string theory as system, suggest that no matter what scale we use to examine a category of *mitzvot*, or a specific mitzvah, there will be a fine structure at a smaller, unseen scale.

But what, exactly, does this mean? Let us focus for a moment on string theory's requirement that there be six tiny, curled-up spatial dimensions in every single element of reality, in addition to the three large dimensions that we commonly experience. This means that whenever we act in the real world, our actions can be understood on two levels. One is the observable level of three large dimensions. I cross from one side of a room to another. I pick up a book and move it to a different shelf. I throw a stone into a pond. These actions can all be perceived as happening in, and affecting, the three-dimensional world with which we are familiar. But they also are happening in, and perhaps affecting, the tiny, curled-up world of the six extra dimensions that we cannot observe. If this is true of crossing a room, moving a book, or tossing a stone, it is equally true for performing *mitzvot*—giving *tzedakah*, comforting mourners, or telling the story of the Exodus from Egypt. Each action has consequences and effects in the observable world of three dimensions, but also in the unobservable world.

If so, we might ask: If the consequences and effects are completely and utterly unobservable, do they matter? Are they important? Should we care? This, I think, can be answered in two different ways, depending largely on the predilection and style of the person making the choice. The pragmatic answer is that wholly unobservable effects of actions can be ignored. If they have no impact on the world that we experience, we need not bother ourselves about them. If your friend is sick and you perform the mitzvah of *bikkur cholim*, or visiting the sick, your action has a whole bunch of consequences. Your sick friend may feel a bit better because he or she knows you care. Your action may serve as an example, influencing others to visit their sick friends. Your sick friend, when he or she recovers, may feel more a part of a caring community and thus may be more likely to respond constructively to the future suffering of others. These are all observable consequences. The pragmatist will argue that these are the important consequences of the mitzvah. If there are other consequences, which no one can ever detect, consequences in the tiny, curled-up dimensions of reality, then we can ignore them.

On the other hand, one could disagree with the pragmatist and claim that it is rather superficial to be concerned only with the large, clearly observed, and easily understood consequences of our actions. This approach claims that any action has a vast array of consequences and results, only some of which can be anticipated, observed, and understood. In our exploration of the implications of the butterfly effect (chapter 3), we saw that, like the flapping of a butterfly's wings, our human behavior can

have huge, unintended, and unanticipated results that seem
vastly out of proportion to the scale of what we thought we
were doing. Being aware of this possibility leads us to consider
our actions and measure our words in a far more careful, inten-
tional, and deliberate manner than we might otherwise do.
Now it seems that our awareness of the tiny, curled-up dimensions hidden inside the normal fabric of reality could lead us to
a similar sense of caution and wonder about what we do. Such
awareness is one of the important goals of a religious life in
which there is a sense that human beings are created in the
image of an aware, conscious God. In my discussion of the
recitation of blessings and the Copenhagen interpretation of
quantum mechanics, I stressed the importance of awareness in
the "creation" of reality. Here we see that reality has many layers of fine structure that are invisible to us. A religious tradition
that sees humans as a reflection of a God who is, if nothing else,
conscious of all things should properly provide mechanisms to
make us aware of the effects of all our actions, even on structural levels hidden from us. When we look at the *tzitzit* and
become aware of its multilayered construction, its symbolic
pointing to the existence of tiny, curled-up dimensions of reality, it serves us well as a reminder of God and our sacred obligations, or *mitzvot*.

THE SHAPE OF GOD

One of the more powerful categories of metaphorical language
used in describing the world and our experiences in it is that of
geometry. As noted earlier, geometrical shapes are idealized and
therefore rarely accurate in their description of reality. But their
idealized qualities make them useful metaphorical frameworks
for describing complex phenomena. A good example of this is
the use of the circle. We speak about a circle of friends, or of
the circle of life, or of a process coming full circle. Because of

our familiarity with this beautifully simple geometric shape, the image of a circle communicates volumes about these situations and processes. Thus a "circle of friends" tells us that the links among the friends are unbroken, that each one is connected to the rest, and that there is a certain uniformity, a smoothness and an equality, among the members of the group. We do not mean that this group of friends is standing in a geometrical pattern that is circular.

I make this rather obvious point because religious metaphors regarding the shape of God are, for some people, quite threatening and disturbing. What shape is God? Many religious thinkers would respond dismissively, "What an absurd—if not downright blasphemous—question! God is not a physical thing; therefore it is meaningless to speak of the shape of God." This response, although common, is not all that ancient. Rather, it can be traced back to the tremendous success of Moses Maimonides's twelfth-century Jewish version of Aristotelian philosophy. In Maimonides's "Thirteen Principles" (which can be found in the morning service in just about any traditional prayer book), we read, "I believe with a perfect faith that the Creator, whose name is blessed, is not a physical form, and that no physical accidents[17] apply to him, and that there is nothing resembling him at all." The popular influence of this position, as well as the other elements of the "Thirteen Principles," was strengthened even more by the composition (probably in Rome in the fourteenth century) of the popular liturgical poem/song *Yigdal*, a clever, rhymed setting of Maimonides's principles. It is hard to avoid accepting the belief in God's incorporeality when you sing this song regularly in synagogue, including the verse, "He has no physical image/nor has He physicality."

But in fact, Maimonides's blanket rejection of anything that even suggested the vaguest possibility of corporeality in speaking of God was not universally accepted. The most remarkable example of a different view is the esoteric mystical doctrine known as *Shiur Komah*. This doctrine, the origin of which goes back to perhaps the second century C.E., speculates about the body of God and was replete with fantastic descriptions of the enormous sizes of God's limbs. It was fueled in general by the highly anthropomorphic God language used in the Bible and in particular by the graphic body descriptions found in the biblical book of Song of Songs. The Song of Songs is a beautiful set of graphic and sensual love poems that describe the passionate relationship between a man (possibly a king) and a lovely dark-skinned woman. But the Rabbis of the talmudic period generally saw the book not as a poem about two human lovers but as a poem about the love between God and Israel. The graphic descriptions of the beloved's body in the book, especially in chapter 5, inspired the descriptions of God's body in *Shiur Komah*. Gershom Scholem describes this aspect of *Shiur Komah* as follows:

> The units of measurement are cosmic; the height of the Creator is 236,000 parasangs[18]—according to another tradition, the height of His soles alone is 30 million parasangs. But "the measure of a parasang of God is three miles, and a mile has 10,000 yards, and a yard three spans of His span, and a span fills the whole world, as it is written: Who hath meted out heaven with the span." Plainly, therefore, it is not really intended to indicate by these numbers any concrete length measurements.[19]

The language of *Shiur Komah* inspired and thrilled the mystics, but it appalled most rationalists. The latter group saw such mystical speculations as an affront to the core biblical principle that God was not to be represented as an image of, in the words of the Ten Commandments, "anything in the heavens above, on the earth below, or in the water under the earth"

(Ex. 20:4). Although this law can be read, in its biblical context, as a prohibition against creating any image of anything and then worshipping that image *instead* of God, most Jewish legal interpretations have taken it more loosely to prohibit also the representation of God as any "thing." This interpretation certainly made sense in a world in which Israel's founding theological fathers were fighting against cultures that saw divinity in mountains, storm clouds, planets, stars, and earthly beasts of all kinds. If one were trying to teach the truth of a new doctrine, with monotheism at its heart, then one would certainly object to the portrayal of God in a recognizable form. For if you can represent God as a calf, then someone else can represent God as a sheep or a goat, and monotheism is out the window. The only monotheistically safe position is that God is absolutely unique and unrepresentable by any image of any thing. This was the position that the proponents of *Shiur Komah* seemed to be attacking. The defense against their attack (and against all similar attempts at representational descriptions of God) was expressed in the kind of absolute terms that Maimonides used: There is nothing corporeal about God whatsoever.

In our era, however, the situation has changed. No longer is there any serious danger that anyone will claim that God is a calf or a mountain. Instead, we find ourselves suffering the opposite danger, namely, an impoverishment of God language such that no description has any real substantial meaning for us. Whereas in ancient times the worry was that God metaphors would become too sharp, real, and concrete, in our day the worry is that they have become too dull, faded, and ethereal to inspire. This worry leads me back to my question: What shape is God? Note that I am not asking, "What thing is God shaped like?" but only, "What is God's shape?" There is a big difference. I am asking, if you will, about the geometry of God. This might seem a strange expression, but we have already spoken several times of the geometry of space-time, so perhaps asking about the geometry of God is not so bizarre! Earlier, I suggested that God is fractal shaped. That suggestion led to some inferences about God's essential qualities that I find helpful. For example, it meant that God is characterized by self-similarity and scaling, so that no matter the scale on which we examine God, we find similar shapes.

I now want to add to the geometric description the possibility that God is Calabi-Yau shaped. This is a much more difficult metaphorical geometry to grasp, however, than that of fractals. Fractals surround us in every part of the natural world. We see them in the branching structure of trees and river systems. As soon as someone points out to us the concept of scaling, we run outside and look at the clouds to see a real-life example. The idea of fractals is not strange. Calabi-Yau shapes, on the other hand, are quite alien. There is nothing in the macroscopic world that resembles them or exhibits their properties. They cannot easily be depicted, drawn, or described, since they are six-dimensional shapes and we live in a world of only three large and visible spatial dimensions. And the mathematics that describes them is certainly vastly more subtle and complex than what most of us nonmathematicians can fathom. Why then do I suggest them as metaphors for the geometry of God? Have I not violated my own rule, namely that to be useful, metaphors must draw on familiar things? Perhaps I have, but the transgression at least deserves some explanation.

One of the most intriguing—and frustrating—parts of the human attempt to think about God is the recurring idea that, by definition, our knowledge and understanding of God is quite limited. While we generally imagine God to be infinite, our knowledge must always remain vague and incomplete because we are finite beings, with a finite range of abilities and experiences. Some have suggested that even when we use the now-familiar tool of metaphorical thought and language, the results are incomplete. Most notably, Maimonides devotes a substantial portion of the first part of his great philosophical work, *The Guide for the Perplexed*, to explaining the biblical use of metaphorical language in speaking of God—God sees, hears, smells, sits, and so on. Maimonides insists that these words must be understood, when they apply to God, as having *nothing whatsoever* to do with the same words when they apply to human beings. In other words, we may say, "God saw" and we may say, "My brother-in-law saw" as long as we understand that that the two instances of the word *saw* are not at all similar.

This approach certainly calls into serious question the usefulness of metaphor in speaking about God! If we apply familiar ideas to God, but then insist that those ideas, when applied to God, bear no resemblance at all to the same ideas as applied to human beings, we come perilously close to undermining the entire theory of the use of metaphor. But by using as metaphor an object so alien and mysterious as a Calabi-Yau shape, we may achieve some deeper understanding of our thinking about God, while avoiding Maimonides's worry that people might confuse the metaphoric language applied to God with the same language when applied nonmetaphorically to other things. Thus, to revisit an old example, when we speak of God as king, Maimonides would be concerned that our use of the word not mislead us into thinking that there is any real similarity between human kings and God. God does not have a head on which a crown or, in more authentically Israelite tradition, anointing oil is placed; God does not sit on a large golden chair encrusted with jewels. We avoid all these mistakes in thinking, however, when we use as a metaphor an object of which we have no common experience. To say, "God is Calabi-Yau shaped" does not create in our minds any mistaken notions that God is similar to a usual object of our experience. But since the whole purpose of metaphor is precisely to explain an unknown thing by likening it to a known thing, how is the Calabi-Yau metaphor useful? My answer is that such a metaphor dances on the very edge of metaphorical usefulness and legitimacy, without—I hope—falling off into oblivion.

What *do* we know about Calabi-Yau shapes? We know, first of all, that they are exceedingly complex. We know that they exist in dimensions of reality that include all the dimensions familiar to us, but that they *also* exist in dimensions of reality that we cannot experience or even imagine. We know that they are all around us, both in the physical matter of our being and the energy that animates us and the whole world, but that we cannot perceive them, even indirectly. We know that artistic renderings of them inspire and awe us, and we are struck by the thought that, if we are inspired and awed by mere two-dimensional suggestions of these six-dimensional shapes, then the real shapes must be vastly more awesome and inspiring. And finally we know that all our "knowing" is not really "knowledge" at all, but rather some inadequate and thin facsimile of knowledge, for we cannot ever really achieve any deep and intuitive understanding of these shapes.

Now go back and reread the previous paragraph, but substitute the word *God* for *Calabi-Yau shapes*. I believe the statements still make sense: What *do* we know about God? We know, first of all, that God is exceedingly complex. We know that God exists in dimensions of reality that include all the dimensions familiar to us, but that God *also* exists in dimensions of reality that we cannot experience or even imagine. This is clearly beyond the typical ways in which we use metaphor. Given one of the root meanings of the prefix *meta-*, namely, "beyond," we might think of this as a meta-metaphor.

TENTATIVENESS

I turn now to one more aspect of string theory that may have great value in restructuring ancient Jewish language and thought. As I read about string theory, I am struck again and again by the tentative and unfinished nature of the whole enterprise. Fascinating as it is, there is no question that it is still quite speculative and that it has by no means been accepted by all, or even most, physicists. Throughout the books and articles on the subject, one is constantly reminded that the theory is a work in progress, that its equations have remained largely unsolved, that none of its assertions have been explored—much less proved!—experimentally, and that it may even be theoretically impossible to prove them. There are large parts of string theory that are based on a level of mathematical approximation (as opposed to precise calculation) that the most enthusiastic string proponents acknowledge to be far too vague to be entirely useful. There are numerous competing versions of string theory and another larger theory, called M theory (no one seems sure what the *M* stands for), that tries to unite them. Loop quantum gravity theory, which goes far beyond my understanding, has also been proposed as an alternative to string theory. I point out this bewildering range of possibilities to clarify a piece of modern scientific methodology that I think has profound implications for religious thought. At the end of a chapter describing the difficulty faced in demonstrating string theory experimentally, Brian Greene makes this observation:

> [I]t's conceivable that one or more generations of physicists will devote their lives to the investigation and development of string theory without getting a shred of experimental feedback. The substantial number of physicists the world over who are vigorously pursuing string theory know that they are taking a risk: that a lifetime of effort might result in an inconclusive outcome.[20]

This feature of science is not generally understood by ordinary folks outside the scientific community. Typically, most people see science as the realm of the true, the kingdom of the proven, and the land of fact. We often think of the literary genre called science fiction as wholly distinct from the other part of science, which is fact. People speak almost reverentially of the fact that science only deals with what is clearly observable and measurable. The image of a serious man, with gray hair and a white lab coat, is an icon of truth that has neither tolerance nor time for speculation or guesswork. There is a pervasive sense of certainty in the whole subject of science. All these common perceptions seem to melt away in string theory (and possibly in other areas of science as well), where we find tentativeness, uncertainty, and theory that is not at all based on what can be observed or measured. We find serious people who are willing to engage in ideas that are not proven and may not even be provable.

Contrast this situation with two well-known statements in Jewish literature. The first, a philosophical/theological creed one section of which we looked at earlier in this chapter, is the "Thirteen Principles" of Maimonides. Each of the thirteen statements begins with a formula: *"Ani ma'amin be'emunah sh'lemah"* (I believe with a perfect faith). They assert the absolute truth of God's existence, unity, incorporeality, and omniscience, as well as the truth of the Torah and the certainty of the coming of the Messiah and the resurrection of the dead. But the specific content of the statements is not my concern here. Rather, I am interested in the absolute certainty with which they are made. Unlike the string theorists, Maimonides permits not a whiff of tentativeness or uncertainty to waft through his creed—"I believe *with a perfect faith*." If the "Thirteen Principles" are to have value, it will only be because they are absolutely true and unquestionable. There is a measure of arrogance in their absoluteness. Now some people claim that what is most interesting about Maimonides's Principles is that they are so unusual in Jewish history. Generally, the claim goes, Judaism has cared far less about what people think or believe, and far more about how people behave. This claim, however, seems to ring hollow in light of a passage from the liturgy of the daily prayer services. The texts that comprise the daily liturgy are designed to be seen and recited by all Jews (or at least all male Jews) every single day from early adolescence onward. As such, they are the bedrock of what the "average Jew" is supposed to internalize. A couple of pages after the *Shema Yisrael* ("Hear, O Israel, the Lord is our God, the Lord is One" is itself a statement of absolute certainty), we find the following passage:

> True and steadfast and correct and eternal and straight and trustworthy and beloved and adored and pleasant and nice and awesome and mighty and set and accepted and good and beautiful is this word [or perhaps "this thing"] for us forever. It is true: God of eternity is our Ruler, the Rock of Jacob is the Shield of our salvation.

This series of sixteen consecutive adjectives (some of which are so similar to one another as to make good translation quite challenging) has the effect of eradicating completely any doubt, any propensity to question. By the time the worshipper has finished reciting all of them, he or she has little choice but to accept wholeheartedly the message of absoluteness and certainty.

Liberal defenders of Jewish tradition claim that Judaism has far more room for argument and questioning than other religious traditions. To a great extent this is an accurate portrayal of the Jewish past. There is, in fact, a venerable tradition of Jews arguing with one another over matters of religious truth. Such arguments form the foundation of the Babylonian Talmud, a massive work filled with disputes among sages about

every imaginable matter of belief, law, and custom. In addition
to arguing with one another, Jews have a long tradition of arguing with God. Abraham challenges God over the impending
destruction of the wicked cities of Sodom and Gomorrah (see
Gen. 18:22–32), and Moses does the same when God threatens
to destroy the Israelites after the building of the Golden Calf
(see Ex. 32:9–14). And the tradition of arguing with God continues throughout Jewish history, notably (but not solely) in the
numerous stories of the late eighteenth-century Hasidic master
Rabbi Levi Yitzchak of Berdichev.[21] Nevertheless, the sacred-
ness of argument reflected in these stories does not alter the
sense of absolute certainty that characterizes much of Jewish
thought and belief. Neither Abraham nor Moses questions
what is right and true. Rather, both question whether what God
has planned to do will be in line with the right and true course
or not. There is never any doubt that there *are* standards for
truth. The questions are always about which course of action
most closely reflects the truth.

In our contemporary world of liberalism, pluralism, and
nonparochialism, the certainty of ancient Jewish tradition (and,
it should be noted, most other ancient religious traditions) often
seems overly arrogant and self-centered. I am concerned and
disturbed, in principle, by any system or proponent of a system
that claims to have absolute truth in its corner. The hubris of
such systems is at best unpleasant and offensive and at worst
highly dangerous, since being convinced that one's system is
absolutely true often leads people to feeling comfortable perse-
cuting or destroying those who cling to other systems. The
metaphor of string theory, replete with a sense of tentativeness,
of we-think-this-is-on-the-right-track-but-we're-not-absolutely-
sure, strikes me as being far more humble and open to real discovery. A religious life grounded in such tentativeness would
more accurately and more ethically reflect the idea that human
beings are finite and imperfect and that our knowledge and

belief systems are therefore also finite and imperfect. Such an approach would be far less likely to lead its proponents to persecute or kill members of other religious groups, since such hostile actions are usually based on a desire to destroy all enemies of the one absolute truth, whatever that truth may be.

INCORPORATING TENTATIVENESS IN JEWISH LIFE

How might such an approach work in Jewish life? At first blush, one might think that the answer is, "Not very well!" After all, Jewish traditions could easily be understood to support the following syllogism: (a) God is one, (b) God is truth, therefore (c) truth is one. The first element of the syllogism is clearly a pillar of ancient Jewish belief. Likewise, the second, the association between God and truth, is well supported. For example, in what is known as the Thirteen Attributes of God (see Ex. 34:6), we read that God has "an abundance of kindness and truth." Similarly, there are numerous biblical descriptions of God as "God of truth" (Jer. 10:10 and Ps. 31:6). If God is one, and God is also closely associated with truth, it is a reasonable (and rather small) logical leap to conclude that truth is one. This statement leads to the unequivocal sense that truth is absolute, complete, and perfect. It all appears to be wrapped up very nicely in a tidy package. If this is so, we might imagine that Jewish life would have little room for notions of partial, incomplete, or approximated truth. Notwithstanding this logic, there are several interesting sources that validate the existence of multiple positions, each of which claims to be true. One of the best known of these is a story in the Talmud about three years of bitter fighting between two groups, Beit Hillel and Beit Shammai (literally, "the House of Hillel" and "the House of Shammai"),[22] over a broad spectrum of Jewish legal issues. The conflict stubbornly resisted resolution until a heavenly voice called out, "These and these [both groups' positions] are the words of the living God!" (*Eruvin* 13b).[23] The story suggests that two human understandings of the world that are diametrically opposed to one another can both reflect elements of divine truth. The fact that the Talmud goes on to rule in favor of Beit Hillel's views on issues of law is a practical, political resolution, but it does not diminish the philosophical importance of the admission that even Beit Shammai's position was, in theory, a piece of the complete truth.

A more modern articulation is found in the writings of Rabbi Abraham Isaac Kook (1865–1935), known more colloquially simply as Rav Kook:

> For the building is constructed from various parts, and the truth for the light of the world will be built from various dimensions, from various approaches, for these and those are the words of the living God.... It is precisely the multiplicity of opinions which derive from variegated souls and backgrounds which enriches wisdom and brings about its enlargement. In the end all matters will be properly understood and it will be recognized that it was impossible for the structure of peace to be built without those trends which appeared to be in conflict.[24]

Rav Kook's formulation is more detailed than the Talmud's brief statement, and a careful reading of the details leads to an important question: What exactly is the comparative status of the conflicting views, for example, the views of Beit Shammai and those of Beit Hillel? There are three possibilities. The first is that the conflicting views may each represent a partial, incomplete human view of what is, from God's perspective, a single, absolute truth. In other words, although there may theoretically be only one absolute truth, we humans are by nature finite and therefore our grasp of that cosmic truth can only be partial. If this is so, each of the conflicting positions would be, in terms of the traditional courtroom oaths, the truth, but not the whole truth. This position has been advocated as a useful method for maintaining respectful disagreement within the Jewish community by Rabbi Reuven Kimelman. In describing the conflict between Beit Hillel and Beit Shammai, he writes:

> By not confusing their claim to the truth with a knowledge of the whole truth, they [i.e., the Hillelites] demonstrated the possibility of total commitment to partial truth. Of course they believed themselves to be more right than the Shammaites. But being more right is not the same as being totally right. The possibility that they had as little as fifty-one percent of the truth permitted them to cede as much as forty-nine percent to the alternative.... While I still believe that any Judaism taking itself seriously has to make truth claims, I no longer hold that such claims have to be necessarily exclusive or absolute.... I can be totally committed to my version of the truth without feeling the need to believe the truth is exhausted by my vision.[25]

Kimelman's position is an interesting interpretation of the process by which human beings struggle to learn about truth. Instead of seeing the process as an all-or-nothing affair, he views it as an incremental one, in which our goal is not to achieve absolute truth but merely to get our hands on as much of the truth as we can. In a dispute between two schools of thought over an issue, be it philosophical, religious, or scientific, this view can tolerate the idea that both positions may have some truth, but that one may have more than the other. In deciding what position to adopt, we always opt for the position that we believe represents the larger piece of the truth pie, but that is not the same thing as claiming that one's own position is the whole truth.

A second possibility for understanding the relative status of two conflicting views is that there is one single, absolute truth and our goal, as human beings, is eventually to grasp it, but that the most useful process for approaching that goal is that of continual argument in which each side's attack forces the other side to sharpen, revise, and refine its position. Thus the dispute between the two sides forces each to approach the truth by stages. This option focuses not on the *amount* of truth claimed by each side, but on the process of argument between the two as a highly effective tool in the search for truth. Such a focus underlies an important passage from *Pirkei Avot*:

> Every dispute which is for the sake of Heaven in the end will be permanently established. And every dispute which is not for the sake of Heaven in the end will not be permanently established. What is an example of a dispute for the sake of Heaven? The dispute between the House of Hillel and the House of Shammai. And what is an example of a dispute that is not for the sake of Heaven? The dispute of Korach and his gang. (*Pirkei Avot* 5:21)

The text distinguishes between two sorts of dispute. A dispute for the sake of heaven will be permanently established in the end, while that which is not for the sake of heaven will, in the end, not be permanently established. The phrase "being permanently established in the end" may seem somewhat unclear, but it accurately reflects the lack of clarity of the Hebrew. What does it mean for the dispute to be "permanently established in the end"? If we were to focus primarily on the outcome of a dispute, that is, on the answer, or the winner, we might think that the text is predicting that answers to disputes "for the sake of Heaven" will be permanently established. But a more fruitful approach, and one that seems better supported by the text itself, is to focus on the *process* of dispute. It is not the resolution of a dispute carried out for the sake of heaven that will be permanently established, but the dispute itself! And conversely, a dispute carried out not for the sake of heaven will not be permanently established: The dispute itself will disappear. The two examples cited by the text of the different kinds of dispute are instructive. The disagreements between the House of Hillel and the House of Shammai, clearly viewed by the text as being for the sake of heaven, are still studied and discussed today wherever students explore talmudic sources. But the biblical rebellion of Korach against the leadership and authority of Moses (see Num. 16) seems, at least in traditional circles, to be a closed issue. After all, it was resolved in the Bible by God's intervention—the earth opened up and swallowed Korach and his co-conspirators, thereby ending the challenge to Moses's position. This approach places great value on the process of disagreement, when the disagreement is motivated not by the ego needs of the disputants to "win" but rather by their deep and sincere desire to seek truth. And although it is admittedly difficult, even in the best of circumstances, to tease apart the desire for truth and the desire to win the argument and be hailed as a hero, the underlying principle is that disagreement in and of itself *can* lead to a more complete picture of truth.

A third possibility is that *there is no absolute single truth*, but rather that all truth is dependent on context and perspective, and therefore the conflicting views are all versions of truth, even though they are opposed to one another. This is the most unsettling, the most challenging possibility of the three. When we are searching for truth, and the search is highly important to our lives, it is deeply comforting to know (or to believe) that there *is* a single truth out there, even if we accept Kimelman's assertion that we may only achieve a partial sense of it. It is perhaps the need for this comfort that gave birth to the liturgical insistence that I cited above: "True and steadfast and correct and eternal and straight and trustworthy and beloved." Even if we know that we don't have full access to God or to God's truth, the composer of the prayer is expressing our sense that it's nice to know they're there, nice to know we can count on them!

Depending on our individual tolerance for such uncertainty, it can be merely unsettling or downright devastating to think that perhaps there just is no absolute truth out there. In many ways, this seems to be a fundamental underlying principle in much of the modern physics that we have explored. Einstein taught that there is no absolute time and no absolute space. The quantum theorists tell us that a particle has no absolute "true" location—just a set of probabilities that describes all the places it might be. If, in fact, our contemporary perception of reality allows for less and less certainty, even at the deepest, most theoretical level, how do we cope with a world built entirely on shifting sands? Here it is crucial to distinguish between two possible interpretations that are often lumped together as one. To say that there is no single, absolute truth but rather that there are multiple truths is *not* the same as saying that there is no truth. The latter possibility is indeed unsettling. If we were to conclude that there is no truth in the universe, but only illusion, then certainly there would be nothing to anchor us, nothing in which we could put our trust. We would not be able to build anything lasting, for the foundation of any creative effort could never be depended upon to remain stable. We could not enter into real relationships, for it would be impossible to count on others. And perhaps worst of all, we would be estranged even from ourselves, for we would have no real, deep confidence in our own convictions. This is all very different from the situation that pertains if we conclude that there are multiple truths in the universe. If there are multiple truths, then we *can* build, we *can* enter relationships, and we *can* trust ourselves. We simply cannot do any of these things with any hint of arrogance, for the truth on which we base each one is, we know, not the only possible truth.

But how can multiple, sometimes conflicting truths emanate from, or be associated with, the God who is one? The question flows directly from the liturgy, for the passage quoted above ("True and steadfast and correct and eternal and straight and trustworthy and beloved") is, structurally speaking, the conclusion to *Shema Yisrael*, the unequivocal declaration that God is one. The underlying logic of this liturgical arrangement was assumed to be beyond question for many centuries. If God is one and God is truth, then truth is one. Simple and clear-cut. But now we find ourselves dealing with a picture of the universe in which assumptions that have long been simple and clear-cut may not be correct. The failure of trusted assumptions may require us to think in radically different, new ways about the reality that surrounds us. If this is the case regarding the physical reality of the universe, then it is so with the philosophical and theological realities of life as well, for they must, in the final analysis, reflect the realities of the universe. In this spirit, we return once more to the fundamentals of string theory. Remember that a major appeal of the theory comes from the fact that it replaces the standard model, a picture of a universe made up of numerous fundamental subatomic particles, with a picture of a universe made up of only one thing, namely, strings. The theory appeals to our yearning for, and belief in, a fundamental unity at the heart of everything. But the one ingredient that makes up the universe, depending on how it vibrates and how tightly it is wound, can be massive or massless, matter or energy. We have felt comfortable for quite a while now, since atomic theory became commonplace, with the knowledge that a mountain and the sheep that graze on its slopes are both made up of the same stuff, on an atomic level. String theory pushes us even further to realize that the mountain, the sheep, the sun, and even the various forms of energy that bind the system together—heat, light, gravity—are *all* the same stuff. The most basic of all physical dualities, the distinction between matter and energy, loses its meaning. It's all strings. In a world described in these terms, we begin to realize that in fact the God who is one *can* be associated with truths that are multiple and even contradictory.

7

PHYSICS IN *SHUL*

Integrating New Metaphors into Traditional Jewish Life

BUT SO WHAT?

There is a popular expression in the culture of traditional yeshiva-style Talmud study: "What's the *nafka mina*?" Although the casual uninitiated listener might think this is an obscure English expression, in fact the expression is Aramaic. *Mai nafka mina* (literally, "What comes out of it?") is a question asked in the Talmud when it's not clear what the implications of a particular discussion are. It is a traditional Jewish way of asking, "So what? What does all this have to do with anything?" We have spent a good deal of time exploring some of the great theories of modern physics and trying to find in them new metaphors by which contemporary Jews might express something about their religious belief and thought. We have looked at the Big Bang, quantum mechanics, fractals, the butterfly effect, special relativity, general relativity, string theory, and other assorted concepts. We now turn to the Talmud's great question: *Mai nafka mina?* What does all this do for us?

ANSWERS EVOLVE IN COMMUNITY

This question can be overwhelming. How do we step out from among the trees and consider the meaning of the forest (note that we can never stop thinking or expressing ourselves in metaphors)? For centuries, there has been a tradition of Jews studying sacred texts by arguing out loud about their meaning. This practice, which may have been borrowed, at least in its essential form, from the Greek Socratic method, is rooted in the belief that ideas develop most fruitfully when they are discussed, batted back and forth, and refined by the process of question and answer, argument and rebuttal. At its core, the method expresses a great deal of faith in the ability of human beings to really function as images of God. How so? In the traditional world of Jewish study, the reigning assumption was that all the texts being studied were, in some fundamental way, divine. For some this meant a rather literalistic view that God had revealed the texts in verbal form to some human scribe who had taken God's dictation. To others, it meant that the human beings who created the texts were somehow inspired by divine wisdom. But one way or the other, the authorship of the texts under consideration was divine. The challenge comes when one tries to interpret a text written by God. How is such a thing possible? One answer is that if we truly regard human beings as having been created in the *image of God*, then discussion of the texts with other human beings is perhaps the next best thing to being able to ask the author questions about what the text means. So when a group of people sits around a table and discusses a text—it could be the weekly Torah portion, or a passage from the Talmud, or the Passover Haggadah (for this is the core activity of the seder)—their goal is to elucidate the text, but also to discuss with other images of God "what God meant" by this text. I believe deeply in the efficacy, the power, and the holiness of this method of study, so when I began to ponder what all these metaphors from physics meant, I turned to this traditional form of sacred argument.

In January 2003, I invited five scholars to join me for a day of discussion and argument. Each received a copy of the manuscript, with instructions to read and think about the material before our meeting. The group included Neil Gillman, rabbi and professor of Jewish philosophy at the Jewish Theological Seminary of America; Michael Paley, rabbi at UJA-Federation of New York; J. Robert "Bob" Dorfman, professor of physics at the University of Maryland; Ilan Chabay, former researcher in laser physics and chemistry, currently a full-time consultant on communicating science to nonscientists, especially through innovative approaches to science museums; and Jim Miller, Presbyterian minister and staff member of DOSER (Dialogue on Science, Ethics and Religion) at the American Association for the Advancement of Science.

We discussed the issues for more than three hours, with a tape recorder rolling. In the weeks that followed, I transcribed the tapes, and parts of the transcription, edited for clarity, are included in the coming pages. Although most of what follows is my own analysis, I could not have come to it without the help of these five scholars.

THE QUESTION OF METAPHOR

The first question to be raised has less to do with any of the particular metaphors discussed in the preceding pages and more to do with the notion of metaphor itself. What is the purpose of metaphor and of metaphorical thinking? How does the metaphor relate to the thing that it is describing? Neil Gillman's view is simple and clear:

GILLMAN: Pictures are very important. Despite the biblical commandment *not* to make pictures of God, the Bible is filled with pictures, verbal pictures, drawn with words. We have to try to read these texts visually. But the trouble is that Jewish tradition is so textual. We take words as words. My feeling is that we have to get the *picture* that's in a text and visualize how God is. Our challenge is to identify the feeling that created the picture, which then was described in words. Then we have to try to go from the words to the picture to the feeling and then begin with our own feelings about the pictures and then get into the words and read the text this way.

Gillman is describing two processes here: the process of authoring a religious text and the process of reading such a text. The first of these includes three steps that an ancient author can be assumed to have gone through, though it is unlikely that the authors were consciously aware of this step-wise process. First, the author develops some feeling, or sense, about God, presumably from his experience of God in the world. Second, he expresses that religious feeling, that sense of God, to himself, visually. In other words, he creates a mental picture by which he can concretize his own understanding of what he has felt or experienced. Finally, he translates the visual image into a verbal description and produces the text that we inherit. Note that this process relies critically on two assumptions. It assumes that the first event in the sequence is some encounter with, or experience of, God. The author sees or hears or experiences something in the world that he identifies as being, or signifying the presence of, God. It further assumes that the most natural way—perhaps the only possible way—for a human mind to make sense of that encounter or experience is pictorially.[1] It is not so much that the author makes a conscious choice to describe the experience of God as a pictorial image, rather than in a different way, but that the encounter with God can *only* be grasped and absorbed as an image. The author has no other way of grasping the experience. It is thus completely natural and understandable that the textual description takes the form of a visual metaphor.

The natural necessity of this process of concrete imagining raises a fascinating question regarding the meaning and purpose of the biblical prohibition, mentioned by Gillman, of making any images of God. I would argue that understanding the commandment as prohibiting image-making is a misinterpretation of the biblical verse. "You shall not make for yourself any sculptured image, or any picture of what is in the heavens above, or on the earth below, or in the water beneath the earth. Do not bow down to them or worship them" (Ex. 20:4-5). If humans think and express themselves metaphorically, the Bible cannot have meant to prohibit our thinking of or describing our experiences of God! Rather, it must mean that we should take great care to remember that the images are metaphors for an indescribable God and to avoid the critical error of worshipping the image in and of itself. To say "God roars like a lion" is fine. To forget the metaphor and create a cult of lion worship is not! This is what the Torah means by "Do not create any sculptured image."

When we read a text created by this process, we are meant to engage in a reverse process. We start with the textual description and, according to Gillman, we must then try to "see" the image that the author had in mind when writing the text. That picture ought to lead us back to some empathic understanding of the state of mind that led the author to the image. In other words, we must use the visual metaphor as a road back to feeling what the author felt when he encountered God. The purpose of this reading process is to use the text, and the feelings about God experienced by its author, to deepen, clarify, or understand our own feelings about God. So ultimately, Gillman is describing a dance between us as readers and the authors of religious text, a dance that serves the goal of helping us with our own religious experience.

This is not the only possible way of understanding the process of reading a religious text. One could as well read the

Bible, for example, or the siddur as historical or anthropological documents, or as literature. But what Gillman is describing is the process by which such texts, intended to be inspirational, were originally *meant* to be read. The psalms could be read to gain insight into ancient Hebrew grammar and poetic style, but they were written to inspire the readers, to help them feel what the psalmist felt and experience God in the world the way the psalmist did.

THE METAPHOR AND THE THING ITSELF

This understanding of the function of religious metaphor fits well with our initial understanding of the broader use of metaphor in all human thought. Metaphor helps us to grasp a reality that would otherwise be out of reach. This notion raises a fundamental question: What is the relationship between the metaphor and the reality that it seeks to evoke or describe? The question leads to different answers, depending on the type of metaphor involved.

With a typical, everyday metaphor, the answer seems straightforward. If we think of the metaphor discussed in the introduction about the taste of frogs' legs, the subject of the metaphor is a real thing that can be experienced. If I *really* want to know what frogs' legs taste like, I can go to a restaurant, order them, and taste them. If I would rather not take that step, I can ask my more gustatorily adventurous friend for a description, and she will probably try to give me the most useful and understandable explanation: They taste like chicken! Then she and her equally adventurous husband may disagree a bit: he claims they taste more like boiled chicken, she insists that they are closer to roasted chicken. But this is clearly only an argument about how best to refine the metaphor for the sake of maximum accuracy. After all is said and done, I can still screw up my courage and taste a plate of frogs' legs at the corner bistro.

If the subject of the metaphor is a scientific one, however, the relationship between the metaphor and the thing itself is less clear. Ilan Chabay and Bob Dorfman discussed two different views of how scientific metaphors work:

CHABAY: I view myself as a translator. I speak the vernacular and I speak the science, and I try to find a way to bridge the two. Now it's important to remember that the metaphor is not the reality. Furthermore, it is context dependent, and it works in some instances, but not in others. There are several ways people misuse metaphor. One is if you really do take it as reality. The other is that you recognize that it's not quite reality, but you don't recognize under what conditions it's valid, or it's meant to be valid. So if I talk to someone about how atoms collide, and I talk about billiard balls, that's just fine. It's a great image. It's a vocabulary for thinking. But if I change the conditions so that the atoms can react with each other and energy can be exchanged, it becomes a lousy metaphor! Now I'd better put Velcro or Silly Putty on the billiard balls. The point is that we have to know not just the metaphor, but the context and limitations that we choose to use in employing that metaphor.

DORFMAN: I want to explain how scientists work in constructing these metaphors. It's a much more pictorial process than nonscientists realize. There's an image of scientists sitting and writing out equations. But behind each and every equation is a mental picture, which is essentially metaphorical. Whether it's colliding billiard balls, or the composition of nuclei in terms of quarks, it's always a little picture. We're always very careful not to say that the world is just a collection of quarks or a collection of billiard balls, but we do have a picture, and it's essential for making progress. We're kind of like dentists—we're always poking at these pictures with a stick, the stick being experiment or some kind of mathematical coherence. So we use these sticks to try and poke holes in the scientific teeth to find out where the weaknesses are.

Chabay's position is that science uses metaphor as a way of making scientific knowledge accessible to nonscientists, the way a translator translates a book, making it accessible to readers unfamiliar with the language of the original. When the language of the original is science, the nonscientist, unlike the reader who could learn a foreign language, cannot master enough science to understand the theory. Short of devoting him- or herself to years of study, he or she has no choice but to learn about the science from metaphors. Given this limitation, Chabay cautions that the nonscientist must bear in mind two things: (1) that the metaphor is not the thing itself (atoms are *not* billiard balls) and (2) that metaphors only work in context (sometimes atoms behave like normal billiard balls, and sometimes they behave like billiard balls that are a little sticky). Failing to bear either of these limitations in mind will lead the nonscientist to a crucial misunderstanding of the thing being described by the metaphor and will thus render the metaphor useless.

Dorfman describes a different use of metaphor in which the scientists themselves use metaphorical (or pictorial) thinking to advance their own understanding of a theoretical structure that cannot be directly observed. They then use the metaphor to test the validity of the theory. The image of dentists probing to find weak spots (again, we find metaphor useful even in describing metaphor!) suggests that, in the case of theoretical physics, the phenomenon under consideration is *not* directly observable and so the metaphor becomes the direct object of the physicist's investigation. So whereas for Chabay the metaphor is a tool used by the scientist to help the nonexpert understand something that without technical expertise is inaccessible to him or her, for Dorfman, the scientist uses metaphor to further his or her expert understanding of a process or a theory. In both cases there is a reality that is separate from the metaphor, but to which there is limited access.

Where religious metaphors, especially metaphors for God, are concerned, however, the question is not so simple. Gillman explains:

GILLMAN: The major issue that I encounter in dealing with and teaching [about religious metaphor] is the attack that says, "The Bible says that God created man, but Gillman, what you're saying is that we really create God." I say, "No, we create the metaphors." "Well, but the metaphors are all we have." "Right." "So we really create God." "No, I think we discover God and then create the metaphors." And sometimes they say, "What comes first?" Sometimes the metaphor enables us to see, but sometimes an experience created the metaphor. So there's a back-and-forth between the metaphor and the experience. The metaphor may lead to an experience, which then modifies the metaphor, which leads to a fluidity of the metaphorical system for God.

The most critical piece of this statement is "the metaphors are all we have." In the case of the human experience of God, I would argue that there can be no direct experience.[2] The religious person certainly may long for such experience and may seek it out through prayer, meditation, and study. But I, as a skeptical, modern Western person, believe that such direct experience is something that always remains just out of our grasp. If that is so, then the use of metaphors for God is radically different from the use of metaphors for the taste of frogs' legs or the structure of an atom. If there can be no direct experience of God, then the metaphors we use actually stand in for a direct knowledge. We may use ancient metaphors—God is a great king, a loving shepherd, a caring parent—or modern ones—God is the Big Bang, but fractal shaped, or perhaps Calabi-Yau shaped. In either case, however, we come face to face with Chabay's caveat about the misuse of metaphor: taking the metaphor as reality. In science, it is a serious error to confuse atoms and billiard balls. What about in religion? Is it a serious error to confuse God with the Big Bang? Or God as father? What we begin to understand here is that metaphors for God function in a way that is significantly different from the ways in which other metaphors function. When my friend tells me that frogs' legs taste like chicken, she is trying to communicate what the taste of frogs' legs actually is. It may even be the case that the chemical composition of frogs' legs has the same (or very similar) effects on the taste buds and olfactory senses as chicken, so that the metaphor is really only a step away from "the thing itself." In the case of atoms and billiard balls, assuming the metaphor is a good one, there may in fact be numerous specific similarities between how billiard balls actually behave and how atoms actually behave. By studying the former, I can actually learn some of the principles that govern the behavior of atoms. But when it comes to God, we cannot claim that our metaphors, be they ancient or modern, reflect the *reality* of God. All we can claim is that they reflect the reality *of our belief* about God. When ancient authors described God as king, they were describing their belief that God is powerful and sovereign and exercises authority over them by issuing laws and so on. When I claim that God is fractal shaped, all I am claiming is that I *believe* that God exhibits features of scaling and self-similarity. I make no claims about what God *actually* is. So it seems that metaphors for God are not properly metaphors for God at all, but rather metaphors for our *beliefs* about God. The difference is a crucial one. For although I do not think we can have direct experience of God, we *do* have direct experience of our beliefs. Each of us is, in fact, the greatest expert on the direct experience of our own beliefs, since beliefs occur inside us.

The problem begins to develop when I try to communicate my belief to someone else. Then I become a scientist trying to describe atoms to a twelve-year-old, and that is when I begin to rely on metaphor.

This being so, we might return to Gillman's statement and suggest a slight modification. Instead of "we discover God and then create the metaphors," it is perhaps more accurate to say that we discover God, then formulate our beliefs about the discovery, then create the metaphors to communicate our beliefs. It is important to remember that the term *belief* here does not necessarily connote some highly abstract, highly theological conceptual theory. It may simply be the mental picture I form in my head to frame, in sensory terms, the experience I have had of God. That mental picture may change depending on the era, the context of the experience, the nature of the individual or group participating in the experience (since these beliefs, and the metaphors they generate, may belong to individuals or to communities), and other factors. This notion is hardly a new one. It has been well understood throughout most of our history. Evidence of this fact can be seen in the following passage from an ancient *midrash* on the Book of Exodus:

> "The Eternal is a man of war, the Eternal is His name" (Ex. 15:3). Why is this said? Because He appeared at the Red Sea as a hero fighting battles.... But He appeared at Mount Sinai as an old man, full of mercy.[3]

A related text is found in the Talmud:

> One biblical verse says, "His garment was white as snow, His hair like clean wool," (Dan. 7:9) and another verse says, "His locks are curly, and black as a raven" (Song of Songs 5:11). There is no contradiction. The first verse refers to God sitting [in judgment], while the second

refers to God in war. As a sage has taught, for sitting [in
judgment] nothing is more fitting than an elder, while
in war nothing is more fitting than a young man.
(*Hagigah* 14a)

In both these texts (and others like them), the Rabbis of
the talmudic period understood that different metaphors for
God are appropriate, needed, and natural in different situations. When God is redeeming Israel from Egyptian slavery and
punishing the Egyptians, the metaphor of "man of war" is
appropriate, whereas when God is revealing Torah to the
Israelites at Mount Sinai, a metaphor that connotes greater age,
maturity, wisdom, and kindness fits the situation better. God
does not change, they would argue, but the way we humans
perceive or imagine God changes, depending on the specific
nature of the interaction at hand.

Another way to say this is that changing times call for
changing God metaphors. When the Israelites' story was one of
escape from Egyptian persecution, they needed metaphors of
strength, energy, and courage—hence, God as "a man of war."
When their story was one of legislation, they needed a
metaphor of God as patient and wise, hence, a sage elder. To
some extent, the communal metaphors used in any period may
be seen as markers for what is going on in the community at
that moment.

What does this insight tell us about our own age? Over the
course of the preceding chapters, I have proposed numerous
new metaphors for God. What do they tell us about ourselves?

All these new metaphors have two features in common.
They are, first of all, strikingly *im*personal. That is to say, that
unlike almost all[4] the metaphors in ancient Jewish texts—God
as father, king, shepherd, master, teacher, and so on—none of
these new metaphors likens God to anything that looks,
behaves, or responds like a human being. They are physical,

natural, and mathematical phenomena. Not only do they not look human, but they have no conscious awareness of humans. Second, these phenomena are entirely universal. It is hard to imagine the Big Bang "choosing" one people over another, or "loving" a people and demonstrating its love by giving the Torah. These two observations are important clues for understanding how our human views of the universe, and our place in it, have changed. Traditional images of God choosing, loving, or protecting us are all rooted in an ancient sense that the universe was somehow centered on us. Ancient cosmology viewed the earth, our home, as the center around which the universe was placed as decoration. This can be seen in the opening verses of the creation story of Genesis, chapter 1. Here is a brief summary:

> Step 1: God begins to create "the heavens and the earth" (v. 1);

> Step 2: God creates light (v. 3);

> Step 3: God creates a domelike empty space (traditionally translated "firmament") to separate "waters above" (rain, snow) from "waters below" (springs, streams, and all subterranean waters) (vv. 6–7);

> Step 4: God gathers all the waters into one place, allowing dry land to appear (v. 9), then creates all sorts of vegetation (vv. 11–12);

> Step 5: God creates the sun, moon, and stars and places them in the sky (vv. 14–18).

The explicit details of step 5—the creation of sun, moon, and stars—are important. The text reads as follows:

> God said, "Let there be lights in the dome of heaven to distinguish between the day and the night, and they

> shall be for signs, and for seasons, for days and for years.
> And they shall be lights in the dome of the heaven, to
> illuminate the earth." And it was so. (Gen. 1:14–15)

The important thing to notice in this passage is not the sequence of creation, which places the sun, moon, and stars in the heavens on the fourth day, after the creation of such uniquely terrestrial objects as vegetation, but rather that these heavenly sources of light have been created to *serve* the needs of the earth and its human inhabitants! The classical eleventh-century French commentator Rabbi Solomon ben Isaac (Rashi) explains the phrase "they shall be for signs" by commenting, "When the lights are eclipsed, it is an evil omen for the world." This view is typical of premodern understandings. The universe was created to provide certain essential services to the earth and its inhabitants.

But in the modern era, our view of the genesis of the universe places the earth, and our own lives, far from the center. We have a deep sense that our sun, our own planet, and our moon are structural phenomena that occur billions of other places in the universe and that our own presence here is a relatively recent addition to the mix.

This shift in perspective is a substantial part of the reason for the shift in tone of the God metaphors I have suggested. The developmental move it represents may be compared to the development in a child's view of his or her father. When the child is very small, his or her entire view of father is "Daddy." In fact, if one asks small children what their parents' names are, often the response will be "Mommy and Daddy." Parents have no existence, importance, or definition outside their overwhelming presence and power in their young children's lives. By the time the young child reaches the age of twenty or thirty, the perspective changes radically, and the young person may say, "My father wanted to be a doctor, but couldn't get into medical school. So he ended up being a pharmacist, with a small pharmacy. But that was bought out by a huge chain store, and by the time he retired, he had been moved from store to store a bunch of times. He never forgot his dream, though, and often read fiction and nonfiction about medicine." In such a description, neither the child nor the family is the center of the father's life. Instead, the child has achieved a perspective that allows for the father to have had an entire life outside the boundaries of family, with a full spectrum of relationships and roles. We modern humans are much like this child. We have grown up and now realize that our childhood view of ourselves as the center of the universe was understandable, but incorrect. Our view of what and who and how God must be now has to shift to fit our new mental map of the universe and our place within it, both temporally and spatially. Seen in this way, we can understand that the metaphor shifts through which we are going now are simply the continuation of a process that has gone on, often in less dramatic form, for many centuries.

METAPHORS AND INSPIRATION

With all this discussion of the role of metaphors in Judaism, and analysis of how and why metaphors change, the question *Mai nafka mina?*—What does all this mean?—still stands. The way in to this question was explored at different points in our roundtable discussion. The two most important statements came from Michael Paley and Bob Dorfman:[5]

PALEY: It's inspiring. The new physics and the expansiveness of the new physics are inspiring in a time when we need inspiration.... The Jewish community is struggling to understand, "What did we survive for? What did we carry around all this stuff for? Torah and monotheism and stuff like that? What was the ultimate purpose of it? ... The Jewish community is grasping for something highly intellectual, highly abstract, that is coherent, and that constitutes a myth that at least has the promise of explaining a wide variety of physical phenomena. It's very powerful.

DORFMAN: I find God in the incredible delicacy and beauty of the way the world is put together. It's a source of inspiration. It is just so incredibly beautiful. That's a feeling, not an intellectual statement. But it's ultimately at the core of what every scientist looks for…. The world, the physical world, is incredibly complex. To me, that notion of beauty is far beyond ordinary science. It's where I hunt for inspiration. One of my answers to my personal feeling about God is that God resides in this incredible beauty in the world. When I say this, you must understand that I am speaking metaphorically. The beauty and delicacy in the universe are not a demonstration that there is a God, as the intelligent-design Christians would have it. Rather, the mathematical precision of the physical world induces a very spiritual response in me.

These two statements seem to point to the same conclusion, though from different directions. Paley, the rabbi, sees the "new physics"[6] as a valuable refuge for a Jewish world desperately searching for meaning. The modern era has been characterized by a sense that many of the assertions and guarantees of traditional religion are false. This sense is most often summed up in the question—perhaps somewhat simplistic but nonetheless anguished and often angry—"Where was God in the Holocaust?" That question, rather than being a specific query about the apparent nonintervention by God in events of great evil, is more a general expression of disappointment that the promises historically made by religion are elusive at best, and false at worst. There seems to be little goodness, little justice, and little truth in the world. The righteous and the wicked seem to suffer or prosper in roughly equal proportions. There seems to be no one "out there" who cares about us. These are clearly not new issues. As we have seen at several points, they go back to our earliest history. Nevertheless, they seem to have acquired a new urgency in our own day. It is not at all uncommon, in these troubled times, to hear people claim that life simply has no meaning. This is the climate to which Paley is responding. His view is that, in times such as ours, metaphors drawn from the new physics—Big Bang, relativity, quantum mechanics, and so on—have the power to convince people that there *is* meaning in the world, and order as well. Note that this response is significantly different from past responses in times of theological or spiritual crisis. The metaphors from physics do not reassure us that the universe really does care, or that the wicked will receive their just deserts in the end. Rather, they only give us the sense that there is structure, beauty, and meaning in the universe, that we do not live in a realm of utter randomness. (We shall return shortly to the question of how this sense of meaning and structure addresses the problem of evil.)

For his part, Dorfman, the physicist, finds inspiration and God in the "delicacy and beauty of the way the world is put together." What he means is that the more minutely and carefully we examine the world, the more remarkable and breathtaking its structure seems to be. His words undermine completely any nonscientist's impression that scientists are primarily interested in *de*mystifying the world, in breaking it down to component parts so that we can inspect it intellectually and rationally, rather than be moved by it emotionally.

Paley's position is far more traditionally Jewish in that it seeks religious meaning for an era in which such meaning seems largely to have evaporated. Dorfman's view, however, is remarkably evocative and reminiscent of the modern Jewish philosophy of Rabbi Abraham Joshua Heschel (1907–1972). Heschel's teaching was grounded in the experience of looking at the world and being filled with what he referred to as "awe" and "radical amazement." These senses are the normal human response to seeing a sky full of stars, or standing on a mountaintop at sunset, or witnessing the power of a storm. They are the feelings that lead us, together with the psalmist, to cry out, "How great are Your works, O Eternal God!" (Ps. 92:6). All Dorfman and his fellow physicists have done is to fine-tune their perceptions so that the inspiration and sense of awe that most of us get from seeing a breathtaking desert panorama or the birth of a baby, they can see in the complex mathematics that describes equally well the fractal branching of a river system and the branching of blood vessels in the human body.

Using the metaphors of physics for inspiration in this fashion raises two fundamental questions. The first is rooted in the questions of God's authority and the concept of *mitzvot*, the second in the question of God's morality and the issue of evil. I certainly cannot offer any straightforward and satisfying solutions to these problems. Nevertheless, it is important to explore them, if for no other purpose than to own up to the thorniness of their challenges.

GOD'S AUTHORITY

Traditional Judaism rests on two fundamental assumptions about God. The first is that God is the creator, responsible for the existence of the world. The second is that God commands, reveals Torah, makes behavioral demands on both the Jewish people and all peoples.[7] The importance of these two forms of divine interaction with the world cannot be overemphasized. In the traditional prayer book, *Shema Yisrael* is framed by three blessings, two before *Shema* and one after. The first of the two blessings before *Shema* reminds the worshipper that God created the world.[8] The second asserts that God showed great love for Israel by giving us the laws of Torah. These assertions are critical elements in the construction of traditional Jewish theology. According to the structure of the prayer book, they lead inevitably to the blessing after *Shema Yisrael*, which tells of God's redemption of Israel from Egyptian slavery. Without creation and revelation, the liturgy claims, there can be no redemption.

The logic of the progression from creation to revelation to redemption is somewhat altered in another element of Jewish life, in which the redemption from slavery leads necessarily to the revelation of God's law. The Exodus is commemorated on Pesach, while the giving of Torah is commemorated seven weeks later on Shavu'ot. This linkage is explained by many as showing the absolute need for the revelation of divine law to complete the process of redemption from Egyptian slavery. A typical formulation is the following explanation, by the nineteenth-century German philosopher Rabbi Samson Raphael Hirsch, of the meaning of the forty-nine-day period known as the Counting of the Omer that is observed between Passover and Shavu'ot:

> Thus … you enumerate seven such weekly periods, linking them with Passover, … and on the day after the seventh such weekly link with Passover you celebrate Shavuot. In this way you declare and firmly establish for all time that Passover finds its culmination in Shavuot, that is to say, that freedom with all its inherent blessings (including the possession of the Holy Land) acquires worth, reality and meaning only through the principles of the Torah. For Israel was delivered from the bondage of Egypt only to serve the Torah, and when Moses was first enjoined to liberate Israel the spiritual purpose of Israel's freedom was declared: 'When thou hast brought forth the people out of Egypt, ye shall serve God upon the mountain. (Ex. 3:12)[9]

Hirsch's claim that the Exodus only finds ultimate value in the giving of Torah, and the prayer book's claim that the giving of Torah is one of the three pillars on which Jewish belief in one God rests, both demonstrate how vital the metaphor of God as lawgiver was for ancient Jewish tradition.

In light of these and many other examples of the traditional prominence of Torah in Jewish thought, one can comfortably argue that Jewish life without a commanding God is not Jewish. The giving of Torah can be seen in many ways. It is sometimes seen as a stern and unavoidable commandment, sometimes as a patiently taught lesson, and sometimes as an expression of divine love. But the end result is always the same: God commands and we are expected to obey.

Now we turn back to the insights raised above in the comments of Paley and Dorfman and ask how this inspiring view of God as the forces that create and order the universe addresses the traditional assumption of God as revealer of Torah. In fact, if we think of God as the sum total of the awesome organization and complexity in the forces of nature, or the amazing delicacy and beauty of the way the world is put together, it is difficult, perhaps impossible, to see how or why such a God would reveal divine will to a particular group of a particular species on a particular planet at one particular time. Indeed, imagining a specific revelation of God's will and law to the Jewish people *requires* the adoption of the old metaphor system, that is, it requires us to imagine God as a benevolent, intelligent being who thinks and feels in ways analogous to the ways human beings think and feel and who resides outside the system, outside the universe that he creates. It further requires that we readopt the sense that we—our planet, our species, and our particular national group—are at the center of the universe, if not physically then at least in terms of importance. Without these regressive steps, it seems impossible to maintain a serious belief in the traditional sense of God's revelation of Torah to Israel.

It seems that we have arrived at a make-or-break crisis point for a certain group of Jewish traditionalists. There are certainly those who would say that, up to this point, all these "new metaphors" have been very interesting, perhaps even somewhat appealing. Since we know, deep down, that the metaphors for God don't really describe God in any concrete or precise way, it has been fun to play with some new kinds of images. But if playing with those images calls into question a pillar of belief as serious as the notion that God commands us and reveals the divine will to us, then that's the point at which this new set of images begins to undermine the very foundation of Judaism and must be abandoned and rejected. Any version of Judaism that leaves no room for the experience of the giving of Torah at Sinai is a failure.

There are several plausible ways around this potentially fatal flaw. Before exploring them, however, it is important to call attention to the extent to which even the formulation of the challenge is inextricably interwoven with traditional metaphors. We might express the challenge this way: *In order to call any system "Judaism" while hoping to maintain any authenticity, the system must include a God who cares enough about humanity in general and Israel in particular to express the divine will through Torah.*

This is not a bad formulation. In fact, it is one with which many Jewish thinkers might agree. But it is entirely dependent on the metaphor of *caring,* which is a function of human relationships. And we tend to forget that such a feature is *only* a metaphor and not a precise description. This is a serious error that we would easily recognize in other situations. In considering a local ecosystem, say a small coral reef, we might marvel colloquially at how remarkable it is that nature cares enough to provide just exactly the right balance of predators and prey to keep the system healthy, but we would be aware that nature does not really "care" in a human sense at all. Rather, predators and prey are kept in balance through highly evolved mechanisms whereby supply and demand regulate the food chain. It is a natural mechanism, more analogous to other laws of nature than to caring. Laws of nature operate without will, in a mechanistic fashion, whereas caring requires volition, emotion, and freedom. When it comes to thinking about God, however, we seem incapable of separating the essential features that we imagine God to exhibit from the human metaphors by which we have conceived of and expressed those features for millennia. It is important for us to be aware of this limitation in our thinking, even if we cannot overcome it.

Now it might be argued that caring is *not* a metaphor but an essential feature of God, that a God who does not *feel* or *care* about the universe and its inhabitants ought not bear the label "God." If one were to stand staunchly by this position, then the new metaphors I have proposed would most likely have to be rejected. That rejection would be a legitimate philosophical choice. What would *not* be legitimate would be the claim that there is no room at all in Jewish thought or belief for a noncaring God. For there have been instances of respected positions in the history of Jewish thought that espoused models of God without caring. Most notable among these are the philosophical systems of Maimonides and Gersonides (that is, Rabbi Levi ben Gershon, 1288–1344). Both took strong positions in the debate that raged among medieval philosophers over whether God's providence (his caring and protection) applies to specific individuals or only to the general structure of the universe. Their response was that God can have no knowledge of particulars and therefore cannot offer providence to them. Rather, individuals receive providential protection as a result of their ability to understand the universe and use their rational faculties to comprehend the laws by which the world functions. This view of divine providence was described by a philosophy professor of mine this way: Providence involves studying meteorology, forecasting the weather, and deciding to bring your umbrella today! God sets up the universe to function according to laws. The more we study those laws, the more "divine protection" we get.[10] Even though this view did not achieve acceptance as the mainstream Jewish view of God's involvement in our lives, it clearly has a respected place in the canon of Jewish philosophy.

There are a few different ways in which we could think about Torah and *mitzvot* without reverting to thinking about God as a human-type figure located outside the system and intervening in it at will. One way starts with the assumption, unheard of in premodern Jewish thought but quite commonly discussed today, that the Torah is a human work. On its face, this assertion can mean several different things. In the nineteenth century, Jewish scholars began considering the suggestion made initially by Christian scholars that the Torah was written by human rather than divine hands. Such scholarship focused on such things as literary style, word usage, ideological and legal positions taken in the text, and awkward "seams" in the text as evidence that the work had been composed by numerous authors, representing various groups, over a significant period of time, and that the whole product had eventually been "stitched together" by some unknown editor.[11] This suggestion was absolutely revolutionary and posed a serious threat to the traditional Jewish view of *Torah Mi-Sinai*—that is, the doctrine that the entire Torah was given by God to Moses on Mount Sinai and is therefore authoritative, immutable, and eternal. Many responded to the new approach by claiming that if the Torah was "merely an ancient literary work," it had historical interest and contained some inspiring ideas, but was no more authoritative or immutable or eternal than any other ancient work of human creativity.

However, the belief that the Torah's divine authority is undermined when it is viewed as a human creation relies on a straightforward and absolute dichotomy between the human and the Divine. Either God wrote it, or else human beings wrote it. There are no other choices. But this dichotomy is not necessarily the only way of understanding revelation. It is possible to see human creativity as the source of Torah and still imagine divine revelation taking place. In a traditional framework, we can imagine that God's revelation takes the form of inspiration in the mind of prophetic leaders, rather than limiting ourselves to the image of God's overwhelming voice booming out over the foothills of Mount Sinai, while the assembled people tremble with fear at the base of the mountain. There is a well-known and oft-repeated debate among classical scholars about what the Israelites actually heard from God's mouth at Sinai. Some say they heard the entirety of the Ten Commandments. Others say they heard only the first two commandments ("I am the Eternal your God" and "You shall have no other gods before me"). Others claimed the content of direct divine revelation was limited to the first commandment. Still others claim that only the first word *Anokhi*, which can mean either "I" or "I am," was heard. But in a marvelously playful yet deeply challenging twist, Menahem Mendel Rymanower, an early nineteenth-century Hasidic teacher, is said to have claimed that the audible part of the divine revelation was limited to the first letter of the first word.[12] That first letter is א *(aleph)*, which, as any beginning student of Hebrew knows, is silent. If the entire content of divine revelation was silent, then where did the *mitzvot* and the endless levels of detailed laws and rules come from? They could only have come from the humans who "heard" the silent *aleph*. The result of such an analysis is that the words of Torah are human words, though the ultimate source of Torah is divine.

In the nontraditional framework of new metaphors from physics, we can also come to an understanding of how a Torah written by humans can nevertheless be divine. First of all, if we express divinity as the principles of organization and complexity that create the universe, then we humans are certainly a part of those principles. The fact that organic life exists, and that our form of that life has become so vastly complex as to develop a culture of storytelling and legislation (not to mention physics and mathematics), is eloquent testimony to the tremendous power of the system that has brought the universe from Big Bang to today. Once we succeed in tearing our religious imagination away from the traditional picture of a wise old God sitting "out there" and deciding to create us and contemplate instead the mind-numbing marvels of structure that govern everything from the smallest quantum processes to the interactions of supergalactic clusters, then it is not hard to see the creativity of human life itself as a part of the system that we call God. Having made this jump, we no longer need to maintain the dichotomy of "either God wrote it or humans wrote it." Revelation is no longer seen as a process by which information from outside the system penetrates the system (especially since there is nothing "outside" the system). Rather, revelation can be understood as the process by which the system expresses itself, whether through the creation of a black hole, or the creation of a butterfly's wings, or the creation of laws and literature.

Another, somewhat more specific way of expressing this is through fractals and their features of scaling and self-similarity. For many classes of fractals, we see pretty much the same thing whether we look at a large or small part of a fractal. Bearing this in mind, if we return to the idea proposed in chapter 3 that God is fractal shaped, we find that any part of the system is similar to and, in a way, representative of the system as a whole. Thus, if the human being is a scaled-down, similar image of the whole system (God), and the human brain is also part of that fractal structure, then the fact that the Torah and its *mitzvot* had their source in the human mind does not lead in any way to the conclusion that they are, therefore, not divine.

UNDERSTANDING EVIL

These two ways of seeing the Divine in human creativity, however, do raise another serious problem: If all creativity, including all human creativity, reflects the creativity of the system that
we may call God, then this must apply to *all* human creations,
not just the ones traditionally seen as "religious." The
Nuremberg Laws as well as Torah, bawdy limericks as well as
psalms, must all be seen equally as products of God. But we are
appalled by this notion! How can anyone possibly think of the
laws of apartheid and the commandment to "Love your neigh-
bor as yourself" as representing the same creative power? Is
there no sense of moral judgment, of right and wrong, of good
and evil involved in religion?

We have seen this question before. It is asked every time
Judaism has to cope with the issue of dualism, that is, the idea
that there are two fundamental realms that control existence, a
good realm and an Evil Realm. Traditional Judaism, committed
as it is to the principle of God's oneness, has almost always
rejected dualism out of hand, choosing instead to see God as the
source of *all* things, good and bad, light and darkness, blessing
and curse. The tradition generally coped with the bad parts of
life by assuming that they were the methods God uses for punishing those who disobey divine will. So the destruction of the
first and second Temples is seen as punishment for the people's
misconduct, as is the exile from the land of Israel and all subsequent misfortunes and catastrophes.

Mordecai Kaplan was one of the few ever to suggest an
alternative to this unswerving commitment to the idea that God
is the source of all things, good and bad. As I have mentioned
before, Kaplan defined God as "the Power that makes for salvation." In other words, when salvation is advanced in the
world, that's God. When such things are not happening, or
when destructive, evil things are happening, God has no part in

that. Kaplan's formulation neatly circumvented the problem of reconciling a belief in a good God with the observation that all of life is not good. But to accept Kaplan's position, one must be prepared to limit God to responsibility for only a portion of the universe's functioning, while leaving out of God's domain anything that is evil, and perhaps much that is morally neutral, or at least that which is morally questionable. For most Jews, limiting God's power is less acceptable than the alternative, namely, somehow coming to grips with how God can be responsible for evil.

It was only in the decades following the Holocaust that Jews for the first time began seriously to question the moral logic of the age-old assumption that God uses evil as a "rod of chastisement" to mete out punishment to those who do not obey the law. The sheer magnitude and utter malevolence of the Holocaust caused various thinkers to undergo a fundamental paradigm shift in the way they saw God and the world. Such questioning found extreme expression in the words of Richard Rubenstein:

> No man can really say that God is dead. How can we know that? Nevertheless, I am compelled to say that we live in the time of "the death of God" … I mean that the thread uniting God and man, heaven and earth, has been broken. We stand in a cold, silent, unfeeling cosmos, unaided by any purposeful power beyond our own resources. After Auschwitz, what else can a Jew say about God?[13]

What is interesting about Rubenstein's statement is that it clearly implies that a change has occurred. He seems to believe, or seems to want to believe, that at some point in the past there was an intact "thread uniting God and man," but that historical events have demonstrated that that thread has been broken.

This is significantly different from the claim that I have made. Rubenstein argues that there used to be a "purposeful power beyond our own resources," and now that purposeful power is silent, or gone, or dead. I am arguing, however, that what has changed is *our experience, perception, and understanding of God!* To say that God is dead is to imagine a change in the fundamental rules by which the cosmos operates. It is to imagine that God used to care about us and protect us but no longer does so. On the other hand, to say that our metaphors for God have changed, and *must* change, is simply to say that our perception of the cosmos has changed, and that we must readjust our God metaphors to account for our new understanding of the universe. The paradigm shift is not in God, but in how we humans understand the universe and our place in it. This view was expressed well in the roundtable discussion by Michael Paley:

PALEY: Any personal providence after the Holocaust is abhorrent. And I don't want any part of it. And therefore what I'm ... searching for is a much bigger image and metaphor of God. Because the first one didn't come through.

When he says "the first one didn't come through," he seems to be saying that the images and metaphors that served Jews for the first 2,500 years (more or less) of their history as a people now seem to be inadequate, given the changes that have occurred in our *sense* of how the world works. The new metaphors that we seek must somehow take into account our understanding of all the data currently available to us.

WHEN AND HOW DO PARADIGMS SHIFT?

I do not mean to minimize the breadth or depth of the challenge that we face in making such a paradigm shift. This is not a case of making minor adjustments to a scheme that is pretty good. What I am suggesting is a fundamental reorientation. Changes on this scale do not happen very often in a system as old, established, and resistant to change as Judaism. They have certainly occurred once in our history, in the transition from the biblical to the rabbinic (or talmudic) era. In the biblical period, the people of Israel lived as a nation on its own land. The primary institutions of community leadership were king and priest, and the primary institution through which the people played out their relationship with God was the Temple. The major ritual act at the heart of the religion was sacrifice—a practice to which a large part of the Torah is devoted. By the time the Babylonian Talmud was completed (roughly 500 C.E.), most Jews lived outside the land of Israel, the roles of king and priest in communal leadership had been replaced by that of rabbi, there was no Temple, and the sacrificial system had long been abandoned. Instead, a system of Halakhah (Jewish law), study of Torah, and lay-led prayer (prayer that does not require an authorized priestly officiant) had assumed the central position for the definition of Jewish life. These are vast, monumental changes that must have shaken the Jewish population to its very core. Unfortunately, since virtually all extant historical records of the period were written by the "winners," it is impossible for us to examine the upheaval that must have occurred. Two factors must be borne in mind, however. First of all, the transformation of biblical religion to rabbinic Judaism took a very long time. It is not unreasonable to mark the destruction of the first Temple by the Babylonians in 586 B.C.E. and the subsequent Babylonian exile as the beginning of the transformation. Even though those events were followed by the building of the second Temple and its functioning for over five hundred years, the seeds of a life without land and without Temple had been planted. If we wish to be far more conservative, we may mark the beginning of the transformation in 70 C.E., when the Romans destroyed the second Temple.

The transformation was well under way by the middle of the talmudic era, roughly around 400 C.E. Thus we are describing a shift that took somewhere between three hundred (if we figure from 70 C.E. to 400 C.E.) and a thousand (if we figure from 586 B.C.E. to 400 C.E.) years to occur. A very long time indeed! Second, it can be argued that the transformation from biblical to rabbinic Judaism was initially sparked by a cataclysmic event, namely the destruction of the Temple (either the first or the second, or both).

If we now compare the fundamental metaphor shifts I have proposed (God as the Big Bang, a fractal- and Calabi-Yau-shaped impersonal creative structure of the physical universe) to the sweeping structural changes that occurred in Judaism in late antiquity, two things become apparent immediately. If there is to be a fundamental shift, we are only in its very early years, and the process of transformation will be a very long one. Even if it will not take as long as the changes from biblical to rabbinic Judaism because of the faster pace of our world and its mass communications, it will still take a very long time. That being so, it is hard to imagine, in these early moments, how the changes will play out. Furthermore, the changes I have discussed are *not* sparked by a single cataclysmic event. Rather, they are (or will be) the product of a long, slow, and quiet revolution in the way we understand the universe and our place in it. In the decades following the destruction of the Temple, it would have been impossible to argue that nothing had changed, unless one were to have staunchly insisted on a rebuilding agenda as the only viable course. The physical absence of Temple, sacrifice, and national sovereignty would have been too harsh a set of realities to ignore. By contrast, in our day, many find it fairly easy to continue using the religious language of the premodern world, while ignoring the mismatch between that language and the generally accepted truths about how our universe came to be and how it operates. The gentleness of the revolution has allowed many to ignore it completely, or to acknowledge it without recognizing its impact. When people talk about cosmology and relate it to the creation story of Genesis by explaining that the term *day* (as in "six days") in the Torah could refer to a much longer period, they are essentially arguing that the intellectual revolution of the last one hundred years can be accepted without threatening the traditional beliefs or language of religion. I see such arguments as desperate attempts to ignore the inevitable paradigm shift. Ultimately, such attempts may delay the shift, but they cannot succeed in preventing it. Nevertheless, it will be a long, long time before we figure out how to reorient our religious language to better reflect our worldview.

IGNORANCE AND ANXIETY

Over the course of the preceding chapters, an interesting theme seems to recur. The theme is ignorance—or, if you find that term a bit harsh, our fundamental inability to know. We can see *almost* all the way back to the Big Bang, but we can't see the event itself, because of the opacity of the first few instants after the bang occurred. We can't see past the event horizon of a black hole because nothing, including electromagnetic signals, can escape its huge gravity. We can't know for certain the future of a quantum system, or of one characterized by deterministic chaos. And even the most fervent proponents of string theory admit that for the time being (and perhaps for a long time to come) their brilliantly elegant theory cannot be proven or demonstrated or tested. We just can't know for sure! This limit to human knowledge came up in the roundtable discussion, in the following comment made by Neil Gillman.

GILLMAN: There is a tendency here toward greater and greater humility about our ability to know anything about anything other than our perception of the world. The most encouraging thing about science that I can see is not its vast achievements, but the fact that the achievements contain an omnipresent escape clause by which we say, "That's what we perceive, but we really don't know anything beyond what we perceive." There's an uncertainty all the way through. I think that the major issue in religion lies between those religionists who say we *do* know and those religionists who say we *don't* know. What religion is all about is the need for absolutes. Then I come in and say there are no absolutes. We don't know what God is, we don't know what God wants, we don't know anything for sure. All that we have is our best perception of what God is, what God wants, how the world makes sense. And when I say that within a religious context, I am echoing what the best of contemporary science is saying in a scientific context. All of this together combines, I think, to create a state of acute anxiety for people who basically do want to know for sure that this is what's out there and this is the way it works and this is what God is and this is what God wants and that's what we have to be. The subversive quality of this book is that you are undermining the need by a lot of people to know that there are absolutes and certainties. It seems to me that you're saying that there are none. That there are none in science, and that there are also none in religion, and that's what's great about both.

When I first heard this comment, I was frankly somewhat shocked. I had honestly never intended to write a subversive book! But the more I have thought about Gillman's insight, the more I have come to recognize its validity. I recently had the opportunity to chat for several hours with a born-again Christian. It was one of those curious, candid, and respectful conversations where we explored one another's faiths by patiently asking questions and listening to the answers, then responding with answers of our own. Over the course of the conversation, a couple of things became very clear, and as they did, they reminded me more and more of Gillman's claim that my writing was "subversive." In the conversation, my Christian friend kept expressing her deep need for certainty from her religious beliefs, pure, simple, uncomplicated certainty. And I, on the other hand, kept expressing the complicated questions that are at the heart of my belief. She was deeply troubled by my claim that there are no absolutes. "If there's no absolute truth," she kept saying, "how can there be *any* truth at all?" I explained that, even in the absence of absolute truth, one could make some important judgments about truth and falsehood. Likewise, even in the absence of absolute right and absolute wrong, one could make some pretty clear judgments about right and wrong. As we talked, I came to realize that one of the fundamental differences between us was this: At the core of her religious world there was pure and certain faith, while at the core of mine there are questions.

That realization brought me back to Gillman's point. Science is about asking questions and developing tentative answers to the questions. But as the answers develop, the researchers are always looking for still better answers, or new ways of asking the questions that will make the previous set of answers a bit less satisfying. Over the past several years, as I have paid close attention to the news about science, I have been struck by the frequency with which the news media report on the question of how much matter the universe contains. The question is important because its answer will have a significant effect on the eventual fate of the universe. If there is less than a certain quantity of matter, such that the total gravitational attraction of all the matter falls below a certain threshold, then the universe could keep on expanding forever and eventually just peter out, as all its energy dissipates. On the other hand, if there is more than a certain quantity of matter, then eventually

the universe might stop expanding and, because of the gravitational attraction of the matter in it, start contracting, leading
eventually to its end in a "big crunch." What I have noticed is
that every time a group of astrophysicists publishes a new study,
the answer changes! I have frankly stopped trying to keep up
and am completely at a loss at this moment to even guess at
what the "latest" theory is. What is clear, however, is that no
matter what the latest theory is, it is just that—a theory based
on the newest thinking that stands ready to be modified or discarded when the next batch of data comes along. This process
stands in sharp contrast to the premodern version of religion, in
which clear and certain revelation yielded absolute and eternal
truths. What I am proposing, based on the metaphor lessons
learned from physics, is that we moderns must begin to get
comfortable with a religious life that is as humble about its
truth claims as our scientific life.

What this means is that the role of religion in human life
must shift. In the past, we were able to see religion as an anchor,
a source of absolute truth and stability in a world beset by
storms and uncertainties. This reliability was perhaps best cap-
tured in a God metaphor that goes all the way back to the
Torah: God as rock, my rock and my redeemer, rock of ages.
These were powerful, comforting, solid images, because our
ancestors could think of nothing more stable or enduring, more
changeless and dependable, than a rock. Of course, we know
now that even the apparent stability and immovability of a rock
are not quite what they seem to be. On an atomic level, rocks
hum with activity and energy, as do all other substances in the
universe. They are composed of various elements that come
together in a variety of ways and can be split apart (as even the
ancients must have known) by a chance lightning strike or by
the freezing of a small amount of water that drips into a crevice.
The ancient sense of "rock" as symbolic of solidity, reliability,
and eternity just doesn't seem as compelling today. We live in a

worldview that sees *nothing* in the universe as static. Motion and change are inescapable, fundamental aspects of all reality. Religion, including both its faith claims and its truth claims, is no exception. In a universe in which, as Einstein taught, there is no absolute time and no absolute space, we must come to terms with the idea that there is no absolute truth either. This notion transforms religion, at least in part, from being a source of comfort to being a source of intellectual and spiritual challenge. It means that the religious life will be one of questions more than of answers. The depth and significance of the shift takes on a whole new meaning when we consider how far we have come from the days of Karl Marx, who disparaged religion as the "opium of the people."

CAN A PHYSICIST PRAY?

I have described God as a fractal-shaped, Calabi-Yau-shaped, multidimensional, creative force in nature. I have suggested that such a view of God makes it hard, if not impossible, to retain traditional language about how God cares for us, or protects us, or loves us, or has conscious awareness. I have claimed that God can be seen either as a part of the system that we call "the universe" or as the system itself, in its totality, but cannot be seen as being outside the system, since, by definition, nothing is outside the system. Given these highly nontraditional assertions, I now want to raise a bottom-line sort of question. Can a physicist pray? To put it somewhat more precisely, since I began this book with the open admission that I am *not* a physicist, can *I*, or anyone else who might hold such radical views, pray?

If we look at the language of the siddur, the traditional Jewish prayer book that has evolved over roughly the last two thousand years, we see statements on every page that contradict most of the claims made in the preceding paragraph. God revealed his will to us at Mount Sinai by giving us the Torah.

God drowned our enemies in the sea. God exiled us from our
land because of our sins. We ask God to rebuild Jerusalem, to
hear our prayers, and to heal us when we are sick.

Some years ago, I was conducting a *Shabbaton*, a weekend
of study and celebration, in Portland, Oregon. On Shabbat
morning we sat in an informal circle for the morning service. I
explained, before we began, that the morning's activity had two
purposes. One was to recite the morning prayers. The other was
to continue our study, which meant that all participants were
welcome to raise questions or make comments at any point during the service. We happened to be using a fairly traditional
prayer book, the kind with the complete traditional Hebrew
text on the right-hand page of every two-page spread, and a
pretty literal English translation across from it, on the left. Well,
about half an hour into what I thought was a lovely mix of
chanting meditative melodies and making insightful comments
about various parts of the liturgy, I was stopped by a partici-
pant. "Can I ask you something?" "Of course," I replied, con-
fident that I could field any response to this process. "I've been
reading the English translation for the last few pages," he said,
"and I just want to know. Do we really believe this crap?" He
had chosen his words for their impact, and he was quite successful! The service ground to a halt and we had a discussion
that ended up taking the rest of the morning. We weren't talking about physics, but it didn't really matter. The question was
the same. He was asking how he could participate in this
liturgy, in good conscience, when many of the statements in its
pages made no sense to him.

This is a profound and difficult question for many modern
human beings. I think, however, that it can be seen as two separate questions that are related but by no means identical. The
first is: Can a modern person, say, a rabbi who reads lots of
nontechnical books about physics, *daven*? That is, can such a
person feel comfortable going to synagogue and participating in

the traditional service? The second question is: Can such a person *pray*? By which I mean, can such a person interact with, or talk to, or find intimacy with God? These are different questions. The first is about participating in a highly ritualized, communal activity that has deep historical and ethnic roots. That activity takes place at prescribed times, often in buildings that, by their décor, push many of our "nostalgia buttons." It is conducted in a traditional language, that is, Hebrew, with familiar, old melodies that evoke memories of childhood. Many participants wear ritual garments—a *kippah* (yarmulke), and *tallit* (prayer shawl), and, on weekdays, *tefillin* (phylacteries). In other words, this activity has all the trappings of a powerfully engaging cultural—one might be tempted to say "tribal"— experience. The second question is about an activity stripped of all the traditional, cultural baggage. It inquires simply about the possibility of a meeting, a tête-à-tête, between a human being and God.

The first question is far easier to answer. Of course a modern Jew can *daven*! Going to synagogue need not be seen as a theological experience at all. Rather, it may be regarded as a cultural and social experience. It is what Jews do and how Jews connect with each other and with the past. It is significant that when the synagogue was invented, during the last century or so of the existence of the Second Temple, it was given the Hebrew name *beit kneset*, a house of gathering (which translates into Greek as *syn-agogue*). It could have been called *beit tefillah*, or house of prayer. It wasn't. I know lots of Jews who go to synagogue regularly, not because they believe the statements in the siddur (most of them have spent little if any time thinking about them!) or because they want to interact with God, but because they enjoy connecting with the community in a traditional environment. They chat with friends; they are touched by the traditional cultural elements of the experience and the memories evoked by them. They may learn something from the rabbi's sermon. And they enjoy the gefilte fish (or tuna salad, at the more contemporary places) at Kiddush. They leave feeling more Jewish, more rooted in a community, and more a part of a tradition. These reinforced feelings are at the heart of the formation and preservation of Jewish identity.

It is the second question, however, that is much more challenging. How can we imagine interacting with, or praying to, an impersonal God who does not choose us, give us commandments, or respond in any significant way to our entreaty? What kind of a relationship can we have with the fractal-shaped, Calabi-Yau-shaped source of all matter, energy, time, and space? In trying to find some framework within which to address these very tough questions, I am drawn to the model of early Hasidism. The claim has been made by many scholars that early Hasidism had profound pantheistic[14] tendencies and that many of its teachers saw God as the vital divine force that suffused every corner of the universe. Such a position is quite similar to the one I have outlined in these pages, with the single difference being my specific use of metaphors drawn from physics. For some of the Hasidim, it led to an approach to prayer that is strictly contemplative. In other words, the purpose of prayer is not for the individual human being to have a dialogue with God, the individual divine being who is out there somewhere, but rather for each person simply to become aware of, tuned in to, and perhaps a part of the ubiquitous flow of divine energy that is present in every single fiber of being that is encountered. One description of this approach in early Hasidism says:

> In the spiritual exercise of the Great Maggid[15] and his school the personal relationship with God is lacking. The Divine is conceived as something impersonal. The divine essence, the *hiyyuth* [life force, vitality], which dwells in all things is a-personal. Indeed, the contemplative mystic renounces even his own personality, since

he aims through the complicated technique of contemplation at attaining a sense of ecstasy in which the "extinction of existence," *bittul hayesh*, the extinction of personality in the self-annihilation of consciousness, is achieved… [P]rayer serves as an occasion for, and as the means of, contemplation and ecstasy. Prayer becomes here a kind of special vehicle of the main contents of the contemplative life.[16]

This description of the Hasidic conception of God is important for three reasons. First, it provides an example of an instance in Jewish history in which the idea of an impersonal God in fact led to a rich personal religious life. Opponents of early Hasidism may well criticize the movement on many grounds, but none could argue that its religious life was anything but vital and compelling. Having argued for religious metaphors that are largely impersonal, I have often been asked whether such a view can lead to any sort of personal religious life. Here we have clear evidence, in a historical precedent, that it can.

Second, the Hasidic model gives us some insight into one particular mystic approach to such an impersonal God, namely the practice known as *bittul hayesh*, or "cancellation of existence." This practice is described by Professor Louis Jacobs as follows:

The Hasid is expected to attain to the state described in Hasidic thought as *bittul ha-yesh*, "the annihilation of somethingness," that is an awareness that God alone is true reality and that all finite things are, as it were, dissolved in His unity. *Bittul ha-yesh* includes the annihilation of selfhood, the soul soaring to God with the ego left behind. This attitude is especially to be cultivated at the time of prayer.[17]

In a system in which God is not seen as a discrete personality, but rather as the life force that suffuses all existence, it
makes some sense to craft a human response that aspires to the
same nonpersonal, egoless state. If God is not thought of as a
"self" distinct from the rest of the universe, then one way for
a human self to approach God is to try to attain a similar
undifferentiated state. It is impossible to achieve a state in
which an individual's self and God's self are in close contact
with each other, since God is not thought of as comprising a
self that is, in any meaningful way, distinct from the whole universe. Thus, an alternative approach is to try in this, as in other
aspects of religious life, to emulate God by dissolving the sense
of selfhood and becoming one with God in the same egoless,
undifferentiated state. Whether or not the approach works for
any given individual, it is nonetheless worth noting that the
fractal concept of self-similarity linking God and human
beings seems inescapable. If God has no discrete "self" separate from the system, then the human being, by virtue of the
fractal phenomenon of scaling, should also seek to reject distinct selfhood.

The third and perhaps most important insight that we
draw from this picture of early Hasidism comes from its teachings about prayer. The goal of the Hasidic prayer referred to
earlier was simply to assist in, experience, and participate in the
unification of all things in God.[18] This overarching goal of unification makes the process a meditative, emotional one, rather
than a logical or analytical one. Jacobs describes one particular
technique as follows:

> The letters of the Hebrew alphabet are, as the Baal
> Shem Tov[19] understands the matter, not mere symbols
> but the expression of metaphysical realities. They are
> the counterpart on earth of God's creative processes
> and are themselves endowed with creating power. The

aim of the Hasid should be to assist the unification of those creative forces and in the process lose himself in the divine. As his mind dwells on each letter separately ..., his soul becomes absorbed in the unification process. The letters are then formed into words and, by reflecting on this, the mind of the Hasid is embraced in an ever higher unification process. Hasidic prayer is, then, an exercise in assisting the divine unification and participating in it, sharing the joy and delight which attend unification as all worlds and all souls become attached to God. The "plain meaning" of the words of the prayers is entirely ignored. All that matters is the unification theme represented by the letters themselves and the way they are grouped together to form words.[20]

We can understand this remarkable description to mean that, for these early Hasidim, the act of prayer was an extended meditation on a single theme, namely, the unification of all things in God. One way this meditation was carried out was by focusing on the individual letters of the words of the liturgy, thereby ignoring the "plain meaning" of the words completely. It is clear that this simple goal is sharply at odds with the apparent purposes of Jewish prayer, as those purposes may be understood by analyzing the traditional liturgy, studying the history of its development, or considering the many earlier sources that define it. Essentially, this Hasidic model constituted a radical redefinition of Jewish prayer! The boldest aspect of this redefinition was the claim that the *meaning of the words of prayer is completely unimportant!*

As I have pondered, discussed, and written about physics-based metaphors during the past few years, I have been troubled by the problem of how to integrate this new language into the traditional practice of Jewish life. At times the prospect has

seemed absurd and amusing, as, for example, in the reformula-
tion of the traditional blessing template: "Blessed art Thou, Big
Bang our God, fractal structure of the universe." But the above-
quoted description of the revolutionary character of some
schools of early Hasidic prayer makes me think that these new
metaphors may, in fact, be more easily integrated than I have
sometimes feared. Taking our cue from the Maggid of Mezritch
and his school, we may think of prayer as contemplative meditation on the themes of the common origin (that is, the original
unity) of all space, time, matter, and energy, the fractal nature of
the universe, the multidimensional character of reality, and so
on. If this is how we understand prayer, then the comment,
which I quoted earlier, by physicist Bob Dorfman suggests an
easy and comfortable way into prayer: "I find God in the incredible delicacy and beauty of the way the world is put together." If
we are willing to consider the Hasidic ploy of declaring the
"plain meaning of the words" to be completely irrelevant, then
we can even bring our sense of God in the universe, crafted as it
is with metaphors from the world of physics, into the synagogue. There we can meditate on the unity of all matter, all
space, all time, and all energy, while chanting the traditional
words of prayer as a sort of mantra designed not to remind us
of a particular message but to allow us to rise above all particular messages to focus on the one universal message: There is
unity, structure, beauty, and meaning in the world. There is no
question that this distillation of Jewish prayer to such a very
simple statement constitutes a radical departure from Jewish tradition. One need only read any good treatment of Jewish
prayer[21] to confirm this. The point is that there is a historical
precedent for such a redefinition, as we have seen from the foregoing comments about early Hasidic prayer. To maintain the
form, and even the language, of Jewish tradition, while assign-
ing such form and language radically new meanings, is allowed,
if we use Jewish history as our guide.

BUT WHY BOTHER?

Having said this, I must confront a further challenge. Even if we accept the fact that Jewish history provides a precedent for radical departures from the "plain meaning" of the language of tradition, one may justifiably ask why we ought to bother. In other words, if our understanding of God, and our relationship with God, are so fundamentally different from at least the bulk of the mainstream of Jewish tradition, why should we perform such mental acrobatics to remain within that tradition? Why search for the obscure views of Maimonides, Gersonides, or some early Hasidim to prove that we are justified in claiming a place within the fold? Why not just admit that our views have developed in such a radical fashion that we are, essentially, no longer inside the system that tradition and history have labeled "Judaism"?

I offer this response to these important questions. First, I believe that human life is far better lived, far more richly and meaningfully lived, in a community. Given the choice between thinking of myself as a free-floating individual, or as a part of humanity as a whole, or as a member of a specific group, I believe deeply that the last option can lead to the greatest fulfillment. A great deal of our sense of identity as human beings involves a sense of belonging. Affiliation with a particular group and its customs, mores, values, and culture enhances my sense of who I am. I make this claim despite the fact that strong allegiance to group identity has been the cause of much (if not all) of the hatred, war, and suffering that have plagued us as a species. These are all terrible consequences of group affiliation, but despite all of them, I think it is extremely difficult, if not impossible, not to see oneself as a member of a particular group. The world is too large and overwhelming for us to be able to confront it comfortably and effectively without the support of a community. This is true, by the way, for affiliation with *any* community; I would make no claim that any one community (the Jewish community, for example) is inherently better, nobler, or more fulfilling than any other. But the Jewish community is *my* community, if for no other reason than by an accident of birth, and as such it is important to me that it be as viable and vibrant as possible. When modern scientific thinking threatens the viability of the Jewish community, as I think it has for many Jews during the past century, I feel it is important to try to reframe Jewishness to keep it accessible, compelling, and fulfilling. Hence, the explorations of the previous pages.

Throughout this book I have carefully avoided employing metaphors taken from the life sciences—biology, genetics, and so on. It was important to me to focus on physics as the most basic of sciences. But at this point the notion of evolution cannot be ignored. It seems, in the course of our planet's history, that any species faces one of two fates: It can adapt, as the conditions of its environment change, or it can perish. In the world of biology, being able to adapt to change is a highly valuable trait. Judaism has been around, in one form or another, for quite a long time. Depending on what we choose as the starting point (and the choice is fairly arbitrary), it is somewhere between 2,500 and 3,500 years old. I have already argued that this lifetime has seen at least one major evolutionary change, namely, the radical redefinition that took place in the centuries following the destruction of the Temple in Jerusalem. But in the last few centuries, there has been a growing sense among many Jews that major changes, radical shifts, are no longer possible in Jewish life. This attitude can only lead to the extinction of the species known as Judaism. Plenty of people may continue to trace their ancestry back to Jews, but the way of life embraced by those forebears will become increasingly irrelevant. My purpose has been to suggest one possible direction for the further evolution of Judaism, a direction that will, I believe, increase its adaptability and thus enhance its viability. As is the case in any evolutionary process, the species may evolve in more than one direction. I am not suggesting that the course I have laid out for developing new metaphors is the only possible one, the only viable one, or even the best one. For me, however, it has provided some fascinating new ways to understand the resources of my Jewish past in the context of some of the most exciting ideas of the contemporary world.

NOTES

I have designed the notes so that if you wish, you can read through the book, never look at the notes at all, and not miss much. The notes are of three sorts. Some give citations of material quoted in the body of the book. Others discuss fine nuances of a particular idea that are not absolutely necessary to understanding the idea, but that may interest the reader who finds fine nuances intriguing. A third sort of note gives suggestions for further reading about an idea that I treat in passing in the book. My purpose in including the notes was not to add something "off-putting" to the book, but rather to take out of the text anything that most readers would find intimidating.

Introduction: Jewish Tradition and Frogs' Legs

1. Chandler Burr, *The Emperor of Scent* (New York: Random House, 2002), pp. 304–305.

2. Also *Avodah Zarah* 36a and *Baba Batra* 60b. In all three cases the tradition is attributed to R. Shimon b. Gamaliel and R. Eliezer b. Zaddok.

3. John D. Barrow, *Theories of Everything* (New York: Fawcett Columbine, 1991), p. 14.

4. Paul Davies, *The Mind of God* (New York: Touchstone/Simon & Schuster, 1992), p. 201.

5. It is ironic that, despite Davies's somewhat sarcastic tone in the comment quoted above, he himself describes in fascinating (metaphorical) detail a particular cosmological theory whereby one universe develops a "bubble" in its space-time, then the neck that attaches that bubble to the universe gets elongated and finally gets "pinched off" to form a new universe. The section in which Davies describes this remarkable theory is entitled "Mother and Child Universes," and in the accompanying diagram, the new universe is labeled "baby universe"! See *The Mind of God*, pp. 70–72.

6. Davies, *The Mind of God*, p. 161.

7. Michael Shermer, *How We Believe: The Search for God in an Age of Science* (New York: W. H. Freeman & Co., 2000), pp. 79–80.

8. Davies, *The Mind of God*, pp. 58–60.

9. Murray Gell-Mann, *The Quark and the Jaguar* (New York: W. H. Freeman & Co., 1994), p. 279.

10. The quotation is from the website of Innernet, www.innernet.org.il/article.php?aid=274. The website credits Rabbi Joseph Elias, *The Artscroll Passover Haggadah* (Brooklyn: Artscroll/Mesorah Publications).

11. Rabbi Blumenkrantz, *The Laws of Pesach: A Digest* (Far Rockaway, N.Y.: Bais Medrash Ateres Yisroel, 1994), pp. 9–16.

12. *Tanakh: The Holy Scriptures* (Philadelphia: Jewish Publication Society, 1985).

13. For an excellent summary of Maimonides's thinking on the matter, as well as that of several other key philosophers of the period, see Isaac Husik, *A History of Medieval Jewish Philosophy* (New York: Atheneum, 1976).

14. The core of Mordecai M. Kaplan's thought, of which this simple sentence is a vast oversimplification, is found in his book *Judaism as a Civilization* (New York: Schocken Books, 1967).

15. I have in mind here the recent proliferation of healing services, books on spiritual routes to healing, organizations devoted to encouraging people to broaden their view of healing and health beyond medical

technology, and even a small but growing number of scientific studies on the effect of prayer on healing.

16. Shermer, *How We Believe*, p. 5.

17. Shermer, *How We Believe*, p. 6.

1 Cosmology and Creation: In Search of Beginnings

1. My purpose here is neither to describe fully nor to analyze the biblical accounts of creation in any depth. There are many excellent descriptions and analyses available in print. Two of the most useful are Jon Levenson, *Creation and the Persistence of Evil* (San Francisco: HarperCollins, 1988) and Nahum Sarna, *Understanding Genesis* (New York: Schocken Books, 1978).

2. There are exceptions to this widespread agreement, including Fred Hoyle's steady-state theory and the Hartle-Hawking no-boundary condition. For descriptions of the former, see Paul Davies, *The Mind of God*, pp. 55–57, and Timothy Ferris, *The Whole Shebang: A State of the Universe(s) Report* (New York: Simon & Schuster, 1997), pp. 111–112. For descriptions of the latter, see Barrow, *Theories of Everything*, p. 91, and Ferris, *The Whole Shebang*, pp. 251ff. Although science does not function democratically (that is, there are noteworthy historical instances in which the lone opinion of a maverick turned out to be correct, despite opposition to it by the vast majority of established experts) for our purposes, the Big Bang model—or some variation on its theme—seems the most likely candidate at this point for an accurate explanation of cosmic origins.

3. Technically, a singularity is defined as "[a] point in space-time at which the space-time curvature becomes infinite." (Stephen Hawking, *A Brief History of Time* [New York: Bantam, 1988], p. 186.) The whole issue of space-time curvature is described in some detail in chapter 5.

4. The universe may, in fact, be larger than 15 billion light-years in size, but since a light-year is the distance light can travel in one year, we cannot know of, or detect in any way, parts of the universe that are more than 15 billion light-years away. If they exist, their light and other signals have not had a chance to reach us yet (assuming that the universe in fact came into existence about 15 billion years ago).

5. I am grateful to Professor Bob Dorfman for showing me the *midrash* in this new light.

6. Davies, *The Mind of God*, p. 57.

7. Although most scientific authors refrain from capitalizing the Bs in the term *Big Bang*, I have deliberately chosen to capitalize them in my discussion, for theological reasons that should now become clear.

8. Occam's razor is a principle stating that given multiple possible explanations, the simplest is usually the best.

9. Davies, *The Mind of God*, p. 59.

10. I am struck by the absurdity of the word *simply* when referring to one of the most complicated and sublime theories of the twentieth century, or, for that matter, of human history. Though the theory itself involves fantastically advanced mathematics, and a precise understanding of it is beyond the ability of most who have not had graduate-level study in math and physics, nevertheless, the equivalence that it suggests between matter and energy is breathtakingly simple and, for me, profound.

11. Ferris, *The Whole Shebang*, p. 32.

12. How, or even whether, to translate such a phrase is an extremely complicated issue. The most common traditional rendering is "Lord of Hosts," though this phrase calls on metaphors and images that we may find troubling for any number of reasons. (For example, "Lord" is explicitly a masculine image. "Hosts," as in "heavenly hosts," means "armies." The difficulties raised by these images are part of the core of my reasons for writing this book.) For the moment, therefore, I shall leave the phrase untranslated.

13. This is often translated as "see My back," but such anthropomorphism is not justified by the context, whereas the translation "see what comes after Me" is more in line with the circumstances.

14. I say "*almost* certainly" because there is one cosmological theory (initially suggested by the Russian meteorologist Alexander Friedmann in the early 1920s) that posits a long, or perhaps endless, series of fluctuations in the size of the universe. In this theory, the universe starts with a Big Bang, expands to a certain size, then collapses in a "big crunch," after which it experiences another Big Bang, and the cycle begins all over again. Even in such an eternally oscillating universe, however, the Big Bangs only occur once in many, many eons, and so the objection raised in this paragraph still requires resolution. For more on Friedmann's theory, see Davies, *The Mind of God*, pp. 50ff.

2 Quantum Mechanics: God in the (Subatomic) Details

1. *Cosmogonic* means "of or relating to cosmogony," that is, the origins of the cosmos. By "myth" I do not mean a fiction or ancient tale, although this is the sense in which the term is often used. Rather, I use the word to mean a story by which people express certain organizing principles of their lives. In this sense, every people, no matter how modern or sophisticated, has myths, and myths themselves can be quite modern and sophisticated. So, for example, both the exploration of the American West and the space race are great American myths; the draining of the swamps by the *chalutzim* is a great Israeli myth, and so on. Their designation as "myths" has more to do with their importance among the people who tell them than with their truth or sophistication.

2. This is perhaps one of Einstein's most famous utterances, though it has, like many well-worn sayings, been corrupted in the transmission. According to Timothy Ferris, the original statement, in a letter from Einstein to friend and colleague Max Born, was "The theory [of quantum mechanics] says a lot, but does not really bring us any closer to the secret of the 'Old One.' I, at any rate, am convinced that *He* is not playing at dice." See Ferris, *The Whole Shebang*, p. 346, n. 34.

3. Hawking, *A Brief History of Time*, p. 89.

4. Ferris, *The Whole Shebang*, p. 97.

5. My translation of excerpts from the Hebrew in Morris Silverman, *High Holiday Prayer Book* (Hartford: Prayer Book Press, 1951), p. 240.

6. It is interesting to note that in Israel, where the story of Hanukkah occurred, the last letter is a *pay*, for *po*, meaning "here."

7. Yehezkel Kaufman, *The Religion of Israel* (Chicago: University of Chicago Press, 1960), p. 92.

8. See note 2 above. Ferris, *The Whole Shebang*, p. 346, n. 34.

9. A "thought experiment" is an experiment that one can imagine doing but that one need not necessarily do. In many cases it is an experiment that could not physically be done (for example, the physicist Kip Thorne repeatedly discusses thought experiments that begin with an astronaut jumping into a black hole. See Kip Thorne, *Black Holes and Time Warps* [New York: W. W. Norton & Co., 1994]), or one that could not be done without violating some very specific ethical

guidelines by which contemporary science is done (the example of this latter situation is precisely what we are about to see).

10. J. P. McEvoy and Oscar Zarate, *Introducing Quantum Theory* (New York: Totem Books, 1996), p. 147.

11. Ferris, *The Whole Shebang,* p. 276.

12. Robert H. March, *Physics for Poets* (New York: McGraw-Hill, 1996), p. 227.

13. March, *Physics for Poets,* p. 228.

14. Babylonian Talmud, *Menachot* 43b.

15. Yosef Stern, ed., *The Pesach Haggadah: With Ideas and Insights of the Sfas Emes* (New York: Mesorah Publications, 1995), p. 161.

16. The startling use of the plural pronoun in this verse raises important questions about whom God intended to address by saying "us" and "our." Explanations include the possibility that God is using the "royal we," that God is consulting with the angels, that God is consulting with all the other things created before the creation of humans and more.

17. These abilities have traditionally been understood in two ways: First of all, human efforts on behalf of the poor, the needy, the sick, the downtrodden, and so on are seen as ways in which we repair the world. Unfortunately, much (though clearly not all—illness comes to mind as an exception) of the "brokenness" that our human activities attempt to mend was initially caused by human thoughtlessness, poor planning, or evil. The second way in which our world-repairing abilities have been understood is by seeing most of technology as a way to upgrade the world. Indeed, technology that improves the length, quality, or dignity of life does seem to qualify as a continuation of the work of creation. The unfortunate fact that many of our technological attempts to improve the world backfire, causing more harm than good, should not blind us to the often noble and creative intentions behind even our most destructive attempts. The disastrous industrial pollution of the last decades was the byproduct of honest attempts to create products and services to make human life better. The environmental degradation that has often resulted from high-tech agricultural methods (the use of DDT, fertilizers, and the like) has been an unanticipated result of honest attempts to feed more people better food at a lower cost. We are, it seems, co-creators in a universe that is far more complicated than we originally gave it credit for being!

18. March, *Physics for Poets,* p. 228.

19. This line is the introduction to *Pesukei D'zimra* (literally, "verses of song"), the second introductory section of the daily morning prayer service.

20. But note that Bryce DeWitt, a major proponent of the many worlds interpretation, wrote in 1971 that it was not necessary to posit an infinite number of parallel universes. Based on his calculations, it is not necessary to assume the existence of more than 10^{100} parallel universes. See Fred Alan Wolf, *Parallel Universes* (New York: Simon & Schuster, 1988), p. 95.

21. Frank J. Tipler, *The Physics of Immortality* (New York: Anchor Books, 1995), p. 169.

22. How seriously we ought to take it is an interesting question. I do not understand any of the mathematics necessary to answer it on my own, so I am forced to compare the analyses of those who do know enough. Murray Gell-Mann cautions us about taking the many worlds interpretation (which he calls "many histories") too seriously:

> In some cases ... [Everett's] choice of vocabulary and that of subsequent commentators on his work have created confusion. For example, his interpretation is often described in terms of "many worlds," whereas we [Gell-Mann is referring to himself and James Hartle] believe that "many alternative histories of the universe" is what is really meant. Furthermore, the many worlds are described as being "all equally real," whereas we believe it is less confusing to speak of "many histories, all treated alike by the theory except for their different probabilities." To use the language we recommend is to address the familiar notion that a given system can have different possible histories, each with its own probability; it is not necessary to become queasy trying to conceive of many "parallel universes," all equally real. (One distinguished physicist, well versed in quantum mechanics, inferred from certain commentaries on Everett's interpretation that anyone who accepts it should want to play Russian roulette for high stakes, because in some of the "equally real" worlds the player would survive and be rich.) (Murray Gell-Mann, *The Quark and the Jaguar,* p. 138)

Based on the strong and clear terms in which others describe the many worlds interpretation (e.g., Tipler and Wolf, and see Tipler's comments on the large proportion of leading theoretical physicists today who feel forced to accept the many worlds interpretation because the mathematics demands it, though they feel uncomfortable with its implications), I wonder if Gell-Mann's cautionary tone here comes from the queasiness that *he* feels when contemplating the weirdness of parallel universes, all equally real! In any event, a sufficient number of respected theoretical physicists describe the many worlds interpretation in sufficiently unambiguous terms that I feel justified in asking what implications flow from a serious acceptance of it. Part of exploring new metaphors for ancient beliefs may involve taking some Dramamine for the queasiness and forging bravely ahead!

23. The entire poem seems to be a *midrash* on the many worlds interpretation of quantum theory. The first three lines and the last three lines are as follows:

> *Two roads diverged in a yellow wood,*
> *And sorry I could not travel both*
> *And be one traveler...*

> *Two roads diverged in a wood, and I—*
> *I took the one less traveled by,*
> *And that has made all the difference.*

From Robert Frost, *The Poetry of Robert Frost.* Edited by Edward Connery Latham (New York: Holt Rhinehart & Winston, 1962).

24. *Midrash Tanhuma* on *Va-yera*, sections 22–23.

25. The whole category was collected and analyzed by Shalom Spiegel in his book *The Last Trial* (Woodstock, VT: Jewish Lights Publishing, 1993).

26. The earliest well-developed version of the story appears in a collection called *The Alphabet of Ben Sira*, a work attributed to the second-century B.C.E. author Ben Sira but thought by most scholars to date from the eleventh century C.E.

27. Wolf, *Parallel Universes*, p. 96. Emphasis added.

28. Wolf, *Parallel Universes*, p. 98.

29. One of the sobering responses to this question is—in good Jewish fashion—a question, one that I have pondered repeatedly without coming to any conclusion: How might we reconcile the notions of

many worlds and many truths with our traditional steadfast belief in one God? I continue to be troubled by this question.

30. Kaplan, *Judaism as a Civilization,* p. 43.

31. Davies, *The Mind of God,* pp. 61–62. I have added the italics for emphasis.

3 Chaos Theory: When Random Things Happen to Regular People

1. *The Tanakh*, Jewish Publication Society.

2. *The Jerusalem Bible* (Garden City, N.Y.: Doubleday & Co., 1968).

3. The Hebrew text can be found in any traditional prayer book, as, for example, in Philip Birnbaum, *Daily Prayer Book* (New York: Hebrew Publishing Co., 1977), p. 13. The translation is mine.

4. The Hebrew text can be found in any traditional Yom Kippur prayer book, as, for example, in Silverman, *High Holiday Prayer Book,* p. 384. The translation is mine.

5. Quoted in Ian Stewart, *Does God Play Dice? The Mathematics of Chaos* (Cambridge, Mass.: Basil Blackwell, 1990), pp. 10, 12.

6. Quoted without further notation of source by James Gleick, *Chaos: Making a New Science* (New York: Viking, 1987), p. 15.

7. Stewart's book does not supply footnotes, but based on the layout of the page this paragraph appears to be Stewart quoting Lorenz.

8. Stewart, *Does God Play Dice?* p. 142.

9. Apparently the sailors, normally thought of as merely background props or "extras" to support the drama between Jonah and God, are truly the unsung heroes of the story!

10. Jonah's motives in the story, both for trying to flee at the outset and for being angry at the people's quick change of heart later on, present complicated moral and psychological questions without clear answers. This may well be the reason that tradition prescribes that the book be read in the afternoon service on Yom Kippur, the Day of Atonement.

11. It is not completely clear what the lesson is about. Compassion? Mercy? In general, the fame and color of the incident in chapter 2 where Jonah is swallowed by a whale (though the original biblical

text credits a fish) has vastly overshadowed and distracted readers from the complexities of the entire story.

12. Harold Kushner, *When Bad Things Happen to Good People* (New York: Schocken Books, 1981), pp. 58–59.

13. These blessings are known more colloquially as the *Amidah* (literally, "standing," from the practice of reciting them in a standing position) or the *Shmoneh Esreh* (literally, "eighteen," perhaps because at one time in the distant past, the weekday version included eighteen blessings, although today it contains nineteen). The blessings are recited three times a day (during the morning, afternoon, and evening services) on regular weekdays, and four times on Shabbat and holidays (because an extra recitation is added in the *Musaf*, or additional, service).

14. Note that the months during which the additional phrase is recited correspond to the months during which the seasonal rains in the land of Israel *must* fall, or else the year's crop will be in danger.

15. Upton Sinclair, *The Jungle* (Cambridge, Mass.: Robert Bentley, Inc., 1971), p. 203.

16. Note that there are two versions of this text extant, one in which the term is *human life,* and the other in which *Jewish life* is substituted (Babylonian Talmud *Sanhedrin* 37a). Although this textual variant raises many intriguing questions about universalism and particularism, and the morality of ethnocentrism, it does not affect the basic point being made here.

17. Margaret Wertheim, *Pythagoras' Trousers* (New York: W. W. Norton & Co., 1997), p. 28.

18. Wertheim, *Pythagoras' Trousers*, p. 22

19. Benoit Mandelbrot, *The Fractal Geometry of Nature* (New York: W. H. Freeman & Co., 1983), p. 1.

20. John L. Casti, *Complexification* (New York: Harper Perennial, 1995), p. 232.

21. Benoit Mandelbrot, "How Long Is the Coast of Britain? Statistical Self-Similarity and Fractional Dimensions," *Science* 155 (1967): 636–638.

22. A typical expression of the power of Maimonides's influence is the following: "the now universally accepted doctrine of the incorporeality of God was by no means accepted as fundamental before him [i.e.,

Maimonides] and was probably an advanced view held by a small group of thinkers and philosophers." Excerpted from Louis I. Rabinowitz, "Maimonides: Biography," in *Encyclopedia Judaica*, vol. 11 (Jerusalem: Keter Publishing, 1972), col. 760.

23. Stewart, *Does God Play Dice?* pp. 167ff.

24. Different editions of Pirkei Avot number sections differently. This passage may appear as Avot 5:9, 5:6, or 5:8. It appears as 5:9 in R. Travers Herford, ed., trans., *Pirke Aboth: The Ethics of the Talmud: Sayings of the Fathers* (New York: Schocken Books, 1969), p. 129.

25. Louis Ginzberg, *The Legends of the Jews*, vol. III (Philadelphia: Jewish Publication Society of America, 1968), pp. 50–54, and notes ad loc.

26. Ginzberg, *The Legends of the Jews*, vol. I, p. 34, and notes ad loc.

27. This is the translation in the version of *Pirkei Avot* found in Philip Birnbaum, ed., *Daily Prayer Book*, p. 516.

28. Stephen Kellert, *In the Wake of Chaos* (Chicago: University of Chicago Press, 1993), p. 14. See also Stewart, *Does God Play Dice?* p. 143.

29. The visual quality of this imagery and the difficulty of describing it in abstract terms are, I think, no coincidence. Mandelbrot claims that, in stark contrast to the highly visual geometry of pre-1875 mathematics, the mathematics of the late nineteenth and early twentieth centuries "seeks to avoid being misled by the graven images of monsters." In other words, the mathematics of the period (and the physics as well—Mandelbrot quotes Paul Dirac in the same vein) was highly suspicious of visual images or the insights they convey. But, he declares, "in the theory of fractals to see *is* to believe." See Mandelbrot, *The Fractal Geometry of Nature*, p. 21.

4 Albert Einstein and Special Relativity: The Cosmic Speed Limit

1. Because this speed is so great, it is usually given as 186,000 miles per second or, in scientific writing, as 3,000,000 meters per second, but since most of the speeds we encounter and calculate in our daily lives are referred to in miles per hour, I find this number a more useful tool for comparative thinking.

2. For the sake of precision, it should be noted that this is the case *in a vacuum* such as that of outer space. In fact, when light passes

through other materials—air, glass, water—there are reductions, but never increases, in its speed.

3. Brian Greene, *The Elegant Universe* (New York: W. W. Norton & Co., 1999), p. 52.

4. According to Gershom Scholem, the term was first used by Isaac the Blind, a major twelfth- to thirteen-century kabbalist from Posquieres in southern France. Gershom Scholem, *Major Trends in Jewish Mysticism* (New York: Schocken Books, 1967), p. 399, n. 8.

5. Karen Armstrong, *A History of God* (New York: Alfred A. Knopf, 1993), p. 244.

6. This is certainly not the place to describe the kabbalistic system of *En Sof* and the *sefirot* in any detail. I urge the interested reader to look at any good introduction to Jewish mysticism for a full treatment of the subject. Probably the most respected scholarly treatment is Gershom Scholem's *Major Trends in Jewish Mysticism*, although there are numerous introductions available that are far more readable.

7. For example, in Christianity, see I John 1:5; in Islam see in the Qur'an, the Sura of Light, 24:35.

8. Note that the last phrase of the verse "but upon you the Lord will shine" is *not* quoted in the *midrash*, but it is quite common for such rabbinic texts to quote only the first part of the verse, apparently assuming that the reader will know, and supply, the rest of the relevant text.

9. *Sifrei BeMidbar* chapter 41 (Horovitz, p. 44, ll. 17–19).

10. *Pesikta DeRav Kahana, Kumi Ori* #29, Buber p. 145.

11. This verse is examined in some more detail in the discussion of the Big Bang as a metaphor for God in chapter 1.

12. Unfortunately, Greenberg has yet to write a systematic and complete description of his theology and philosophy. Most of his teachings, however, are clearly articulated in his numerous public lectures. I learned of the concepts described here over the course of a dozen years studying with and listening to him.

13. Archibald MacLeish, *J.B.* (Boston: Houghton Mifflin, 1956), p. 11.

14. Mordecai M. Kaplan, *Judaism Without Supernaturalism* (New York: Reconstructionist Press, 1967), p. 25.

15. Kaplan, *Judaism Without Supernaturalism*, p. 110.

16. The rest of this paragraph is my summary of Brian Greene, *The Elegant Universe,* pp. 37–41.

17. Greene, *The Elegant Universe,* p. 391, n. 3.

18. Ancient Israelite culture divided the night into three equal periods, or watches, so that in a season in which there was a twelve-hour night, a watch would be four hours.

19. A. Cohen, ed., trans., *The Psalms* (London: Soncino Press, 1945), p. 298.

20. Greene, *The Elegant Universe,* pp. 50–51.

21. Scholem, *Major Trends in Jewish Mysticism,* p. 270.

22. Gershom Scholem, *Kabbalah* (Jerusalem: Keter Publishing House, 1974), pp. 141ff.

23. Scholem, *Kabbalah,* p. 269.

24. H. L. Ginsberg claims that the phrase was *not* originally intended as an epithet for God, but that its interpretation as such resulted from a mistranslation in the King James Bible. This claim seems to me highly unlikely, especially in light of several talmudic references to God using the exact same Aramaic phrase as the one used by Daniel. For example, in trying to explain a somewhat obscure phrase in Isaiah 23:18, the Talmud comments, "This refers to one who conceals the things [or "words"] which the *atik yomin* [Ancient of Days] concealed. What are they? The secrets of the Torah" (Babylonian Talmud, Pesachim 119a). Explaining this statement, the twelfth-century commentary of Samuel ben Meir (known as Rashbam) clarifies the term *atik yomin:* "This is the Holy Blessed One, as it is written (Daniel 7), 'The *atik yomin* was sitting ...'" (*Rashbam on Pesachim* 119a). It is hard to see how Rashbam, in twelfth-century France, could have been misled by the King James version of the Bible, which first appeared in England in 1611! Even Ginsberg admits, however, that the fact that this usage originated in a mistranslation "does not constitute an objection to the liturgical use of it as such in English (in which it has a solemn and singularly beautiful ring)." See H. L. Ginsberg, "Ancient of Days," in *Encyclopedia Judaica,* vol. 2 (Jerusalem: Keter Publishing House, 1972) cols. 940–941.

25. From the JPS translation.

26. It is important to note that there is another sociopolitical objection to this metaphor. Many people feel strongly that it is not the

anthropomorphism per se that is the problem, but rather the fact that it portrays the Creator as a male, thereby creating and reinforcing a male-dominance paradigm in the universe, much to the detriment of women's roles and rights in the history of humankind. Similarly, when the "old-man-with-beard" image gets translated onto artists' canvas, the old man is invariably white (although the text describes only his garments as being white, not his skin), thus leading to a similar sense of the "divine and natural" dominance of white races.

27. Greene, *The Elegant Universe*, p. 51.

28. Cohen, *The Psalms*, p. 298.

5 General Relativity: Jewish Meaning in Curved Space

1. This quotation appears in Greene, *The Elegant Universe*, p. 57. Greene cites the source as A. Motte and Florian Cajori, trans., *Sir Isaac Newton's Mathematical Principle of Natural Philosophy and His System of the World*, vol. I (Berkeley: University of California Press, 1962), p. 634.

2. In the four years that I have been working on this book, understanding the thought process by which Einstein figured out general relativity has been the single most difficult part of this entire project. To the extent that I have *any* grasp of it, I am indebted to a modest little book, Martin Gardner, *Relativity Simply Explained* (New York: Dover Publications, 1967). First published in 1962 (by Macmillan, New York) under the title *Relativity for the Million*, this unpretentious work is by far the most user-friendly explanation I have found.

3. Gardner, *Relativity Simply Explained*, pp. 72–73.

4. Interestingly, Copernicus's revolutionary work was anticipated centuries earlier by the Pythagorean Aristarchus of Samos (310–230 B.C.E.). See Milton K. Munitz, *Theories of the Universe* (New York: The Free Press, 1957), pp. 6–7.

5. Martin Buber, *Tales of the Hasidim: Later Masters* (New York: Schocken Books, 1966), pp. 249–250.

6. As I research these ideas, because of my general interest in Jewish issues, I try to keep track of which of the players happen to have been Jewish. Although much has been written on Einstein's Jewish back-

ground and his religious beliefs, relatively little seems to have been said about Minkowski. His appearance in the (1972) *Encyclopedia Judaica* (vol. 12, cols. 34–35) suggests that he was Jewish. (Why else would he appear there? After all, neither Newton nor Galileo has an entry!) But, curiously, the short article is silent about Minkowski's Jewishness! It appears, according to Cecil Roth and Geoffrey Wigoder, eds., *The New Standard Jewish Encyclopedia* (Garden City, N.Y.: Doubleday & Co., 1970, col. 1345), that the reason for the silence is that Minkowski, although born Jewish, was baptized.

7. Quoted in Julian Barbour, *The End of Time* (Oxford: Oxford University Press, 2000), p. 138, as well as in Greene, *The Elegant Universe*, p. 66; Gardner, *Relativity Simply Explained*, p. 85; and others.

8. Thorne, *Black Holes and Time Warps*, p. 131.

9. This description of the history and mechanism of black holes is largely paraphrased from Thorne, *Black Holes and Time Warps*, ch. 3. The lucidity and readability of his writing is remarkable.

10. Many leading researchers actually think that, because of some very complicated quantum processes occurring just at or just outside the event horizon, some signals can be emitted from a black hole. In Stephen Hawking's memorable words, which appear as the title of chapter 7 of his *A Brief History of Time*, "Black Holes Ain't So Black." For the purpose of ordinary, colloquial understanding, however, it seems reasonable to picture black holes as emitting no signals whatsoever, thus being completely "sealed off" from and inaccessible to the outside universe.

11. This anecdote is recounted by Stephen Hawking (*A Brief History of Time*, p. 134).

12. For a succinct and thorough analysis of the biblical expression, see Richard Elliott Friedman, "The Biblical Expression *Mastir Panim*," *Hebrew Annual Review* I (1977): 139–148.

13. See Martin Buber, *Eclipse of God* (New York: Harper & Row, 1957).

14. Buber, *Eclipse of God*, p. 23.

15. David Birnbaum, *God and Evil* (Hoboken, N.J.: KTAV Publishing House, 1989), pp. 130–131.

16. Scholem, *Major Trends in Jewish Mysticism*, p. 12.

6 String Theory: Tying It All Together

1. A note regarding methodology: For every other chapter, I have read and cited numerous works, partly because I was never able to grasp an idea fully by reading its treatment by just one author, and partly because I believe it to be important, in principle, to get a broad picture of authoritative views, lest any one not be a fair or balanced treatment. Unfortunately, in the case of string theory, that is not possible. The history of the theory's development begins in the late 1960s and early 1970s, but the bulk of its insights seem to have been worked out in the mid-1990s. So far, there is, to my knowledge, only one book accessible to the nontechnical reader that treats the theory thoroughly, namely, the brilliantly lucid *The Elegant Universe* by Brian Greene. Although it bothers me to do so, I have used this fine book as my only source for the physics in this chapter.

2. Greene credits John Wheeler with having coined this evocative term. See Greene, *The Elegant Universe*, p. 127.

3. John Barrow, *Theories of Everything*, pp. 20–21.

4. Greene, *The Elegant Universe*, p. 130

5. This courtroom imagery first appears in the Talmud but is then found regularly throughout Jewish literature. Perhaps its best-known examples are found in the writings of the modern Yiddish author Isaac Leib Peretz (1852–1915), who described the court and its personnel in great detail in such stories as *Bontsche Shveig* (*Bontsche the Silent*) and *The Three Gifts*.

6. The clearest and most concise summary of twentieth-century work on elementary particles, their forces, and the various theories of their interactions that I have found is in Stephen Hawking, *A Brief History of Time*, ch. 5.

7. Greene, *The Elegant Universe*, p. 156. Italics in original.

8. Specifically, when only three spatial dimensions were assumed, string theory yielded negative quantum probabilities. Probabilities, by definition, can only be between 0 and 1. These negative values were canceled out when a system of more than three spatial dimensions was adopted. See Greene, *The Elegant Universe,* pp. 201–203.

9. We should note, although we will not explore the fact in any detail, that more recent string theorists, proponents of something called M theory, suggest that the approximations involved in the original string theory calculations caused the physicists carrying them out to

miss one spatial dimension. Thus M theory proposes ten spatial dimensions and one temporal dimension, for a total of eleven! See Greene, *The Elegant Universe*, pp. 203ff, and ch. 12.

10. For an explanation of why only three spatial dimensions expanded, leaving the other six curled up, see Greene, *The Elegant Universe*, ch. 14, and specifically pp. 359–360.

11. Greene, *The Elegant Universe*, p. 207.

12. *Katan* means "small" or "a minor." The name comes from the fact that in some traditions, especially those of Eastern Europe, a man does not wear a *tallit* until he is married. His unmarried state, however, does not relieve him of his obligation to fulfill the commandment of wearing *tzitzit*, which applies to him when he reaches the age of legal majority, so he wears a *tallit katan*, that is, a *tallit* for a young, unmarried man. In any event, many traditional Jewish men continue to wear the *tallit katan* throughout their lives, even if they are married, since the *tallit* is only worn during the prayer service, while the *tallit katan* can be worn all day long.

13. For an excellent survey of the history and meaning of the *tzitzit* and of *tekhelet* in ancient times, see Jacob Milgrom, *The JPS Torah Commentary: Numbers* (Philadelphia: Jewish Publication Society of America, 1990), pp. 410–414. In 1993, an organization was established in Israel to manufacture and distribute *tekhelet*. See the organization's website, www.tekhelet.com, for more information, including more historical information on the rediscovery of the authentic *tekhelet* dye.

14. The number 613 as the sum of all the Torah's commandments is hallowed by tradition, going back to earliest talmudic times, but is not necessarily an accurate count of the biblical injunctions. In fact, it is very difficult, if not impossible, to get a truly accurate count of the biblical commandments, since this would require numerous judgment calls about how many commandments each specific complex legal passage constitutes.

15. The significance of the numbers of coils (7, 8, 11, 13) lies, once again, in the numerical value of words: $7 + 8 + 11 = 26$, which is the numerical value of the Hebrew word *YHWH*, which is the unpronounceable biblical name of God, and 13 is the numerical value of the Hebrew word *echad*, or "one." So the system of 7, 8, 11, and 13 coils "spells out" the important message "God is one."

16. This description is from the Internet site of the Higgins Wool Company of Australia, www.higginsinsulation.com/au/wool.htm#1TheFibre.

17. The word *accidents,* when used as a philosophical term, refers to any condition or specific quality.

18. A *parasang* is an ancient Persian unit of length, estimated at about four miles.

19. Scholem, *Major Trends in Jewish Mysticism,* p. 64.

20. Greene, *The Elegant Universe,* p. 226.

21. See, for example, Martin Buber, *Tales of the Hasidim: The Early Masters* (New York: Schocken Books, 1972), pp. 209ff.

22. It is not clear what these groups were historically. They seem to have been a combination of what we would identify today as political parties, philosophical traditions, and religious sects that traced their views loosely to Hillel and Shammai, two of the leading scholars of the early first century C.E.

23. The "resolution" of the conflict actually comes in the next part of the text, namely, "but let the law be decided in accordance with the rulings of Beit Hillel." This practical resolution, no doubt the reflection of a tradition originating from Beit Hillel, is less important for us here than the theoretical assertion that both of the conflicting views represent "the words of the living God."

24. *Olat Raya,* vol. I, p. 330.

25. Reuven Kimelman, "Taking Risks for Jewish Unity," *Journal of Jewish Communal Service 65,* no. 3 (Spring 1989): p. 198.

7 Physics in *Shul:* Integrating New Metaphors into Traditional Jewish Life

1. We should not limit our understanding of the word *pictorially* to visual pictures; pictures painted through other senses would fit the process just as well. So, for example, when the prophet Hosea wrote, "The Lord will roar like a lion" (Hosea 11:10), the picture is auditory rather than visual, but the same process is taking place.

2. This claim might well be disputed by some religious thinkers, especially of the more mystical variety. For them, the direct experience of God is the entire goal of religious life. But even when they achieve that goal, they are forced to resort to metaphor if they wish to describe their experience to others. This fact can be seen by perusing the first chapter of the prophet Ezekiel, either in Hebrew or in any translation. The classic mystical vision of God, the throne, and the

chariot is filled with metaphors: "something that looked like burning coals of fire" (Ezek. 1:13), "gleamed like beryl" (1:18), "gleam as of crystal" (1:22), "Like the appearance of the bow which shines in the clouds" (1:28), and more (all these from the Jewish Publication Society translation, 1978).

3. J. Z. Lauterbach, ed., *Mekhilta de-Rabbi Ishemael,* vol. II (Philadelphia: Jewish Publication Society of America, 1933), p. 31. The English translation is my own, not Lauterbach's. Most scholars believe this compilation dates from the third to fourth century C.E.

4. The one exception to this broad generalization is the rabbinic term *makom* meaning "place" as an epithet for God. See the discussion in chapter 1.

5. Note that although these two comments came from roughly the same section of the discussion, they were not consecutive, that is, Dorfman's comment is not a direct response to Paley's.

6. It is unclear where and when the term *the new physics* was first used. It has come to connote all the fields addressed in the previous chapters and, more generally, the major innovations in physics starting with relativity and quantum theory and moving forward through the twentieth and now the twenty-first centuries. See Paul Davies, ed., *The New Physics* (Cambridge, England: Cambridge University Press, 1989), especially Davies's preface and chapter 1.

7. The question of what Jewish tradition sees as God's commandments to gentiles is a complex and fascinating one. Clearly, non-Jews are not required or expected (or, according to some, even permitted) to observe the commandments of Judaism—such as Shabbat, *kashrut* (dietary laws), holidays. But there is an idea that goes back at least as far as the early talmudic period that all humans are obligated to follow the laws given by God to Noah after the flood. For a thorough treatment of the subject, see David Novak, *The Image of the Non-Jew in Judaism: A Historical and Constructive Study of the Noahide Laws* (Lewiston, N.Y.: Edwin Mellen Press, 2002).

8. This blessing has a different text in the morning and the evening, with the morning version focusing on God as creator of light, while the evening version focuses on God as the one who brings on the evening and orders the stars in their heavenly courses. Both, however, are concerned ultimately with God the creator.

9. Samson Raphael Hirsch and I. Grunfeld, trans. *Horeb* (New York: Soncino Press, 1962), p. 122.

10. I am grateful to Professor Leonard Kravitz, of Hebrew Union College–Jewish Institute of Religion, for first introducing me to this medieval debate many years ago and for referring me to Gersonides as the most eloquent proponent of the position I am describing.

11. Good summary accounts of this development in modern biblical scholarship can be found in the introduction to Nahum Sarna, *Understanding Genesis* (New York: Schocken Books, 1970), and in Yehezkel Kaufman, *The Religion of Israel*, ch. 5. A highly popular and readable, if somewhat controversial, account can also be found in Richard E. Friedman, *Who Wrote the Bible?* (San Francisco: HarperSanFrancisco, 1997).

12. This tradition is discussed in Gershom Scholem, *On the Kabbalah and Its Symbolism* (New York: Schocken Paperback edition, 1969), p. 30.

13. Rubenstein, *After Auschwitz*, p. 151.

14. "Pantheism" is a philosophical position that claims that everything is God, and God is everything. Some scholars argue that Hasidism did not espouse pantheism precisely, but panentheism, a variant that claims not that God *is* everything but that God is *in* everything. This distinction strikes me as an unnecessary splitting of hairs for the purposes of this analysis.

15. That is, Rabbi Dov Baer, known as the Great Maggid (preacher) of Mezritch (d. 1772), the successor to the Baal Shem Tov (the founder of Hasidism).

16. Joseph Weiss, "Contemplative Mysticism and 'Faith' in Hasidic Piety," in Joseph Weiss and David Goldstein, ed., *Studies In Eastern European Jewish Mysticism* (New York: Littman Library/Oxford University Press, 1986), pp. 43–55. In the article, the author describes and contrasts two basic schools of Hasidic thought, one represented by Rabbi Dov Baer, the Maggid of Mezritch and the Habad school, and the other represented by Rabbi Nachman of Breslov. It is to the former school that the quoted passage refers. I am grateful to Rabbi Lawrence Kushner for making me aware of this astonishing article.

17. Louis Jacobs, *Hasidic Prayer (*New York: Jewish Publication Society of America/Schocken Books, 1975), p. 21.

18. Note that this was not true for all Hasidic groups. In fact, the whole point of the article by Joseph Weiss (see note 16) is a comparison of two basic Hasidic systems. The system developed by Dov Baer, the

Maggid of Mezritch, is contemplative and pantheistic, while that developed by Reb Nachman of Breslov is highly theistic and sees prayer as an attempt by the human self to draw closer to the divine self.

19. The "Baal Shem Tov" is the name given to Rabbi Israel ben Eliezer (d. 1760), the founder of Hasidism.

20. Jacobs, *Hasidic Prayer,* p. 76.

21. For example, Hayim Halevy Donin, *To Pray as a Jew: A Guide to the Prayer Book and the Synagogue Service* (New York: Basic Books, 1991), which presents a highly traditional view, or Lawrence A. Hoffman, *My People's Prayer Book* (Woodstock, VT: Jewish Lights Publishing, 1999), which presents the material from a much broader perspective.

DISCUSSION GUIDE

1. In the introduction, the author claims that virtually all religious language and all religious thought is metaphorical in nature. But in the last chapter, there is a discussion about the importance of distinguishing between a metaphor and the "thing itself"—the reality the metaphor seeks to evoke or describe. Bearing both of these claims in mind, is there a point at which, as old Jewish metaphors are deemed obsolete and new Jewish metaphors are created, the metaphor system ceases to be something that can be justifiably called "Judaism"? If you think there is such a point, does it appear in this book? Where? If, on the other hand, you do not think there comes a point where the metaphor system ceases to have a solid claim to be called "Judaism," then what do you see as the essential elements of Judaism that persist despite the discarding of old metaphors and the creation of new ones? In other words, if the metaphors are not at the core of Judaism, what is?

2. As you think about the relationship between the metaphors of religion and the essence of religion (the "thing itself"), what effect does this book have on more typical recent controversies about traditional God metaphors? Specifically, it has become commonplace in liberal Jewish circles in the past couple of decades to delete all gender-specific God metaphors, such as "father," "king," and "Lord." Some have even proposed the addition of female God metaphors to augment, or correct, the traditional male language. What, if any, relationship do you see between those arguments over gender-specific metaphors and the proposals made in this book about new metaphors?

3. Many authors have addressed the question about God and scientific views of creation. A typical example of this may be seen in Timothy Ferris's *The Whole Shebang: A State-of-the-Universe(s) Report.*

> So it seems reasonable to ask what cosmology, now that it is a science, can tell us about God. Sadly, but in all earnestness, I must report that the answer as I see it is: Nothing. Cosmology presents us neither the face of God, nor the handwriting of God, nor such thoughts as may occupy the mind of God.

Does Ferris's view constitute an attack on the claims made in chapter 1 of this book?

4. In chapter 1, God is likened to the Big Bang—a tiny point of vast energy. Although it was initially the source of everything that would exist in the subsequent history of the universe, the Big Bang itself was utterly simple; it had no particular structure or complexity. The discussion of fractals in chapter 4 suggests that we human beings, in our astounding complexity, are similar to God (that is, we are images of God). If both of these claims are correct, then God must have *developed* or

evolved starting from the first instant of the universe's existence, continuing through our own era, and extending into the future. Does the possibility of the evolution or development of God raise questions or problems? How does it affect the way we understand ancient and modern interpretations of the relationship between God and human beings?

5. At the end of chapter 2, physicist Paul Davies is quoted as saying that "the spontaneous appearance of a universe is not such a surprise, because physical objects are spontaneously appearing all the time—without well-defined causes—in the quantum microworld."

   Does the possibility of such spontaneous appearances of physical objects, including the universe as a whole, seem to constitute an assault on a fundamental tenet of traditional religion? If so, can you imagine how people with different views than your own might respond? A religiously conservative person? A liberal?

6. In chapters 3 and 6, the author describes metaphors for the shape of God. This notion may be rather foreign to most readers, and many may be put off by it. A negative reaction probably originally stems from Maimonides's assertion that God has neither physical body nor any semblance of physicality. Do you find these notions of the shape of God useful? If so, how? If not, why? How are they antagonistic to the very core of Jewish belief? What ways can you find to incorporate them into your way(s) of thinking about God?

7. A recurring theme throughout the book is the limitation on knowledge, both human and divine. To what extent do you require, or crave, certainty in your spiritual life? Is there room in your belief system for uncertainty? How does uncertainty weaken or undermine religion?

8. Most of the new God metaphors suggested by the author do not personify God; they do not give God human characteristics and descriptions. Big Bang, light, fractals, gravity—all these are phenomena of nature. Although they are impressive—perhaps even awe-inspiring—they do not inspire love or adoration from us. Yet, we live in a world in which religious individuals focus more and more on having personal relationships with God. Do you think that religion in general, or Judaism in particular, can flourish if our sense of God is not personified?

9. We often imagine scientific people and religious people at opposite ends of the spectrum in terms of how they live their lives. For example, some people would imagine that religious ritual behavior, a fundamental element of religious life, would have little, if any, relevance to, or place in, scientific life. Yet the author makes a case for the importance and meaning of at least three specific pieces of Jewish ritual, namely, reciting *berakhot* (blessings), baking challah (twisted egg bread eaten on Shabbat and holidays), and wearing *tzitzit* (tassels on the prayer shawl). How has this book affected your view of, and attitude toward, personal religious ritual observance?

10. One way of looking at this book is to see it as an attempt to facilitate a conversation between religion and science. Yet, Michael Shermer points out in his book *How We Believe: Science, Skepticism and the Search for God,* "If science is the art of the soluble, religion is the art of the insoluble." This statement might be taken to suggest that religion and science function in such different realms, and with such different goals, that there can be no useful conversation between them. Before you read this book, what possibilities did you see for such a conversation? Has this book changed your view? If so, in what ways?

SUGGESTIONS FOR FURTHER READING

Physics

Barrow, John D. *Theories of Everything*. New York: Ballantine Books, 1992.

Davies, Paul. *The Mind of God: The Scientific Basis for a Rational World.* New York: Simon and Schuster, 1992.

Ferris, Timothy. *The Whole Shebang: A State of the Universe(s) Report.* New York: Simon and Schuster, 1998.

Gardner, Martin. *Relativity Simply Explained.* New York: Dover Publications, 1997.

Greene, Brian. *The Elegant Universe: Superstrings, Hidden Dimensions, and the Quest for Ultimate Theory.* New York: Vintage Books, 2000.

Hawking, Stephen. *A Brief History of Time: From the Big Bang to Black Holes.* New York: Bantam Books, 1998.

Stewart, Ian. *Does God Play Dice? The Mathematics of Chaos.* Cambridge, MA: Blackwell Publishers, 1990.

Judaism

Ariel, David S. *The Mystic Quest: An Introduction to Jewish Mysticism.* New York: Schocken Books, 1992.

Berkovits, Eliezer. *Major Themes in Modern Philosophies of Judaism.* New York: KTAV, 1975.

Frank, Daniel H. and Leaman, Oliver, eds. *The Cambridge Companion to Medieval Jewish Philosophy.* New York: Cambridge University Press, 2003.

Frankiel, Tamar. *The Gift of Kabbalah: Discovering the Secrets of Heaven, Renewing Your Life on Earth.* Woodstock, VT: Jewish Lights Publishing, 2001.

Gillman, Neil. *The Way Into Encountering God in Judaism.* Woodstock, VT: Jewish Lights Publishing, 2004.

———. *Sacred Fragments: Recovering Theology for the Modern Jew.* Philadelphia: Jewish Publication Society, 1992.

Green, Arthur. *Ehyeh: A Kabbalah for Tomorrow.* Woodstock, VT: Jewish Lights Publishing, 2004.

Greenberg, Irving. *The Jewish Way: Living the Holidays.* New York: Touchstone, 1993.

Kushner, Lawrence. *Honey from the Rock: An Introduction to Jewish Mysticism.* Woodstock, VT: Jewish Lights Publishing, 2000.

———. *The Way Into Jewish Mysticism.* Woodstock, VT: Jewish Lights Publishing, 2001.

Matt, Daniel. *God and the Big Bang: Discovering Harmony between Science and Spirituality.* Woodstock, VT: Jewish Lights Publishing, 1998.

Steinsaltz, Adin. *A Guide to Jewish Prayer.* New York: Schocken Books, 2000.

ILLUSTRATION CREDITS

Figures 1.1A, 1.1B, 3.3, 4.1, 4.2 are courtesy of Adin M. J. Nelson.

Figure 3.1 is courtesy of Professor Harold Hastings of the Physics Department, Hofstra University, Long Island, New York.

Figure 3.2 is courtesy of Professor Larry Riddle, Department of Mathematics, Agnes Scott College, Atlanta, Georgia.

Figure 6.1 is a rendering in Mathematica by Stewart Dickson after the mathematical formulation by Andrew Hanson. Dickson is a visualization researcher at the Computer Science and Mathematics Division of Oak Ridge National Laboratory, Oak Ridge, Tennessee.

Figure 6.2 is courtesy of Marcie Cooperman.

Figure 6.3 is courtesy of Dr. Herb Benkel of Woodcliff Lake, New Jersey.

Figure 6.4 is reprinted with the permission of CSIRO Textile and Fibre Technology, Australia.

Figure 6.5 is reproduced with the permission of CSIRO Textile and Fibre Technology, Australia.

INDEX

Inspiration

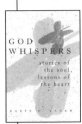

God in All Moments
Mystical & Practical Spiritual Wisdom from Hasidic Masters
Edited and translated by Or N. Rose with Ebn D. Leader
Hasidic teachings on how to be mindful in religious practice and cultivating everyday ethical behavior—*hanhagot*. 5½ x 8½, 192 pp, Quality PB, ISBN 1-58023-186-1 **$16.95**

Our Dance with God: Finding Prayer, Perspective and Meaning in the
Stories of Our Lives *By Karyn D. Kedar*
Inspiring spiritual insight to guide you on your life journeys and teach you to live and thrive in two conflicting worlds: the rational/material and the spiritual.
6 x 9, 176 pp, Quality PB, ISBN 1-58023-202-7 **$16.99**

Also Available: **The Dance of the Dolphin** (Hardcover edition of *Our Dance with God*)
6 x 9, 176 pp, Hardcover, ISBN 1-58023-154-3 **$19.95**

The Empty Chair: Finding Hope and Joy—Timeless Wisdom from a Hasidic Master,
Rebbe Nachman of Breslov *Adapted by Moshe Mykoff and the Breslov Research Institute*
4 x 6, 128 pp, 2-color text, Deluxe PB w/flaps, ISBN 1-879045-67-2 **$9.95**

The Gentle Weapon: Prayers for Everyday and Not-So-Everyday Moments—
Timeless Wisdom from the Teachings of the Hasidic Master, Rebbe Nachman of Breslov
Adapted by Moshe Mykoff and S. C. Mizrahi, together with the Breslov Research Institute
4 x 6, 144 pp, 2-color text, Deluxe PB w/flaps, ISBN 1-58023-022-9 **$9.99**

God Whispers: Stories of the Soul, Lessons of the Heart *By Karyn D. Kedar*
6 x 9, 176 pp, Quality PB, ISBN 1-58023-088-1 **$15.95**

An Orphan in History: One Man's Triumphant Search for His Jewish Roots
By Paul Cowan. Afterword by Rachel Cowan. 6 x 9, 288 pp, Quality PB, ISBN 1-58023-135-7 **$16.95**

Restful Reflections: Nighttime Inspiration to Calm the Soul, Based on Jewish Wisdom
By Rabbi Kerry M. Olitzky & Rabbi Lori Forman 4½ x 6¼, 448 pp, Quality PB, ISBN 1-58023-091-1 **$15.95**

Sacred Intentions: Daily Inspiration to Strengthen the Spirit, Based on Jewish Wisdom
By Rabbi Kerry M. Olitzky and Rabbi Lori Forman 4½ x 6¼, 448 pp, Quality PB, ISBN 1-58023-061-X **$15.95**

Kabbalah/Mysticism/Enneagram

Awakening to Kabbalah: The Guiding Light of Spiritual Fulfillment
By Rav Michael Laitman, PhD
A distinctive, personal and awe-filled introduction to this ancient wisdom tradition.
6 x 9, 192 pp, Hardcover, ISBN 1-58023-264-7 **$21.99**

Seek My Face: A Jewish Mystical Theology
By Dr. Arthur Green
This classic work of contemporary Jewish theology, revised and updated, is a profound, deeply personal statement of the lasting truths of Jewish mysticism and the basic faith claims of Judaism. 6 x 9, 304 pp, Quality PB, ISBN 1-58023-130-6 **$19.95**

Zohar: Annotated & Explained
Translation and annotation by Dr. Daniel C. Matt. Foreword by Andrew Harvey
Offers insightful yet unobtrusive commentary to the masterpiece of Jewish mysticism. 5½ x 8½, 160 pp, Quality PB, ISBN 1-893361-51-9 **$15.99** *(A SkyLight Paths book)*

Cast in God's Image: Discover Your Personality Type Using the Enneagram and Kabbalah
By Rabbi Howard A. Addison
7 x 9, 176 pp, Quality PB, Layflat binding, 20+ journaling exercises, ISBN 1-58023-124-1 **$16.95**

Ehyeh: A Kabbalah for Tomorrow *By Dr. Arthur Green*
6 x 9, 224 pp, Quality PB, ISBN 1-58023-213-2 **$16.99;** Hardcover, ISBN 1-58023-125-X **$21.95**

The Enneagram and Kabbalah, 2nd Edition: Reading Your Soul
By Rabbi Howard A. Addison 6 x 9, 192 pp, Quality PB, ISBN 1-58023-229-9 **$16.99**

Finding Joy: A Practical Spiritual Guide to Happiness *By Dannel I. Schwartz with Mark Hass*
6 x 9, 192 pp, Quality PB, ISBN 1-58023-009-1 **$14.95**

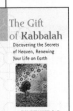

The Gift of Kabbalah: Discovering the Secrets of Heaven, Renewing Your Life on Earth
By Tamar Frankiel, Ph.D.
6 x 9, 256 pp, Quality PB, ISBN 1-58023-141-1 **$16.95;** Hardcover, ISBN 1-58023-108-X **$21.95**

The Way Into Jewish Mystical Tradition *By Lawrence Kushner*
6 x 9, 224 pp, Quality PB, ISBN 1-58023-200-0 **$18.99;** Hardcover, ISBN 1-58023-029-6 **$21.95**

Holidays/Holy Days

Yom Kippur Readings: Inspiration, Information and Contemplation
Edited by Rabbi Dov Peretz Elkins with section introductions from Arthur Green's These Are the Words
An extraordinary collection of readings, prayers and insights that enable the modern worshiper to enter into the spirit of the Day of Atonement in a personal and powerful way, permitting the meaning of Yom Kippur to enter the heart.
6 x 9, 348 pp, Hardcover, ISBN 1-58023-271-X **$24.99**

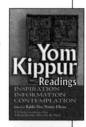

Leading the Passover Journey
The Seder's Meaning Revealed, the Haggadah's Story Retold
By Rabbi Nathan Laufer
Uncovers the hidden meaning of the Seder's rituals and customs.
6 x 9, 208 pp, Hardcover, ISBN 1-58023-211-6 **$24.99**

Reclaiming Judaism as a Spiritual Practice: Holy Days and Shabbat
By Rabbi Goldie Milgram
Provides a framework for understanding the powerful and often unexplained intellectual, emotional, and spiritual tools that are essential for a lively, relevant, and fulfilling Jewish spiritual practice. 7 x 9, 272 pp, Quality PB, ISBN 1-58023-205-1 **$19.99**

7th Heaven: Celebrating Shabbat with Rebbe Nachman of Breslov
By Moshe Mykoff with the Breslov Research Institute
Explores the art of consciously observing Shabbat and understanding in-depth many of the day's spiritual practices. 5⅛ x 8¼, 224 pp, Deluxe PB w/flaps, ISBN 1-58023-175-6 **$18.95**

The Women's Passover Companion
Women's Reflections on the Festival of Freedom
Edited by Rabbi Sharon Cohen Anisfeld, Tara Mohr, and Catherine Spector
Groundbreaking. A provocative conversation about women's relationships to Passover as well as the roots and meanings of women's seders.
6 x 9, 352 pp, Quality PB, ISBN 1-58023-231-0 **$19.99**; Hardcover, ISBN 1-58023-128-4 **$24.95**

The Women's Seder Sourcebook
Rituals & Readings for Use at the Passover Seder
Edited by Rabbi Sharon Cohen Anisfeld, Tara Mohr, and Catherine Spector
Gathers the voices of more than one hundred women in readings, personal and creative reflections, commentaries, blessings, and ritual suggestions that can be incorporated into your Passover celebration.
6 x 9, 384 pp, Quality PB, ISBN 1-58023-232-9 **$19.99**; Hardcover, ISBN 1-58023-136-5 **$24.95**

Creating Lively Passover Seders: A Sourcebook of Engaging Tales, Texts & Activities
By David Arnow, Ph.D. 7 x 9, 416 pp, Quality PB, ISBN 1-58023-184-5 **$24.99**

Hanukkah, 2nd Edition: The Family Guide to Spiritual Celebration
By Dr. Ron Wolfson. Edited by Joel Lurie Grishaver.
7 x 9, 240 pp, illus., Quality PB, ISBN 1-58023-122-5 **$18.95**

The Jewish Family Fun Book: Holiday Projects, Everyday Activities, and Travel Ideas
with Jewish Themes *By Danielle Dardashti and Roni Sarig. Illus. by Avi Katz.*
6 x 9, 288 pp, 70+ b/w illus. & diagrams, Quality PB, ISBN 1-58023-171-3 **$18.95**

The Jewish Gardening Cookbook: Growing Plants & Cooking for
Holidays & Festivals *By Michael Brown* 6 x 9, 224 pp, 30+ illus., Quality PB, ISBN 1-58023-116-0 **$16.95**

The Jewish Lights Book of Fun Classroom Activities: Simple and Seasonal
Projects for Teachers and Students *By Danielle Dardashti and Roni Sarig*
6 x 9, 240 pp, Quality PB, ISBN 1-58023-206-X **$19.99**

Passover, 2nd Edition: The Family Guide to Spiritual Celebration
By Dr. Ron Wolfson with Joel Lurie Grishaver 7 x 9, 352 pp, Quality PB, ISBN 1-58023-174-8 **$19.95**

Shabbat, 2nd Edition: The Family Guide to Preparing for and Celebrating the Sabbath
By Dr. Ron Wolfson 7 x 9, 320 pp, illus., Quality PB, ISBN 1-58023-164-0 **$19.95**

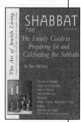

Sharing Blessings: Children's Stories for Exploring the Spirit of the Jewish Holidays
By Rahel Musleah and Michael Klayman
8½ x 11, 64 pp, Full-color illus., Hardcover, ISBN 1-879045-71-0 **$18.95** *For ages 6 & up*

Life Cycle
Marriage / Parenting / Family / Aging

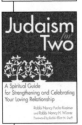

Jewish Fathers: A Legacy of Love
Photographs by Lloyd Wolf. Essays by Paula Wolfson. Foreword by Harold S. Kushner.
Honors the role of contemporary Jewish fathers in America. Each father tells in his own words what it means to be a parent and Jewish, and what he learned from his own father. Insightful photos. 9½ x 9⅞, 144 pp with 100+ duotone photos, Hardcover, ISBN 1-58023-204-3 **$30.00**

The New Jewish Baby Album: Creating and Celebrating the Beginning of a Spiritual Life—A Jewish Lights Companion
By the Editors at Jewish Lights. Foreword by Anita Diamant. Preface by Sandy Eisenberg Sasso.
A spiritual keepsake that will be treasured for generations. More than just a memory book, *shows you how—and why it's important*—to create a Jewish home and a Jewish life. 8 x 10, 64 pp, Deluxe Padded Hardcover, Full-color illus., ISBN 1-58023-138-1 **$19.95**

The Jewish Pregnancy Book: A Resource for the Soul, Body & Mind during Pregnancy, Birth & the First Three Months
By Sandy Falk, M.D., and Rabbi Daniel Judson, with Steven A. Rapp
Includes medical information, prayers and rituals for each stage of pregnancy, from a liberal Jewish perspective. 7 x 10, 208 pp, Quality PB, b/w illus., ISBN 1-58023-178-0 **$16.95**

Celebrating Your New Jewish Daughter: Creating Jewish Ways to Welcome Baby Girls into the Covenant—New and Traditional Ceremonies
By Debra Nussbaum Cohen 6 x 9, 272 pp, Quality PB, ISBN 1-58023-090-3 **$18.95**

The New Jewish Baby Book, 2nd Edition: Names, Ceremonies & Customs—A Guide for Today's Families *By Anita Diamant* 6 x 9, 336 pp, Quality PB, ISBN 1-58023-251-5 **$19.99**

Parenting As a Spiritual Journey: Deepening Ordinary and Extraordinary Events into Sacred Occasions *By Rabbi Nancy Fuchs-Kreimer* 6 x 9, 224 pp, Quality PB, ISBN 1-58023-016-4 **$16.95**

Judaism for Two: A Spiritual Guide for Strengthening and Celebrating Your Loving Relationship *By Rabbi Nancy Fuchs-Kreimer and Rabbi Nancy H. Wiener*
Addresses the ways Jewish teachings can enhance and strengthen committed relationships. 6 x 9, 208 pp, Quality PB, ISBN 1-58023-254-X **$16.99**

Embracing the Covenant: Converts to Judaism Talk About Why & How
By Rabbi Allan Berkowitz and Patti Moskovitz 6 x 9, 192 pp, Quality PB, ISBN 1-879045-50-8 **$16.95**

The Guide to Jewish Interfaith Family Life: An InterfaithFamily.com Handbook
Edited by Ronnie Friedland and Edmund Case 6 x 9, 384 pp, Quality PB, ISBN 1-58023-153-5 **$18.95**

Introducing My Faith and My Community
The Jewish Outreach Institute Guide for the Christian in a Jewish Interfaith Relationship
By Rabbi Kerry M. Olitzky 6 x 9, 176 pp, Quality PB, ISBN 1-58023-192-6 **$16.99**

Making a Successful Jewish Interfaith Marriage: The Jewish Outreach Institute Guide to Opportunities, Challenges and Resources
By Rabbi Kerry M. Olitzky with Joan Peterson Littman 6 x 9, 176 pp, Quality PB, ISBN 1-58023-170-5 **$16.95**

The Creative Jewish Wedding Book: A Hands-On Guide to New & Old Traditions, Ceremonies & Celebrations *By Gabrielle Kaplan-Mayer*
Provides the tools to create the most meaningful Jewish traditional or alternative wedding by using ritual elements to express your unique style and spirituality. 9 x 9, 288 pp, b/w photos, Quality PB, ISBN 1-58023-194-2 **$19.99**

Divorce Is a Mitzvah: A Practical Guide to Finding Wholeness and Holiness When Your Marriage Dies *By Rabbi Perry Netter. Afterword by Rabbi Laura Geller.*
6 x 9, 224 pp, Quality PB, ISBN 1-58023-172-1 **$16.95**

A Heart of Wisdom: Making the Jewish Journey from Midlife through the Elder Years
Edited by Susan Berrin. Foreword by Harold Kushner. 6 x 9, 384 pp, Quality PB, ISBN 1-58023-051-2 **$18.95**

So That Your Values Live On: Ethical Wills and How to Prepare Them
Edited by Jack Riemer and Nathaniel Stampfer 6 x 9, 272 pp, Quality PB, ISBN 1-879045-34-6 **$18.99**

Meditation

The Handbook of Jewish Meditation Practices
A Guide for Enriching the Sabbath and Other Days of Your Life
By Rabbi David A. Cooper
Easy-to-learn meditation techniques. 6 x 9, 208 pp, Quality PB, ISBN 1-58023-102-0 **$16.95**

Discovering Jewish Meditation: Instruction & Guidance for Learning an Ancient
Spiritual Practice *By Nan Fink Gefen, Ph.D.* 6 x 9, 208 pp, Quality PB, ISBN 1-58023-067-9 **$16.95**

A Heart of Stillness: A Complete Guide to Learning the Art of Meditation
By Rabbi David A. Cooper 5½ x 8½, 272 pp, Quality PB, ISBN 1-893361-03-9 **$16.95**
(A SkyLight Paths book)

Meditation from the Heart of Judaism: Today's Teachers Share Their
Practices, Techniques, and Faith *Edited by Avram Davis*
6 x 9, 256 pp, Quality PB, ISBN 1-58023-049-0 **$16.95**

Silence, Simplicity & Solitude: A Complete Guide to Spiritual Retreat at Home
By Rabbi David A. Cooper 5½ x 8½, 336 pp, Quality PB, ISBN 1-893361-04-7 **$16.95**
(A SkyLight Paths book)

The Way of Flame: A Guide to the Forgotten Mystical Tradition of Jewish
Meditation *By Avram Davis* 4½ x 8, 176 pp, Quality PB, ISBN 1-58023-060-1 **$15.95**

Ritual/Sacred Practice/Journaling

The Jewish Dream Book: The Key to Opening the Inner Meaning of
Your Dreams *By Vanessa L. Ochs with Elizabeth Ochs; Full-color illus. by Kristina Swarner*
Instructions for how modern people can perform ancient Jewish dream practices
and dream interpretations drawn from the Jewish wisdom tradition. For anyone
who wants to understand their dreams—and themselves.
8 x 8, 120 pp, Full-color illus., Deluxe PB w/flaps, ISBN 1-58023-132-2 **$16.95**

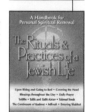

The Jewish Journaling Book: How to Use Jewish Tradition to Write
Your Life & Explore Your Soul *By Janet Ruth Falon*
Details the history of Jewish journaling throughout biblical and modern times,
and teaches specific journaling techniques to help you create and maintain a vital
journal, from a Jewish perspective. 8 x 8, 304 pp, Deluxe PB w/flaps, ISBN 1-58023-203-5 **$18.99**

The Book of Jewish Sacred Practices: CLAL's Guide to Everyday & Holiday
Rituals & Blessings *Edited by Rabbi Irwin Kula and Vanessa L. Ochs, Ph.D.*
6 x 9, 368 pp, Quality PB, ISBN 1-58023-152-7 **$18.95**

Jewish Ritual: A Brief Introduction for Christians
By Rabbi Kerry M. Olitzky and Rabbi Daniel Judson
5½ x 8½, 144 pp, Quality PB, ISBN 1-58023-210-8 **$14.99**

The Rituals & Practices of a Jewish Life: A Handbook for Personal Spiritual
Renewal *Edited by Rabbi Kerry M. Olitzky and Rabbi Daniel Judson*
6 x 9, 272 pp, illus., Quality PB, ISBN 1-58023-169-1 **$18.95**

Science Fiction/
Mystery & Detective Fiction

Mystery Midrash: An Anthology of Jewish Mystery & Detective Fiction
Edited by Lawrence W. Raphael. Preface by Joel Siegel.
6 x 9, 304 pp, Quality PB, ISBN 1-58023-055-5 **$16.95**

Criminal Kabbalah: An Intriguing Anthology of Jewish Mystery & Detective Fiction
Edited by Lawrence W. Raphael. Foreword by Laurie R. King.
6 x 9, 256 pp, Quality PB, ISBN 1-58023-109-8 **$16.95**

Wandering Stars: An Anthology of Jewish Fantasy & Science Fiction
Edited by Jack Dann. Introduction by Isaac Asimov.
6 x 9, 272 pp, Quality PB, ISBN 1-58023-005-9 **$16.95**

More Wandering Stars: An Anthology of Outstanding Stories of Jewish Fantasy and
Science Fiction *Edited by Jack Dann. Introduction by Isaac Asimov.*
6 x 9, 192 pp, Quality PB, ISBN 1-58023-063-6 **$16.95**

Spirituality

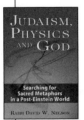

Does the Soul Survive? A Jewish Journey to Belief in Afterlife, Past Lives & Living with Purpose   *By Rabbi Elie Kaplan Spitz. Foreword by Brian L Weiss, M.D.*
Spitz relates his own experiences and those shared with him by people he has worked with as a rabbi, and shows us that belief in afterlife and past lives, so often approached with reluctance, is in fact true to Jewish tradition.
6 x 9, 288 pp, Quality PB, ISBN 1-58023-165-9 **$16.99**; Hardcover, ISBN 1-58023-094-6 **$21.95**

First Steps to a New Jewish Spirit: Reb Zalman's Guide to Recapturing the Intimacy & Ecstasy in Your Relationship with God
By Rabbi Zalman M. Schachter-Shalomi with Donald Gropman
An extraordinary spiritual handbook that restores psychic and physical vigor by introducing us to new models and alternative ways of practicing Judaism. Offers meditation and contemplation exercises for enriching the most important aspects of everyday life.   6 x 9, 144 pp, Quality PB, ISBN 1-58023-182-9 **$16.95**

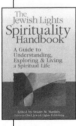

God in Our Relationships: Spirituality between People from the Teachings of Martin Buber   *By Rabbi Dennis S. Ross*
On the eightieth anniversary of Buber's classic work, we can discover new answers to critical issues in our lives. Inspiring examples from Ross's own life—as congregational rabbi, father, hospital chaplain, social worker, and husband—illustrate Buber's difficult-to-understand ideas about how we encounter God and each other. 5½ x 8½, 160 pp, Quality PB, ISBN 1-58023-147-0 **$16.95**

Judaism, Physics and God: Searching for Sacred Metaphors in a Post-Einstein World   *By Rabbi David W. Nelson*
In clear, non-technical terms, this provocative fusion of religion and science examines the great theories of modern physics to find new ways for contemporary people to express their spiritual beliefs and thoughts.
6 x 9, 352 pp, Quality PB, ISBN 1-58023-306-6 **$18.99**; Hardcover, ISBN 1-58023-252-3 **$24.99**

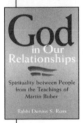

The Jewish Lights Spirituality Handbook: A Guide to Understanding, Exploring & Living a Spiritual Life   *Edited by Stuart M. Matlins*
What exactly is "Jewish" about spirituality? How do I make it a part of my life? Fifty of today's foremost spiritual leaders share their ideas and experience with us.
6 x 9, 456 pp, Quality PB, ISBN 1-58023-093-8 **$19.95**; Hardcover, ISBN 1-58023-100-4 **$24.95**

Bringing the Psalms to Life: How to Understand and Use the Book of Psalms
By Dr. Daniel F. Polish
6 x 9, 208 pp, Quality PB, ISBN 1-58023-157-8 **$16.95**; Hardcover, ISBN 1-58023-077-6 **$21.95**

God & the Big Bang: Discovering Harmony between Science & Spirituality
By Dr. Daniel C. Matt 6 x 9, 216 pp, Quality PB, ISBN 1-879045-89-3 **$16.95**

Godwrestling—Round 2: Ancient Wisdom, Future Paths
By Rabbi Arthur Waskow 6 x 9, 352 pp, Quality PB, ISBN 1-879045-72-9 **$18.95**

One God Clapping: The Spiritual Path of a Zen Rabbi   *By Rabbi Alan Lew with Sherril Jaffe*
5½ x 8½, 336 pp, Quality PB, ISBN 1-58023-115-2 **$16.95**

The Path of Blessing: Experiencing the Energy and Abundance of the Divine
By Rabbi Marcia Prager 5½ x 8½, 240 pp., Quality PB, ISBN 1-58023-148-9 **$16.95**

Six Jewish Spiritual Paths: A Rationalist Looks at Spirituality   *By Rabbi Rifat Sonsino*
6 x 9, 208 pp, Quality PB, ISBN 1-58023-167-5 **$16.95**; Hardcover, ISBN 1-58023-095-4 **$21.95**

Soul Judaism: Dancing with God into a New Era
By Rabbi Wayne Dosick 5½ x 8½, 304 pp, Quality PB, ISBN 1-58023-053-9 **$16.95**

Stepping Stones to Jewish Spiritual Living: Walking the Path Morning, Noon, and Night   *By Rabbi James L. Mirel and Karen Bonnell Werth*
6 x 9, 240 pp, Quality PB, ISBN 1-58023-074-1 **$16.95**; Hardcover, ISBN 1-58023-003-2 **$21.95**

There Is No Messiah ... and You're It: The Stunning Transformation of Judaism's Most Provocative Idea   *By Rabbi Robert N. Levine, D.D.*
6 x 9, 192 pp, Quality PB, ISBN 1-58023-255-8 **$16.99**; Hardcover, ISBN 1-58023-173-X **$21.95**

These Are the Words: A Vocabulary of Jewish Spiritual Life   *By Dr. Arthur Green*
6 x 9, 304 pp, Quality PB, ISBN 1-58023-107-1 **$18.95**

Spirituality/The Way Into... Series

The Way Into... Series offers an accessible and highly usable "guided tour" of the Jewish faith, people, history and beliefs—in total, an introduction to Judaism that will enable you to understand and interact with the sacred texts of the Jewish tradition. Each volume is written by a leading contemporary scholar and teacher, and explores one key aspect of Judaism. *The Way Into...* enables all readers to achieve a real sense of Jewish cultural literacy through guided study.

The Way Into Encountering God in Judaism   *By Neil Gillman*
6 x 9, 240 pp, Quality PB, ISBN 1-58023-199-3 **$18.99**; Hardcover, ISBN 1-58023-025-3 **$21.95**

Also Available: **The Jewish Approach to God: A Brief Introduction for Christians**
By Neil Gillman 5½ x 8½, 192 pp, Quality PB, ISBN 1-58023-190-X **$16.95**

The Way Into Jewish Mystical Tradition   *By Lawrence Kushner*
6 x 9, 224 pp, Quality PB, ISBN 1-58023-200-0 **$18.99**; Hardcover, ISBN 1-58023-029-6 **$21.95**

The Way Into Jewish Prayer   *By Lawrence A. Hoffman*
6 x 9, 224 pp, Quality PB, ISBN 1-58023-201-9 **$18.99**; Hardcover, ISBN 1-58023-027-X **$21.95**

The Way Into Judaism and the Environment   *By Jeremy Benstein, PhD*
6 x 9, 225 pp (est.), Hardcover, ISBN 1-58023-268-X **$24.99**

The Way Into *Tikkun Olam* (Repairing the World)   *By Elliot N. Dorff*
6 x 9, 320 pp, Hardcover, ISBN 1-58023-269-8 **$24.99**

The Way Into Torah   *By Norman J. Cohen*
6 x 9, 176 pp, Quality PB, ISBN 1-58023-198-5 **$16.99**; Hardcover, ISBN 1-58023-028-8 **$21.95**

Spirituality and Wellness

Aleph-Bet Yoga
Embodying the Hebrew Letters for Physical and Spiritual Well-Being
By Steven A. Rapp. Foreword by Tamar Frankiel, Ph.D., and Judy Greenfeld. Preface by Hart Lazer
7 x 10, 128 pp, b/w photos, Quality PB, Layflat binding, ISBN 1-58023-162-4 **$16.95**

Entering the Temple of Dreams
Jewish Prayers, Movements, and Meditations for the End of the Day
By Tamar Frankiel, Ph.D., and Judy Greenfeld
7 x 10, 192 pp, illus., Quality PB, ISBN 1-58023-079-2 **$16.95**

Jewish Paths toward Healing and Wholeness: A Personal Guide to Dealing
with Suffering   *By Rabbi Kerry M. Olitzky. Foreword by Debbie Friedman.*
6 x 9, 192 pp, Quality PB, ISBN 1-58023-068-7 **$15.95**

Minding the Temple of the Soul
Balancing Body, Mind, and Spirit through Traditional Jewish Prayer, Movement, and
Meditation   *By Tamar Frankiel, Ph.D., and Judy Greenfeld*
7 x 10, 184 pp, illus., Quality PB, ISBN 1-879045-64-8 **$16.95**
Audiotape of the Blessings and Meditations: 60 min. **$9.95**
Videotape of the Movements and Meditations: 46 min. **$20.00**

Spirituality/Lawrence Kushner

Filling Words with Light: Hasidic and Mystical Reflections on Jewish Prayer
By Lawrence Kushner and Nehemia Polen
Reflects on the joy, gratitude, mystery and awe embedded in traditional prayers and blessings, and shows how you can imbue these familiar sacred words with your own sense of holiness. 5½ x 8½, 176 pp, Hardcover, ISBN 1-58023-216-7 **$21.99**

The Book of Letters: A Mystical Hebrew Alphabet
Popular Hardcover Edition, 6 x 9, 80 pp, 2-color text, ISBN 1-879045-00-1 **$24.95**
Collector's Limited Edition, 9 x 12, 80 pp, gold foil embossed pages, w/limited edition silkscreened print, ISBN 1-879045-04-4 **$349.00**

The Book of Miracles: A Young Person's Guide to Jewish Spiritual Awareness
6 x 9, 96 pp, 2-color illus., Hardcover, ISBN 1-879045-78-8 **$16.95** *For ages 9–13*

The Book of Words: Talking Spiritual Life, Living Spiritual Talk
6 x 9, 160 pp, Quality PB, ISBN 1-58023-020-2 **$16.95**

Eyes Remade for Wonder: A Lawrence Kushner Reader *Introduction by Thomas Moore*
6 x 9, 240 pp, Quality PB, ISBN 1-58023-042-3 **$18.95;** Hardcover, ISBN 1-58023-014-8 **$23.95**

God Was in This Place & I, i Did Not Know
Finding Self, Spirituality and Ultimate Meaning 6 x 9, 192 pp, Quality PB, ISBN 1-879045-33-8 **$16.95**

Honey from the Rock: An Introduction to Jewish Mysticism
6 x 9, 176 pp, Quality PB, ISBN 1-58023-073-3 **$16.95**

Invisible Lines of Connection: Sacred Stories of the Ordinary
5½ x 8½, 160 pp, Quality PB, ISBN 1-879045-98-2 **$15.95**

Jewish Spirituality—A Brief Introduction for Christians
5½ x 8½, 112 pp, Quality PB Original, ISBN 1-58023-150-0 **$12.95**

The River of Light: Jewish Mystical Awareness 6 x 9, 192 pp, Quality PB, ISBN 1-58023-096-2 **$16.95**

The Way Into Jewish Mystical Tradition
6 x 9, 224 pp, Quality PB, ISBN 1-58023-200-0 **$18.99;** Hardcover, ISBN 1-58023-029-6 **$21.95**

Spirituality/Prayer

Pray Tell: A Hadassah Guide to Jewish Prayer
By Rabbi Jules Harlow, with contributions from Tamara Cohen, Rochelle Furstenberg, Rabbi Daniel Gordis, Leora Tanenbaum, and many others
Enriched with insight and wisdom from a broad variety of viewpoints.
8½ x 11, 400 pp, Quality PB, ISBN 1-58023-163-2 **$29.95**

My People's Prayer Book Series

Traditional Prayers, Modern Commentaries *Edited by Rabbi Lawrence A. Hoffman*
Provides diverse and exciting commentary to the traditional liturgy, helping modern men and women find new wisdom in Jewish prayer, and bring liturgy into their lives. Each book includes Hebrew text, modern translation, and commentaries from all perspectives of the Jewish world.

Vol. 1—The *Sh'ma* and Its Blessings
7 x 10, 168 pp, Hardcover, ISBN 1-879045-79-6 **$24.99**
Vol. 2—The *Amidah*
7 x 10, 240 pp, Hardcover, ISBN 1-879045-80-X **$24.95**
Vol. 3—*P'sukei D'zimrah* (Morning Psalms)
7 x 10, 240 pp, Hardcover, ISBN 1-879045-81-8 **$24.95**
Vol. 4—*Seder K'riat Hatorah* (The Torah Service)
7 x 10, 264 pp, Hardcover, ISBN 1-879045-82-6 **$23.95**
Vol. 5—*Birkhot Hashachar* (Morning Blessings)
7 x 10, 240 pp, Hardcover, ISBN 1-879045-83-4 **$24.95**
Vol. 6—*Tachanun* and Concluding Prayers
7 x 10, 240 pp, Hardcover, ISBN 1-879045-84-2 **$24.95**
Vol. 7—Shabbat at Home
7 x 10, 240 pp, Hardcover, ISBN 1-879045-85-0 **$24.95**
Vol. 8—*Kabbalat Shabbat* (Welcoming Shabbat in the Synagogue)
7 x 10, 240 pp, Hardcover, ISBN 1-58023-121-7 **$24.99**
Vol. 9—Welcoming the Night: *Minchah* and *Ma'ariv* (Afternoon and Evening Prayer) 7 x 10, 272 pp, Hardcover, ISBN 1-58023-262-0 **$24.99**

Theology/Philosophy

Aspects of Rabbinic Theology
By Solomon Schechter. New Introduction by Dr. Neil Gillman.
6 x 9, 448 pp, Quality PB, ISBN 1-879045-24-9 **$19.95**

Broken Tablets: Restoring the Ten Commandments and Ourselves
Edited by Rachel S. Mikva. Introduction by Lawrence Kushner. Afterword by Arnold Jacob Wolf.
6 x 9, 192 pp, Quality PB, ISBN 1-58023-158-6 **$16.95**; Hardcover, ISBN 1-58023-066-0 **$21.95**

Creating an Ethical Jewish Life
A Practical Introduction to Classic Teachings on How to Be a Jew
By Dr. Byron L. Sherwin and Seymour J. Cohen
6 x 9, 336 pp, Quality PB, ISBN 1-58023-114-4 **$19.95**

The Death of Death: Resurrection and Immortality in Jewish Thought
By Dr. Neil Gillman 6 x 9, 336 pp, Quality PB, ISBN 1-58023-081-4 **$18.95**

Evolving Halakhah: A Progressive Approach to Traditional Jewish Law
By Rabbi Dr. Moshe Zemer
6 x 9, 480 pp, Quality PB, ISBN 1-58023-127-6 **$29.95**; Hardcover, ISBN 1-58023-002-4 **$40.00**

Hasidic Tales: Annotated & Explained
By Rabbi Rami Shapiro. Foreword by Andrew Harvey, SkyLight Illuminations series editor.
5½ x 8½, 240 pp, Quality PB, ISBN 1-893361-86-1 **$16.95** *(A SkyLight Paths Book)*

A Heart of Many Rooms: Celebrating the Many Voices within Judaism
By Dr. David Hartman 6 x 9, 352 pp, Quality PB, ISBN 1-58023-156-X **$19.95**

The Hebrew Prophets: Selections Annotated & Explained
Translation & Annotation by Rabbi Rami Shapiro. Foreword by Zalman M. Schachter-Shalomi
5½ x 8½, 224 pp, Quality PB, ISBN 1-59473-037-7 **$16.99** *(A SkyLight Paths book)*

Keeping Faith with the Psalms: Deepen Your Relationship with God Using the
Book of Psalms *By Daniel F. Polish* 6 x 9, 320 pp, Quality PB, ISBN 1-58023-300-7 **$18.99**;
Hardcover, ISBN 1-58023-179-9 **$24.95**

The Last Trial
On the Legends and Lore of the Command to Abraham to Offer Isaac as a Sacrifice
By Shalom Spiegel. New Introduction by Judah Goldin.
6 x 9, 208 pp, Quality PB, ISBN 1-879045-29-X **$18.95**

A Living Covenant: The Innovative Spirit in Traditional Judaism
By Dr. David Hartman 6 x 9, 368 pp, Quality PB, ISBN 1-58023-011-3 **$20.00**

Love and Terror in the God Encounter
The Theological Legacy of Rabbi Joseph B. Soloveitchik
By Dr. David Hartman
6 x 9, 240 pp, Quality PB, ISBN 1-58023-176-4 **$19.95**; Hardcover, ISBN 1-58023-112-8 **$25.00**

The Personhood of God: Biblical Theology, Human Faith and the Divine Image
By Dr. Yochanan Muffs; Foreword by Dr. David Hartman
6 x 9, 240 pp, Hardcover, ISBN 1-58023-265-5 **$24.99**

The Spirit of Renewal: Finding Faith after the Holocaust
By Rabbi Edward Feld 6 x 9, 224 pp, Quality PB, ISBN 1-879045-40-0 **$16.95**

Tormented Master: *The Life and Spiritual Quest of Rabbi Nahman of Bratslav*
By Dr. Arthur Green 6 x 9, 416 pp, Quality PB, ISBN 1-879045-11-7 **$19.99**

Your Word Is Fire: The Hasidic Masters on Contemplative Prayer
Edited and translated by Dr. Arthur Green and Barry W. Holtz
6 x 9, 160 pp, Quality PB, ISBN 1-879045-25-7 **$15.95**

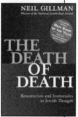

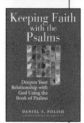

I Am Jewish
Personal Reflections Inspired by the Last Words of Daniel Pearl

Almost 150 Jews—both famous and not—from all walks of life, from all around
the world, write about Identity, Heritage, Covenant / Chosenness and Faith,
Humanity and Ethnicity, and *Tikkun Olam* and Justice.

Edited by Judea and Ruth Pearl

6 x 9, 304 pp, Deluxe PB w/flaps, ISBN 1-58023-259-0 **$18.99**; Hardcover, ISBN 1-58023-183-7 **$24.99**
Download a free copy of the *I Am Jewish Teacher's Guide* at our website:
www.jewishlights.com

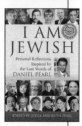

About Jewish Lights

People of all faiths and backgrounds yearn for books that attract, engage, educate, and spiritually inspire.

Our principal goal is to stimulate thought and help all people learn about who the Jewish People are, where they come from, and what the future can be made to hold. While people of our diverse Jewish heritage are the primary audience, our books speak to people in the Christian world as well and will broaden their understanding of Judaism and the roots of their own faith.

We bring to you authors who are at the forefront of spiritual thought and experience. While each has something different to say, they all say it in a voice that you can hear.

Our books are designed to welcome you and then to engage, stimulate, and inspire. We judge our success not only by whether or not our books are beautiful and commercially successful, but by whether or not they make a difference in your life.

For your information and convenience, at the back of this book we have provided a list of other Jewish Lights books you might find interesting and useful. They cover all the categories of your life:

Bar/Bat Mitzvah
Bible Study / Midrash
Children's Books
Congregation Resources
Current Events / History
Ecology
Fiction: Mystery, Science Fiction
Grief / Healing
Holidays / Holy Days
Inspiration
Kabbalah / Mysticism / Enneagram

Life Cycle
Meditation
Parenting
Prayer
Ritual / Sacred Practice
Spirituality
Theology / Philosophy
Travel
Twelve Steps
Women's Interest

Stuart M. Matlins, Publisher

Or phone, fax, mail or e-mail to: **JEWISH LIGHTS Publishing**
Sunset Farm Offices, Route 4 • P.O. Box 237 • Woodstock, Vermont 05091
Tel: (802) 457-4000 • Fax: (802) 457-4004 • www.jewishlights.com
Credit card orders: (800) 962-4544 (8:30AM–5:30PM ET Monday–Friday)
Generous discounts on quantity orders. SATISFACTION GUARANTEED. Prices subject to change.

For more information about each book, visit our website at www.jewishlights.com